LOCAL JUSTICE

LOCAL JUSTICE

*How Institutions Allocate Scarce Goods
and Necessary Burdens*

Jon Elster

RUSSELL SAGE FOUNDATION / NEW YORK

The Russell Sage Foundation

The Russell Sage Foundation, one of the oldest of America's general purpose foundations, was established in 1907 by Mrs. Margaret Olivia Sage for "the improvement of
social and living conditions in the United States." The Foundation seeks to fulfill this
mandate by fostering the development and dissemination of knowledge about the
political, social, and economic problems of America.

The Board of Trustees is responsible for oversight and the general policies of the
Foundation, while administrative direction of the program and staff is vested in the
President, assisted by the officers and staff. The President bears final responsibility for
the decision to publish a manuscript as a Russell Sage Foundation book. In reaching
a judgment on the competence, accuracy, and objectivity of each study, the President
is advised by the staff and selected expert readers. The conclusions and interpretations
in Russell Sage Foundation publications are those of the authors and not of the Foundation, its Trustees, or its staff. Publication by the Foundation, therefore, does not imply
endorsement of the contents of the study.

Library of Congress Cataloging-in-Publication Data

Elster, Jon, 1940-
    Local justice / by Jon Elster.
        p.   cm.
    Includes bibliographical references and index.
    ISBN 0-87154-231-5
    1. Distributive justice.   2. Resource allocation.   I. Title.
    HB523.E45   1992   91-39717
    330—dc20   CIP

The paper used in this publication meets the minimum requirements of American
National Standard for Information Sciences—Permanence of Paper for Printed Library
Materials, ANSI Z39.48-1984.

RUSSELL SAGE FOUNDATION
112 East 64th Street, New York, NY 10021

10 9 8 7 6 5 4 3 2 1

Contents

v

For Kathy, Lorraine, and Minnie

Preface
and Acknowledgments

This work has two main flaws, and one possible virtue. I am acutely aware of the fact that I am stretching my competence thinly over a large number of areas. It is not just that my treatment of the issues is selective: my knowledge is based on what may well be, in some cases, idiosyncratically chosen, unrepresentative, or dated sources. Although I could have gathered more, and more accurate, information, this would not have made much of a difference for the main purpose of the book, which is to sketch a framework for the study of the in-kind allocation of goods and burdens.

Unfortunately, that framework turned out to be messy and ugly. I have been unable to respect the standards of simplicity and parsimony that many readers will feel they have a right to expect. It may be that I just lack the ability or the inclination to cut through the bewildering surface variety of local justice phenomena and find the underlying principles that would bestow intelligibility on them all. Or it might be that there are no such principles to be found, and that the messiness is inherent in the object. Most probably, there is some truth in both hypotheses.

I hope that some readers, nevertheless, will share my delight and exhilaration in observing the endless variety and inventiveness of human institutions. The details are not incidental to the story I am telling: they are its essence. I am sure I could have told the story better, and perhaps a better sort of story could have been told; but I hope there may still be some instruction and entertainment in what follows.

My main intellectual debts are to my collaborators in the Local Justice Project at the University of Chicago: Patricia Conley, Michael Dennis, Steve Laymon, and Stuart Romm. Through our exchanges over the last few years they have provided me with invaluable factual information as well as conceptual arguments and innovative explanatory suggestions. In the present book I have drawn extensively on their working papers on transplantation, layoffs, and college admission. I have also benefited greatly from their detailed written comments on the present manuscript and its various antecedents. The extent of their contributions will become clear in subsequent publications from the Local Justice Project. I want to emphasize, however, that their share in the project goes well beyond that of research assistance as usually conceived. If I had been able to pin down exactly which of the ideas developed below originated in their suggestions, scores of references would have been required. Since it is hard to identify the origin of ideas that arise in the give and take of discussion, this collective and nonspecific acknowledgment will have to do.

I have also benefited enormously from my collaboration with Fredrik Engelstad, Nicolas Herpin, and Volker Schmidt, who are responsible for the Local Justice Projects in Norway, France, and Germany, respectively. With them, too, I experienced the exciting interplay between information-gathering on the one hand, and conceptual and causal analysis on the other.

On the several occasions that I taught courses on the empirical study of distributive justice at the University of Chicago I have ended up getting as much as I was giving. I am especially grateful to Karen Lembcke, Gerry Mackie, David McIntyre, and Monica Toft for what I learned from their papers on prison crowding, immigration, and adoption.

For comments on various working papers that eventually turned into this book I am indebted to G. A. Cohen, Hans Fredrik Dahl, Torstein Eckhoff, Dagfinn Føllesdal, Miriam Golden, Aan-

und Hylland, Raino Malnes, and Cass Sunstein. Craig Calhoun, Willem Hofstee, David Laitin, Claus Offe, and John Roemer made detailed comments on the whole manuscript, which resulted in substantial changes and, I hope, improvements.

I am grateful to the Russell Sage Foundation for financial support of the project. Additional support has been provided by the Spencer Foundation, the College Board, the Center for Ethics, Rationality, and Society at the University of Chicago, and the Norwegian Research Council. A fellowship from the John Simon Guggenheim Foundation in 1989 provided me with time to read and think when I needed it most. I wish to thank them all.

A final acknowledgment is due to Steven Laymon and Sven Linblad for competent and imaginative bibliographical assistance.

I dedicate this book to Kathy Anderson, Lorraine Dwelle, and Minnie Seahom in the Political Science Department at the University of Chicago, for their invariable helpfulness and competence.

1 / Introduction

A classical definition of economics is that it deals with the allocation of scarce resources with alternative uses. An equally well-known definition of politics is that it is about "who gets what, when, and how." According to these definitions, the issues raised in this book belong equally to economics and to politics. Among many others, I discuss questions such as the following:

- Who gets a kidney for transplantation?
- Who is admitted to selective colleges?
- Who is selected for layoffs?
- Who is chosen for military service?
- Who is allowed to adopt children?
- Who shall be allowed to immigrate?

Yet, although these issues would seem to be part of economics as well as of politics, neither economic theory nor political science has much to say about them. I hasten to say that in one sense this is a bit of an exaggeration. The issues discussed in the book have indeed been extensively examined by economists, political scientists, and scholars from other disciplines. But my point is that there have been virtually no attempts to study the whole range of questions of this kind, and to develop a conceptual and theoretical framework to describe and explain how institutions allocate goods and burdens. Nor have philosophers been much concerned with the normative aspects of these issues—except, once again, on a case-by-case basis.

I find this neglect puzzling. The life chances of the citizen in modern societies do not depend exclusively on market choices or on governmental decisions. To an increasing extent, they also depend on allocations made by relatively autonomous institutions, beginning with admission or nonadmission to nursery school and ending with admission or nonadmission to nursing homes. One could write the fictional biography of a typical citizen, to depict his life as shaped by successive encounters with institutions that have the power to accord or deny him the scarce goods that he seeks. Many of these encounters are relatively insignificant. Although my life is affected by the decision of my university to allot or deny me a parking space, the issue is hardly a vital one. Other encounters decide matters of life and death, such as the allocation of scarce medical resources and the induction into military service in wartime. Be the issues small or big, the sum total of all such decisions can rival the market and the state in their importance for shaping our lives. They deserve, I think, no less careful consideration.

In Chapter 2, I shall explain in more detail the issues that fall under the heading of "local justice." Some remarks may be useful at this point, however, concerning each of the two central terms, "local" and "justice."

I can explain what I mean by "local" by saying something about the relation of this monograph to the research project in which it is embedded. A few years ago, I set out to study allocative practices in three sectors or, as I shall often call them, *arenas* of American society: health, education, and work. Eventually, the focus became narrower: organ transplantation, college admission, job layoffs. Each of these arenas follows different principles and procedures for selecting recipients of goods and burdens. *Need* is central in allocating organs for transplantation, *merit* in admitting students to college, and *seniority* in selecting workers for layoffs.

In one sense of "local," then, the word refers to the fact that different institutional sectors use different substantive principles of allocation.

Later, similar projects were undertaken in Norway, France, and West Germany, with emphasis on the same (or similar) allocative issues.[1] A project in Brazil is just starting up. By enabling cross-national comparisons, these projects suggest a different sense of "local": allocative principles and practices can differ across countries, as well as across arenas. In many European countries, need (as measured by number of family dependents) can be a factor in deciding which workers to lay off. Access to higher education is sometimes decided by a lottery. The allocation of scarce medical resources is frequently regulated by queuing. Thus we can ask (and perhaps answer) questions such as the following: Is the allocation of medical resources in France more similar to the allocation of medical resources in the United States or to the allocation of university places in France? More generally, to what extent is allocation goods-specific and to what extent is it country-specific?

Later, a third sense in which allocative decisions are "local" has become clear. Initially, I assumed that in most cases the practices within a given arena in a given country were relatively uniform. For instance, the scheme for kidney allocation in the United States (laid down by the United Network for Organ Sharing) is stated so as to apply to all transplantation centers. On closer inspection, however, it turned out that local centers can and do ask UNOS for permission to apply their own variants of the general scheme. More obviously, private colleges differ quite widely in their admission policies and in the ways they implement them. Collective bargaining agreements differ extensively in the relative importance they assign to seniority and ability as criteria for retaining workers in layoff situations.

These empirical studies focus, then, on three specific allocative questions, as they are resolved in different countries. The results will be reported in subsequent publications. The present mono-

---

[1]Layoffs and the allocation of kidneys are studied in all four countries. The difference in educational systems makes it impossible, however, to find exact analogues to the college admission situation. Instead, other selective institutions of higher education are examined.

graph has a different character. Since it is largely theoretical in character, I discuss case studies to illustrate general points and not for their own sake. Also, I go beyond the three arenas of health, work, and education to include a number of other allocative issues. I also range more freely in time and space, to achieve a higher degree of conceptual and theoretical generality.

Local justice can be contrasted with global justice. Roughly speaking, globally redistributive policies are characterized by three features. First, they are designed centrally, at the level of the national government. Second, they are intended to compensate people for various sorts of bad luck, resulting from the possession of "morally arbitrary properties." Third, they typically take the form of cash transfers. Principles of local justice differ on all three counts. They are designed by relatively autonomous institutions which, although they may be constrained by guidelines laid down by the center, have some autonomy to design and implement their preferred scheme. Also, they are not compensatory, or only partially so. A scheme for allocating scarce medical resources may compensate patients for bad medical luck, but not for other kinds of bad luck (including the bad luck of being turned down for another scarce good). Finally, local justice concerns allocation in kind of goods (and burdens), not of money. Thus, for instance, I do not consider wage determination by firms as a problem of local justice. Although this delimitation may appear arbitrary, it is justified by the fact that in modern societies wages enter indirectly into the global redistributive system, through comprehensive schemes of collective bargaining, progressive taxation, pension schemes, and the like.[2]

The notion of "justice" is used here mainly for explanatory rather than normative purposes. My goal is not to evaluate allocative practices by some particular standard of justice. Some of my own ideas about distributive justice will no doubt come across as I go along, especially in what I say about commonsense conceptions of justice in Chapter 6. But in the main body of the book these ideas play no role. Rather, I consider the conceptions of

---

[2] For a study of monetary allocations that are *not* connected with the global redistributive system see Kellerhals, Coenen-Huther, and Modak, "Justice and the Family."

justice held by actors who are in a position to influence the selection of specific procedures or criteria to allocate scarce resources.

These actors include four main groups. At the core of the process we find individuals in the institution that is charged with the allocative task: admission officers, personnel managers, transplantation surgeons, members of local draft boards, housing authority officials. These individuals usually have a clear idea of what constitutes a fair or, more generally, an appropriate allocation; a first-best principle which they would like to implement were it not for practical difficulties (costs of implementation, information problems, incentive effects, and the like) or for the opposition of other actors. Doctors want to allocate medical resources to those who need them most. (But see Chapter 3 for some ambiguities in this concept.) Admission officers want to select students according to their scholastic performance. Draft boards want to select for mental and physical fitness. Firms want to retain the most productive workers. Immigration services often prefer the applicants who would blend best into the country.

Political actors can also shape allocative principles, through their control over the scarce resources used by the institution and through other forms of leverage. Often, their conceptions of justice differ from those of allocative officers. As a rough generalization, they are more concerned with the efficient use of the resources than with a fair allocation. At the same time as they are trying to handle pressure from above, institutions have to cope with claims from below, that is, from potential recipients of the scarce good. They, too, will often express their claims in terms of justice and fairness, an appeal that may or may not be sincere. Some invocations of justice are little more than rationalizations of self-interest. Yet the claims will not be successful unless they embody a bona fide ideal of distributive justice. A concept of fair distribution cannot be manipulated if it is never invoked for other than manipulative purposes.[3]

Institutions, political actors, and claimants form three well-defined groups. In addition we must consider the diffuse and pervasive force of *public opinion,* often crystallized in the media. Here, too, conceptions of fairness come to the forefront, especially

[3]Cp. my *The Cement of Society,* pp. 128, 234.

through intermittently occurring *scandals.* Sometimes public opinion forms spontaneously; in other cases it is manipulated by one of the three other groups (or by the media). Whatever its origin, it can bring about a change in allocative principles, by forcing political actors to make the institutions mend their ways.

There is a terminological point that may usefully be discussed here. Assume that a doctor advocates the allocation of kidneys that maximizes the sum total of quality-adjusted life years. Many would say that this proposal reflects a concern for efficiency rather than for justice. By contrast, they would say, the proposal to use time on the waiting list for transplantation as a criterion embodies a recognizable, albeit controversial, principle of justice. I shall not use this language. Instead, I shall use the term "justice" in a broad sense that includes the allocation of scarce goods for the purpose of maximizing some aggregate of features of the recipients or, more generally, of all citizens.[4] In the special case where this feature is utility, my usage implies that utilitarianism qualifies as a theory of distributive justice. I do not think this implication counts against the proposal; and in any case nothing substantive is at stake. When I want to emphasize aspects of justice unrelated to efficiency I shall use the terms "fairness" or "equity."

I said earlier that the general set of issues I discuss in this book have not, as far as I know, received any systematic treatment. It is time to discuss some important, if partial, exceptions to this statement. First, however, let me repeat that there are many valuable case studies of individual instances of local justice. Without these, the present book could not have been written. Robert Klitgaard's *Choosing Elites*—a study of admissions policies at Harvard—is an excellent example. Another is John Chambers's *To Raise an Army,* a history of the draft in the United States. I have also been much helped by Henry Aaron's and William Schwartz's *The Painful Prescription,* a comparative study of the allocation of scarce medical resources in Britain and the United States. In addition, I refer the reader to the books and articles cited in subsequent chapters.

To my knowledge, the first author to raise the general issue of goods-specific allocation was James Tobin, in a brief article from

---

[4]Note that this excludes profit-maximizing as a principle of justice.

1970 entitled "On Limiting the Domain of Inequality." The article is organized around the contrast between two ways of achieving equality.[5] On the one hand, there is the "general egalitarianism" advocated by economists. To the extent that economists are egalitarians at all, they want to achieve their aim by providing individuals with cash, to be used any way they might want to. On the other hand, there are the "specific egalitarians" who believe that "certain specific scarce commodities should be distributed more equally than the ability to pay for them." In Tobin's words,

> While concerned laymen who observe people with shabby housing or too little to eat instinctively want to provide them with decent housing and adequate food, economists instinctively want to provide them with more cash income. Then they can buy the housing and food if they want to, and if they choose not to, the presumption is that they have a better use for the money.[6]

As examples of specific egalitarianism Tobin considers wartime rationing, voting, the draft, the right to bear children, education, medical care, food stamps, and subsidized housing. His general characterization of the reasons why such goods are withheld from the market, and allocated instead by (nontransferable) ration tickets, vouchers, and the like, is "paternalism," a term that is clearly intended to have negative connotations. He admits, however, that "It does make sense in some cases to adopt nonmarket egalitarian distributions of commodities essential to life and citizenship," namely, when "the scarcity of the commodity cannot be overcome by drawing resources from the general economy."[7]

Being short and programmatic, Tobin's article does not go into a great deal of detail, and several necessary distinctions are obscured. For instance, it seems much more plausible to view the prohibition against vote-buying as a solution to a collective-action problem than as a form of paternalism. The main value of the article lies in the analysis of various economic aspects of in-kind

---

[5] I am indebted to an anonymous reviewer for directing my attention to Tobin's article.

[6] Tobin, "On Limiting the Domain of Inequality," pp. 264–265. Since Tobin limits himself to egalitarian principles, the scope of his article is narrower than that of the other works discussed below (and of the present work).

[7] Ibid., pp. 276–277.

allocation. For one thing, Tobin observes that the case for nonmarket distribution is stronger the more inelastic the supply. For another, he argues that in some respects transferable vouchers are superior both to unalloyed egalitarianism (nontransferable vouchers) and to a pure market system. The following passage, in particular, is thought-provoking:

> Although equality of [military service] could be achieved in current circumstances by short enlistment, too rapid a turnover would make it impossible for the armed forces to accomplish their mission. In these circumstances a lottery, with no deferments, is the only egalitarian device available. Forbidding the exchange of a vulnerable draft number for a safe number is conceptually equivalent to prohibiting the sale of votes or of ration tickets—once again a paternalistic insistence on an egalitarian distribution takes precedence over the standard economist's presumption that a voluntary exchange increases the welfare of both parties. . . . A volunteer army is subject to the same objections on egalitarian grounds as a free market in negotiable military obligations. It is just a more civilized and less obvious way of doing the same thing, that is, allocating military service to those eligible young men who place the least monetary value on their safety and on alternative uses of their time. There is one important difference, however. With a voluntary army, the general taxpayer must provide the funds necessary to draw into military service the number of soldiers needed. With a free market in draft obligations, much of this burden is picked up by the draftees who are buying substitutes, or by their families. The general taxpayer bears only the costs of the official soldiers' pay, which in a draft system is of course below the market supply price. Young men who escape the obligation are, in effect, taxed to pay the young men who take it on. It is certainly not obvious that the volunteer army solution, whatever its other merits, is the more equitable of these two arrangements.[8]

Two more synoptic studies deserve a fuller discussion. *Tragic Choices* by Guido Calabresi and Philip Bobbit focuses on an important subset of the cases discussed here; those, roughly, which we may think of as "life-and-death decisions." Their main examples are the allocation of dialysis, the draft, and the allocation of procreation rights. The last example is largely hypothetical, and

---

[8] Ibid., p. 270.

mainly used as a vehicle for various thought experiments.[9] To their list of "tragic choices" we may add those of real and hypothetical lifeboat cases,[10] the allocation of places in intensive care units,[11] the allocation of sperm for artificial insemination,[12] and the provision of emergency food supplies in disaster situations.[13] The authors do not claim that the criteria and mechanisms adopted in tragic choices differ systematically from those used in nontragic choices. Rather, their reason for singling out this subset of allocative issues is that whatever criteria are adopted tend to be unstable, unless they somehow succeed in obscuring their own operation. Because tragic choices do not stand the light of day, they cannot be made by principles conforming to the *condition of publicity* (Chapter 6) that constrains allocation in democratic societies.

Calabresi and Bobbit consider four main allocative procedures: the market, accountable political decisions, lotteries (and their close relative, "first-come, first-served"), and what they call "the customary or evolutionary approach," which more or less amounts to "fudging rather than facing" the choice.[14] The focus is not descriptive or explanatory (as in the present book), nor squarely normative (as in Walzer's *Spheres of Justice,* considered below). Rather, the authors discuss how each approach or solution creates (or could create) problems of its own, mainly by imposing "process costs" on participants or observers. Their conclusions are generally negative, suggesting that the best society can do is to muddle through in a way that obscures the fact that some are selected to live and others to die (or not to be born).

The book is an important pioneering effort. It makes some im-

---

[9]Sometimes, however, the authors confuse the actual and the hypothetical. At one point, for instance, they claim that "societies *often* refuse to permit the production of the full amount of the scarce resource that could be made available without creating other unacceptable scarcities" (*Tragic Choices,* p. 21, italics added), and then go on to use a purely hypothetical example concerning population control.

[10]Simpson, *Cannibalism and the Common Law.*

[11]Singer et al., "Rationing Intensive Care."

[12]Herpin, "Le don de sperme."

[13]Tong, "Allocation of Disaster Relief in China's Qing Dynasty."

[14]For this expression, see Barry, "Review of *Tragic Choices.*"

portant analytical points, such as the distinction (further discussed in Chapter 5) between first-order determinations of the total amount to be allocated and the second-order allocation of the good among claimants. It is constantly and acutely insightful on a number of details. I shall return to these at the appropriate places below. Here I just want to emphasize that for anyone with a serious interest in issues of in-kind allocation, *Tragic Choices* remains obligatory reading.

The analysis is also, however, unsatisfactory in several ways. First, the indulgence in hypothetical and often farfetched examples removes much of the poignancy of the alleged "tragic choices." Second, I agree with Brian Barry when he says that the excessive emphasis on symbolic or process costs "infects the whole analysis with a kind of fundamental irrationalism."[15] Third, the constant references to what "society" does or desires make for an extreme form of functionalism. (In Chapter 5, I discuss whether it is possible to provide rational foundations for this functionalist approach.) The authors claim, for instance, that "If a society wants market pressures to win out but wishes to pretend otherwise, corruption can become an accepted way of life."[16] But how can we identify what "society wants"? And how are these wants channeled into action? Or again, they argue that a scheme that uses both money and time as criteria for allocation "is often used precisely because it renders imperceptible the bases of both the market and the collective elements of the allocation."[17] Used by whom?[18]

In several places, Calabresi and Bobbit claim that the actual number of children born in the United States can be viewed as the result of a "customary nonmarket first-order determination." To the obvious objection that this number is more plausibly seen as the unintended outcome of decentralized and uncoordinated individual choices, they respond that "such a view would require that, were the number of children born in the United States today suddenly to increase or decrease dramatically, we would still be

---

[15] Ibid.

[16] *Tragic Choices*, p. 123.

[17] Ibid., p. 98.

[18] For further discussions of functionalist explanations in the social sciences I refer the reader to Chapter 2 of my *Explaining Technical Change*.

content with the result."[19] The view requires nothing of the sort, however. One might just as well argue that because a ball rolling down a path between two walls *would be* prevented by the walls from leaving the path were it to deviate from its course, those walls actually *do* keep it on the path. The fact that society would not tolerate a very high or a very low population size does not mean that it tolerates, and even less that it decides, the current size.

The title of Michael Walzer's *Spheres of Justice* is obviously a forerunner of the phrase "local justice." Moreover, Walzer deals with many of the issues that are raised in later chapters of the present book: military service, immigration, medical care, education. The main difference is that Walzer's focus is mainly normative. Whereas I shall show that different goods are, as a matter of fact, regularly allocated by different principles, Walzer wants to show that they ought to be thus allocated. At times, one gets the impression that he advocates a principle of goods-specificity according to which the nature of the good requires a certain principle of distribution. Thus medical goods should be given to the medically needy,[20] specialized education to the talented,[21] and so on. At other times, it is more natural to read him as proposing a principle of country-specificity, according to which the just allocation depends on the meaning of the good in the society in question. "One can conceive of a society in which haircuts took on such central cultural significance that communal provision would be morally required."[22] Walzer would probably say that the two views are reconciled by his assumption that goods are *constituted* by their social meaning.[23] I remain unconvinced. Does the fact that higher education is rationed by grades in Norway and by queuing in France mean that we are dealing with two different goods? But this is not the place to pursue the matter. Nor shall I try to decipher his views on the relationship between the "common understanding" and the beliefs that people actually hold.

---

[19] *Tragic Choices*, p. 174; cp. also p. 46.
[20] Walzer, *Spheres of Justice*, p. 86.
[21] Ibid., p. 211.
[22] Ibid., p. 88 n.
[23] Ibid., p. 7.

From his brief comments on the caste system[24] one might get the impression that empirically observable beliefs do not constitute a common understanding unless they are "autonomously" or "authentically" held,[25] but the problem is not fully confronted.

Perhaps the most interesting parts of *Spheres of Justice* are the analyses of *blocked exchange*. Walzer notes that "money seeps across all boundaries,"[26] unless proper care is taken to block the exchange of money against votes or against the obligation to do military service.[27] He goes on to provide a list—intended to be exhaustive—of the things that cannot be had for money "in the United States today" (i.e., in 1983).[28] For some reason, medical resources are not on the list, in spite of his claim that "care should be proportionate to illness and not to wealth."[29] I assume this is simply an oversight.[30] Nor does he cite the fact that academic degrees are not for sale, except for a brief comment that "Nor can professional standing be bought, insofar as this is regulated by the community, for doctors and lawyers are our secular priests; we need to be sure about their qualifications."[31] Since I cannot believe Walzer would condone the sale of Ph.D.s in, say, assyriology, I believe this omission, too, must be an oversight.

Walzer does not provide any arguments to show that these items ought to be withheld from the market, beyond the flat assertion that their marketization would violate our shared understand-

---

[24] Ibid., pp. 313–314.

[25] These are my terms, not Walzer's. For a discussion of what they might mean, see Geuss, *The Idea of a Critical Theory*.

[26] Ibid., p. 22.

[27] Similarly, Calabresi and Bobbit note that "Every time a system of allocation other than a pure market is established in a society in which the danger continues to operate in other areas, there is danger that the nonmarket allocation will be altered by market pressures" (*Tragic Choices*, p. 122). They go on to make a valuable distinction between two ways in which this can happen: "Those with money are tempted to buy the resources by bribing the deciders or by paying the recipients of the resource to sell it" (ibid.).

[28] After the passage of the National Organ Transplant Act in 1984, the prohibition of the sale of organs has to be added to the list.

[29] *Spheres of Justice*, p. 86.

[30] As Walzer is exploring our shared understanding of what goods *should be* withheld from the market, the omission cannot be explained by reference to the fact that in reality medical goods are disproportionately available to the rich.

[31] *Spheres of Justice*, p. 101.

ings. But I think we can do better. In some cases, the prohibition against sale can be justified on purely conceptual grounds. A proposal to buy love, prizes, honors, or divine grace is not so much objectionable as conceptually incoherent. In other cases the prohibitions are justified on grounds of paternalism, to exclude "exchanges born of desperation" such as selling oneself into slavery. Arguments for overruling private preferences can also be grounded in lack of information, weakness of will, the social shaping of individual wants, and similar phenomena.[32] In still other cases the prohibition is needed to prevent free riding and overcome a collective-action problem: no single citizen would be materially hurt if he were to sell his vote, but all would be hurt if all did so.[33] The reason why people cannot buy a medical degree is, as Walzer says, that we need to be sure that our doctors are qualified to treat us: a straightforwardly utilitarian argument. Thus, whenever Walzer's claims are plausible, they can be backed by arguments that are more powerful and specific than the blanket appeal to "shared understandings." And whenever they find no such backing, they are not very plausible. I see no reason, for instance, why the rich should not be allowed to buy medical treatments that are not available to others, provided they pay the full social costs.[34] To refuse them the right to do so would be a form of sumptuary legislation, based on barely disguised envy.[35] I return to this set of issues in Chapter 6.

The need to block some market exchanges illustrates Walzer's general thesis: injustice arises when goods are inappropriately converted into other goods, by a transgression of "spheres." By comparison, he argues, unequal distribution of goods within a sphere need not be objectionable. We can accept that some are richer or more powerful than others, but not that the rich should use their wealth to buy votes or the powerful use their position

[32] See Sunstein, "Legal Interference with Private Preferences."

[33] Cp. G. A. Cohen's argument against Robert Nozick in "Robert Nozick and Wilt Chamberlain."

[34] In practice, of course, the rich are often able to use the political power that their wealth confers on them to get the resources at less than their full social costs. But since Walzer would block the use of money to purchase influence, he cannot invoke such practices to justify blocking the use of money to purchase medical goods.

[35] Pauly, "Equity and Costs," p. 173. See also my "Envy in Social Life."

to ensure jobs for their relatives.[36] Similarly, the wall between church and state is designed both to protect religions from state intervention and to protect politics from theocratic transgressions. Once again, these plausible views are capable of much more powerful and general justifications than can be provided by the appeal to common meanings and shared understanding. John Rawls's *A Theory of Justice*, for instance, appeals to the notion of choice behind the veil of ignorance to argue for equality of opportunity and religious toleration. The conclusion is backed by a rational argument, and not simply by reference to a factual shared understanding that this is the way things should be.

As a philosophical argument, *Spheres of Justice* is disappointingly vague. As a phenomenology of moral life, it is strikingly insightful. Compared with most other treatments, including the present one, it has the advantage of placing issues of microallocation in their historical and social context. There *is* a danger in the unthinking assumption that institutions like "military service" or "medical care" must have the same meaning at all times and places, and Walzer's work provides a splendid antidote to such mechanical reasoning. I simply cannot accept the concomitant argument that the normative analysis itself has to be a contextual one.

The present book does not propose a "theory of local justice," that is, a set of conditions—necessary, sufficient, or both—for the application of a particular allocative principle. I am not sure a theory of this kind will ever be forthcoming, and I certainly have no idea of what it might look like. When I embarked on the study of local justice, I entertained what I now believe to be chimerical ideas about the kinds of generalizations and theories that might emerge. Let me quote from an earlier publication:

> The empirical study of local justice may be conceived of as filling in the cells in a three-dimensional matrix. Along one dimension one would enumerate various goods and burdens to be allocated. Along another, one would list various mechanisms and criteria of

[36] Walzer is inconsistent on the practice of using power to reward "cronies." Endorsed on p. 163 of *Spheres of Justice*, it is condemned on p. 283.

allocation. Along a third dimension one would enumerate past and contemporary societies in which scarce goods have been allocated formally by institutions, rather than informally allocated by tradition or dictatorially imposed from above. Obviously, most of the cells would be empty. A typical example of a non-empty cell would be the observation that in seventeenth-century France recruitment to the militia was done by randomly selecting one young man in each village. The theoretical study of local justice consists in explaining the pattern of empty and non-empty cells in this matrix.[37]

Within this framework, one might hope for answers to questions such as the following. For a given good A, is there any principle X that is never used to allocate it? For a given principle X, is there any good A such that X is never used to allocate A? Are there pairs (A, X) such that A is always allocated by X? Are there patterns of covariation, such that if a society uses principle X to allocate good A it will use principle Y to allocate good B? If generalization of this kind could be established, the next step would be to look for causal explanations that could support them. My inclination was to look toward economics and social psychology, that is, toward accounts capable of providing microfoundations for the observed patterns of macro-allocation.

Since then, my closer acquaintance with issues of local justice, as well as a more skeptical approach toward social science explanation in general, has persuaded me that this research program is unfeasible. I do not think the study of local justice will ever yield much by way of robust generalizations. As will become clear from later chapters, local justice is above all a very messy business. To a large extent it is made up of compromises, exceptions, and idiosyncratic features that can be understood only by reference to historical accidents. Thus the statement about the French militia in the seventeenth century, although not exactly false, is misleading in that it fails to mention that young men could and did avoid having their name put into the pool by joining religious orders.

This is not to say that since no theory is available, we have to stay content with mere description. The dichotomy between the-

---

[37] "Local Justice," p. 134.

ory and description seems to me a profoundly inadequate approach to the methodology of the social sciences. Between theory and description (including "thick description") there exists the intermediary category of a *mechanism*—an identifiable causal pattern that comes into play under certain, generally unknown, conditions. I have argued briefly for this view of the social sciences elsewhere,[38] and hope to offer a more comprehensive account on some later occasion. In the present context it suggests that we try to establish a list of allocative principles together with a repertoire of mechanisms that can lead to their adoption. This is, roughly speaking, the line taken in the present work.

In Chapter 2, I first characterize problems of local justice and make some basic distinctions, emphasizing the properties of scarcity, homogeneity, and divisibility of goods and distinguishing between situations of selection, admission, and placement. I then illustrate the notion of local justice through a number of examples, taken mainly from contemporary Western societies. The list of examples, although long, obviously is not exhaustive.

In Chapter 3, I go on to construct a different kind of list: an enumeration of principles, mechanisms, and procedures of allocation. The list, again, is long and this time *is* intended to be roughly exhaustive. Although actual procedures of allocation vary infinitely, they all appear to be mixtures or combinations of some two or three dozen pure principles.

In Chapter 4, I point to three consequences of local principles of allocation. First, a principle may have a *disparate impact* on various social groups, so that individuals with characteristics not explicitly mentioned in the principle are de facto excluded from the good. Next, principles can set up *incentive effects* that in some cases have far-reaching social implications. Finally, I argue that the sum total of many locally fair decisions may be to generate *global injustice*.

In Chapter 5, I move on from description to explanation. To explain why an institution selects a particular principle of allocation we have to consider preference formation as well as preference aggregation. On the one hand, we must try to understand

---

[38] See notably my *Nuts and Bolts for the Social Sciences;* also Chapter 1 of my *Political Psychology.*

how the various actors identified above come to prefer and advocate specific principles. On the other hand, we must study the processes of bargaining and coalition formation by which these preferences are aggregated to yield the final principle.

In Chapter 6, finally, I survey issues of local justice in the light of philosophical theories of global justice. First, I discuss a number of methodological problems common to all or most of these theories, with a view to displaying their relevance to issues of local justice. Next, I discuss three major contemporary theories of justice: utilitarianism, John Rawls's *A Theory of Justice,* and Robert Nozick's *Anarchy, State and Utopia.* Here, too, the exposition is guided by the special problems of local justice. In the same vein, I finally consider what I believe to be the "commonsense conception of justice" held by professional all-round decision makers in Western societies.

The book revolves around a stock of examples of allocative practices. The reader will come to know many of them quite well, since they are discussed over and over again from different angles and in increasing depth and breadth. Chapter 2, where the most important examples of allocative problems are introduced, is largely descriptive and stays at a low level of abstraction. Chapter 3 reshuffles the same problems and quite a few others, so as to organize them around the principles that are used in solving them. Chapter 4 looks at the secondary or unintended consequences that may flow from these solutions. In Chapter 5 the same examples are used to bring out some varieties of causal mechanisms that can explain the adoption of specific solutions to specific problems, and in Chapter 6 they are used to illustrate some larger normative issues. My hope is that by proceeding in this way I can help the reader get a feel for the phenomenology of local justice. No two cases are alike, and yet all are similar in ways that defy concise summary.

2 / Problems of Local Justice

In this chapter I survey some central cases of local justice. Needless to say, the list of allocative situations that fall under the heading of local justice is endless, especially when we range farther in space and time than I do here. Most of my examples are taken from current American practices, with excursions into other periods and societies. They have been selected partly because of their substantive importance, as measured by their impact on any given individual and by the number of individuals concerned,[1] partly for their conceptual interest.

In this chapter, and in the book as a whole, I only consider goods that are allocated to *individuals*. Similar problems, however, can arise in allocating goods and burdens to supra-individual entities, such as firms, communities, and states. Examples include the allocation of airport slots to air carriers,[2] the allocation of quotas

---

[1] In Chapter 5, I return to these two dimensions of local justice—the number of individuals concerned and the urgency or importance of the issue for each of them—and their role in explaining the adoption of specific allocative principles.

[2] Grether, Isaac, and Plott, *The Allocation of Scarce Resources*.

for the emission of greenhouse gases,[3] and the selection of sites for toxic and nuclear waste.[4] The reason for not including these issues on a par with those that involve individuals is partly lack of space and competence, partly, and more importantly, my wish to develop a coherent conceptual framework. It is not at all clear what notions of "need," "desert," and the like would mean if applied to organizations or communities. For some further remarks related to this issue, I refer the reader to the discussion of ethical individualism in Chapter 6.

CONCEPTUAL PRELIMINARIES

First, however, I have to state the criteria by which something counts as a problem of local justice. Basically, it is a matter of matching goods (including exemptions from burdens) with recipients. In this chapter, I assume that both the amount of the good and the number of individuals who would benefit from it are given. In later chapters, I consider how the choice of an allocative principle can have an impact on the supply of the good as well as on the demand for it.

Formally, we need not distinguish between the allocation of goods and the allocation of burdens, since the exemption from a burden always counts as a good. Instead of inquiring into the criteria for doing military service, we can ask about the criteria for exemption. This formal symmetry of goods and burdens does not, however, destroy the real asymmetry between the allocative decisions that make some people better off and nobody worse off, and those that make some people worse off and nobody better off.[5] This difference might affect the method chosen to select the recipients. In a survey of the use of lotteries in allocative situa-

---

[3] Young, "Sharing the Burden of Global Warming."

[4] Kasperson (ed.), *Equity Issues in Radioactive Management Waste*.

[5] Allocation of a good might well make some people worse off compared to the status quo, however. By denying a person a liver for transplantation one may effectively be condemning him to death. In such cases the appropriate baseline for comparison is the state in which there is nothing to allocate at all. The person would have died in any case had there been no livers to allocate. (And of course allocation of a good will make the nonrecipients worse off compared to a situation in which they receive the good. But this counterfactual baseline is not the one envisaged in the text.)

tions,[6] I suggested, for instance, that they are more frequently used to allocate burdens than goods, a conjecture that was partially confirmed in a subsequent experimental study.[7]

It is not always clear whether something is a good or a burden. Are voting and jury service rights or obligations? Workers who are offered early retirement schemes often perceive them as a mixed blessing, as do women with respect to the maternal presumption for child custody. In both cases, the formal right easily turns into an informal obligation. For members of the ethnic majority, military service is usually seen as a burden, but for minority members it is sometimes perceived as a good.[8] In a marriage, each spouse may argue that tasks assigned to the other, such as reading to the children, are goods rather than burdens. Being laid off is sometimes seen to be a good—a paid vacation—rather than a burden. Thus in the United States, almost one fourth of the collective bargaining agreements in a Bureau of Labor Statistics sample allow an employee to waive his seniority rights and take layoff.[9] The assignment of work duties in a cooperative provides a case in which "the entities being distributed are considered goods by some and bads by others, or where they are considered goods only up to a point and bads thereafter."[10]

Even when a task, such as serving a prison sentence or doing military service, is unambiguously a burden, the following problem can arise. Sometimes not all who have been selected for the task can assume it immediately. The prisons may be full, or the army unable to accommodate all those who have passed the fitness tests. To alleviate the scarcity, various solutions, further discussed below, are possible. Here I shall only consider queuing, or more generally, the imposition of some delay between the time of selection and the time of service. Is this delay to be considered a good or an extra burden? Some individuals will want to postpone the service for as long as possible, acting on the general

---

[6] See my *Solomonic Judgements*, pp. 104–105.

[7] Hofstee, "Allocation by Lot." The confirmation is only partial, since the study deals with perceptions of fairness rather than with actual practice.

[8] Petersen, "Rationality, Ethnicity and Military Enlistment."

[9] Bureau of Labor Statistics, *Layoff, Recall, and Worksharing Procedures*, Bulletin 1425–13, 1972.

[10] Yaari and Bar-Hillel, "On Dividing Justly," p. 2.

principle that the present impact both of future pains and future pleasures decreases with time. Others will want to have it over and done with as soon as possible, either because they want to get on with the business of planning their lives or because they find the prospect of waiting for a bad thing almost as unattractive as the bad thing itself.[11] In the case of military service, it would make sense to admit the latter category before the former. In the case of prison sentences, the question seems more ambiguous.

Allocative issues may be classified according to the presence or absence of scarcity, indivisibility, and homogeneity.[12] That a good is scarce means that there is not enough of it to satiate all individuals. Scarcity can be (weakly or strongly) natural, quasi-natural, or artificial. Strong natural scarcity arises when there is nothing anyone could do to increase the supply. Paintings by Rembrandt are an example. Weak natural scarcity arises when there is nothing anyone could do to increase the supply to the point of satiating everybody. The provision of oil is an example; the supply of cadaver organs is another.[13] Quasi-natural scarcity arises when the supply could be increased, possibly to the point of satiation, only by the uncoerced actions of citizens. The supply of children for adoption and of sperm for artificial insemination are examples.[14]

---

[11] For the latter argument, see G. Loewenstein, "Anticipation and the Valuation of Delayed Consumption."

[12] In addition, we may distinguish between reusable goods (such as dialysis machines) and nonreusable goods (such as kidneys). As observed by Kilner, *Who Lives? Who Dies?*, pp. 83, 149, certain dilemmas take a different form (or disappear) when the good to be allocated is reusable. For instance, the problem of giving scarce goods to the elderly is less acute when the goods can be used by others after their death. In allocating dialysis machines, the same total number of life years will be saved regardless of the age of the recipients. I disagree, however, with Kilner's claim that this argument also applies to the allocation of intensive care beds. The conclusion would follow only if we assume, implausibly, that expected prolongation of life is proportional to length of time spent in the intensive care unit.

[13] Of course the government could decide to kill randomly selected individuals to get enough organs for all who need them. (Cp. Harris, "The Survival Lottery" for a proposal to this effect.) In this sense the distinction between natural and artificial scarcity is blurred. I shall assume that minimal respect for the autonomy of individuals and families precludes such moves.

[14] Since the government can increase the supply of such goods by offering incentives for the citizens to provide them, the distinction between quasi-natural and artificial scarcity is also somewhat blurred.

Artificial scarcity arises when the government could, if it so decided, make the good available to everyone to the level of satiation. Exemption from military service and provision of places in kindergarten are examples.

A good is indivisible if it is impossible for more than one person to receive it. It is not clear, for instance, what it would mean to divide the right to procreate or to adopt a child. Also, a good may be classified as indivisible if division would virtually destroy its value, as in Solomon's proposal to cut the contested child in two. A related phenomenon arises when the good has increasing marginal utility. Many divorcing parents oppose joint custody because they feel that being a full-time parent is much more satisfying than being part of a joint custody scheme. If they are risk neutral, they would rather flip a coin than share the time. If they are sufficiently risk averse, they may nevertheless agree on a time-sharing scheme. When goods are indivisible, allocation decisions take the form of saying Yes or No to the candidates, rather than awarding them some variable amount of the good. An implication is that principles of the form "To each according to his X" have no application to indivisible goods. *Equity theory*, for instance, which says that goods are to be allocated such that the ratio between contribution and reward is the same for all claimants,[15] does not apply to core issues of local justice such as layoffs, immigration, college admission, or the allocation of organs for transplantation.[16]

That a good is homogeneous means, in the case of strictly indivisible goods, that all units are indistinguishable, at least with respect to the features that make them desirable; and, in the case of divisible goods, that any two equal-sized amounts are similarly indistinguishable. Even when burdens are unequal, exemptions

[15] See Harris, "Pinning Down the Equity Formula."

[16] Strictly speaking, this conclusion is too strong. Even in the case of indivisible goods, the *probability* of getting them might be made proportional to earlier contributions. John Broome argues ("Fairness and the Random Distribution of Goods") that such *weighted lotteries* ought to be the basic principle for allocating scarce resources. (In discussing the determinants of the weights, he does not, however, limit himself to prior contributions.) In practice, such lotteries are rare, the main exception being the system of admission to medical school in the Netherlands. In later chapters I return to various aspects of this system.

are homogeneous. Some forms of military service are more onerous than others, and yet it makes no sense to say that one would
rather be exempt from a more onerous branch than from a less
onerous one.[17]

For many indivisible goods—durable consumer goods, procreation rights, and custody rights are exceptions—satiation occurs
with the first unit of the good. Scarcity then reduces to the fact
that there are more individuals who could benefit from the good
than there are units to go around. The allocation of kidneys, the
admission of students to selective colleges, and the layoff of workers all fit this pattern. Another pattern arises in the allocation of
scarce, divisible goods. Energy, water, land, and production quotas illustrate this case. A third pattern arises when the good, although not scarce, is heterogeneous in relevant respects. The allocation of offices among workers in a firm or the assignment of
students to dormitories both illustrate this case. Everybody is as-
sured of a place; and nobody could use more than one place; but
some places are better than others.

To proceed in a slightly more systematic manner, we may note
that three dichotomous distinctions yield a total of eight possible
cases. Not all combinations are observed, however, because non-
scarce goods are in practice also indivisible. Also, goods that are
non-scarce and homogeneous do not pose allocative problems.
Hence five relevant combinations remain: (a) The good is not
scarce but heterogeneous in aspects that matter for how it is evaluated by recipients. When Congress assigns members to committees, firms allocate offices to employees, or universities assign
college students to dormitories, conflicts of interest frequently
arise.[18] (b) The good is scarce, indivisible, and homogeneous. Durable consumer goods or admission to Harvard college are examples. (c) The good is scarce, indivisible, and heterogeneous. Examples include kidneys, hearts, and livers for transplantation.
(d) The good is scarce, divisible, and homogeneous. Water, energy, and most consumer goods are examples. (e) The good is

---

[17] Cp. the old chestnut of a menu: "Sandwich with ham: $2. Sandwich
with cheese: $1. Sandwich without ham: 50¢. Sandwich without cheese: 25¢."

[18] For a study of such allocation problems, see Hylland and Zeckhauser,
"The Efficient Allocation of Individuals to Positions." See also the comments
in Chapter 4 on the market for interns.

scarce, indefinitely divisible, and yet heterogeneous. Land is a good example.

In these cases we are dealing with a total that, for whatever reason, is limited in quantity or variable in quality. Even if it might have been possible to produce enough of the good to satiate everybody at the same, optimal level of quality, I assume that there is in fact sufficient scarcity or heterogeneity to create a conflict of interest. Thus the allocation of dialysis sets up a problem of local justice in Britain, where such treatment remains scarce, but not in the United States, where it is accessible to all. Access to kindergarten is an issue of local justice in Norway, but not in France. In these situations, the conflict of interest has to be solved by a procedure that matches goods and recipients. A detailed examination of such procedures and the principles underlying them is undertaken in the next chapter. Here, I want to sketch a brief formal classification of procedures that arises naturally out of the classification of goods offered above.

Following Willem Hofstee,[19] I distinguish between selection, admission, and placement.[20] A selection procedure compares individuals against each other, usually by producing a ranking list, and accepts them by starting at the top and going down the list until the good is exhausted. An admission procedure compares individuals against an absolute threshold, and offers the good to all those and only those who exceed the threshold. A placement procedure regulates the allocation of non-scarce, heterogeneous goods, ensuring that each individual ends up with some unit of the good. Clearly, admission procedures are unsuitable for the allocation of scarce, indivisible goods that exist in rigidly fixed quantities. Because the relevant features of individuals tend to vary stochastically, the number of applicants exceeding the threshold can fall short of the number of units of the good, in which case valuable resources might be wasted. Alternatively, there may be more qualified recipients than there are units of the good, in which case the allocators have to start all over again,

---

[19] Hofstee, "Allocation by Lot."

[20] Selection and admission correspond to what Calabresi and Bobbit (*Tragic Choices*, p. 72 ff.) call allocation on the basis of, respectively, relative and absolute worthiness.

either using a different threshold or moving to a selection system. (Imagine that a firm adopted the standing policy that in layoffs all workers who have more than eight years of seniority will be retained.)

Admissions procedures fall into two categories. First, there are what I shall call pure admissions procedures, in which the threshold is chosen because it is in some sense substantially appropriate. Second, there are impure admissions procedures, in which admission is used as a proxy for selection, with the threshold being chosen with a view to match the number of applicants with the number of places. Impure admissions procedures make sense in two main cases. First, the good may be easily divisible, so that after the fact one can adjust the amount of the good allocated to each qualified recipient. Second—and this seems to be the more frequent case—the good may be easily expandable (through a first-order decision). Universities, for instance, can easily handle a slightly smaller or slightly larger class than expected. Similarly, placement procedures often require some first-order flexibility.

Complex examples of admission policies are found in the procedures used by firms in offering early retirement schemes to their workers, often to avoid layoffs. Usually, offers are made to all workers satisfying joint requirements of age and length of service. Thus in 1987 IBM augmented an already existing early retirement scheme with the following program, for which 10,000 US employees signed up. Normally, to be eligible for early retirement an employee must be fifty-five years or older with fifteen years of service, or have thirty or more years of service. Under the plan, IBM added five years to both the age and the service length of an employee in calculating eligibility and benefits.[21] A similar plan at Xerox added an incentive to take the plan—employees could take their time deciding—but for each year that they waited to decide, one year was subtracted from the five that would have been added to their age and service.[22] Some of these plans fail to attract the expected number of workers, and thus must be supplemented by layoffs. Others, notably in the steel industry, have overshot

[21] "Early Retirement: Companies Move to Window Plans in Efforts to Stay Competitive." *BNA Pension Reporter* 14 (January 5, 1987), p. 8.
[22] Ibid.

by attracting too many workers and creating great financial burdens for the firms. These problems could have been avoided by using a selection system, based on age and seniority aggregated according to some formula. One may speculate about the reasons why nevertheless an admission system was used. Perhaps management calculated that the scheme would not appear attractive unless early retirement was formulated as an entitlement.

Issues of local justice *stricto sensu* arise only in the presence of scarcity and heterogeneity. I shall occasionally, however, discuss problems in which neither feature is present. Consider, for instance, extensions or restrictions of the suffrage. It is perfectly feasible to extend the right to vote to everyone, including children. Yet as a matter of fact not everybody is allowed to vote. Similarly, I believe there is nothing in Christian theology to suggest that God is unable to offer salvation to everybody, including the most hardened sinners. If some are condemned to eternal pain, it is not because of lack of space in heaven. Yet although God is not forced by circumstances to choose some and reject others, this is what he is supposed to do. The criteria used in regulating suffrage and salvation are also used in some contexts of local justice: age and gender in the case of suffrage, desert in the case of salvation. Hence we can see such cases as lying on the periphery of local justice, capable of illuminating the core cases as well as of being illuminated by them.

Suffrage and salvation are pure admission problems. First, one decides what the criteria should be, and then one accepts all those and only those who satisfy them. The criteria represent intrinsic worthiness rather than a convenient method for matching applicants with scarce goods. In local justice cases, admissions procedures tend to be impure. When more goods become available, the threshold is lowered. Yet intrinsic worthiness can also matter in local justice problems. The use of high school grades in admitting students to medical school does not simply serve to regulate numbers: it probably also reflects the view that doctors ought to have a certain level of competence. Similarly, the use of physical fitness in selecting soldiers is not just an indefinitely expandable or compressible device for ensuring that the right number of young men are called up. The decision whether to allow the mentally handicapped to have children is a pure admissions problem, unless it is part of a policy that aims at an overall target size of the population.

These remarks suggest the use of two-step procedures. First, an absolute threshold might be set that reflects the minimal degree of substantive acceptability. Next, if there are more acceptable candidates than goods to be allocated or places to be filled, a selection procedure might be applied. The criterion used in ranking the acceptable candidates may or may not be related to the criterion used in determining who is acceptable. In layoff cases, ability is sometimes used to form the pool and seniority for choosing from the pool. In allocating kidneys for transplantation, age has sometimes been a limiting factor for getting on the waiting list, but has not been used as a criterion for being selected from the list. Income is used to screen adoptive parents, but of two couples that pass the threshold the one that earns more is not more likely to be chosen. When the two steps use different criteria, it is often the case that the first step reflects a concern for efficiency, the second a concern for equity. I return to such mixed schemes in the next chapter.

In what I have called the core cases of local justice, or local justice *stricto sensu*, the relevant good is allocated—and the principle for allocating it chosen—by a relatively autonomous institution. Paradigm cases are draft boards, admissions offices, transplantation teams. Again, however, it is often useful to consider peripheral cases. American immigration principles are decided by Congress, with relatively little autonomy being granted to the immigration authorities.[23] (By contrast, Australian and Canadian immigration policies give extremely wide discretion to immigration officials.)[24] Child custody is decided by the courts. The allocation of household tasks is unilaterally imposed by one family member or by bargaining among all members. The suffrage is regulated by the central political authorities. Salvation and damnation are in the hands of God. Once again, however, these peripheral cases suggest conceptual distinctions that help us understand the core cases. Hence in this chapter and in the following I shall

[23] This is no doubt why "immigration law is one of our largest and most complex bodies of legislation, perhaps exceeded only by the tax code" (Hutchinson, *Legislative History of American Immigration Policy*, p. xiii).

[24] Briggs, *Immigration Policy and the American Labor Force*, p. 93.

be relatively liberal in what I accept as instances of local justice. In Chapter 5, where the focus is on explanation rather than conceptual analysis, I shall mainly (but not exclusively) be concerned with the central cases.

Some Examples

In this section I present the empirical basis for the book as a whole, by describing selected aspects of the following allocative issues:

- military service in wartime
- demobilization from the army
- allocation of kidneys
- selection of workers for layoffs
- access to higher education
- allocation of sperm for artificial insemination
- selection of adoptive parents
- award of child custody
- admission to kindergarten
- division of household work
- allocation of prison space
- immigration
- rationing in wartime

Military service in wartime. The selection of soldiers for active military service is perhaps the most important problem of local justice in modern societies.[25] Being a life-and-death issue, the stakes are extremely high for the young men and women directly involved. Unlike other such issues, e.g. the allocation of organs for transplantation, it affects huge numbers of people. In fact, it affects everybody, since the fate of the country itself may be at stake. The procedures of selection vary a great deal across countries and periods. Here, I shall limit myself to some American practices, as described by John Chambers in *To Raise an Army* and,

---

[25] It is one of the two distributive issues that are discussed both in *Tragic Choices* and in *Spheres of Justice* (immigration is the other).

for the more recent period, by James Gerhardt in *The Draft and Public Policy*.

People join the army in two ways: because they volunteer or because they are forced to. Currently the United States has an all-volunteer army, a system that until the Gulf War of 1991 had never been used in wartime. I shall not consider it further. To raise soldiers for war, one has relied either on a combination of volunteering and drafting or just on drafting. From colonial times up to 1973, the tendency has been from relying largely but not exclusively on volunteers, toward an increasing and finally exclusive reliance on drafting.

In the War of Independence, the Continental army was composed of paid, long-term (two or three years) enlistees. When this system proved insufficient, it was supplemented by the draft, but in a way that really was a form of enlistment. "When not enough citizen-soldiers volunteered, local militia officers drafted the more affluent citizens who, in turn, hired men to serve as substitutes. This selective draft functioned mainly as a kind of tax for raising individual enlistment bounties."[26]

During the Civil War, the North relied largely on volunteers, who made up more than 92 percent of the 2,100,000 who served in the Union army.[27] Attempts to use the draft were made, but unsuccessfully: "Of the 300,000 men summoned [in 1863] by draft authorities, 40,000 failed to report for examination, 165,000 were examined and then exempted because of physical or other disability or dependency, 52,000 escaped service by paying the commutation fee (contributing $15 million to the federal bounty fund), 26,000 provided substitutes, and only 10,000 were held to personal services."[28] Even low-paid unskilled workers were able to buy substitutes, since the states provided them with grants to do so.[29] By contrast, the Confederate army was largely based on conscription. "Although only 21 percent of the one million Confederate soldiers were obtained through the draft, the Conscription Acts had been used to keep in the service for the duration the

[26] Chambers, *To Raise an Army*, pp. 20–21.
[27] Ibid., p. 42.
[28] Ibid., p. 57.
[29] Ibid., p. 61.

79 percent who had first entered as volunteers."[30] Also the South, unlike the North, soon prohibited substitution.

In the First World War, drafted soldiers outnumbered the volunteers. Toward the end of the war, voluntary enlistment was actually prohibited, because it was seen as an obstacle to efficient planning: "Many of the volunteers were more useful to the nation in their civilian occupation."[31] Also, there was a widespread feeling that volunteerism was inequitable (see Chapter 5 for more details). To organize the draft, the government first toyed with the idea of giving blanket exemptions to certain occupational categories needed for the war effort as well as to married men (so as to relieve taxpayers of the need to support their families). "The secretary of war quickly realized, however, that occupational group exemptions were unacceptable. They would be seen as unfair because there would be individuals within such groups who did not warrant exemption."[32] A similar objection was made to the idea of a general exemption for married men. The government decided, therefore, to let exemptions and deferment be made on a case-by-case basis by local draft boards, operating under general guidelines. The order of selection was determined by a lottery. Quotas were assigned to each state, with credits for residents who had volunteered. Thus non-volunteers in different states had different chances of being drafted, depending on the number of volunteers. Although violating individual-level equality, the system promoted equity among the states by ensuring that no state had a larger proportion of its residents serving in the army than any other. The system also violated individual equality in another respect: since the draft quotas were based on total population, "citizens in a community or neighborhood in which there were many aliens had to furnish not only their own proportion of conscripts, but supply the quota assessed against the considerable numbers of non-declarant aliens who were legally exempt."[33]

Ever since the First World War up to the introduction of an all-volunteer army in 1973, local draft boards have played a major role in deciding who would actually have to fight. Although con-

[30] Ibid., p. 46.
[31] Ibid., p. 187.
[32] Ibid., p. 142.
[33] Ibid., p. 227.

strained by central guidelines, these boards had considerable autonomy in deciding on inductions, exemptions, and deferments. In World War I, for instance, "disgruntled wives sometimes brought troublesome or abusive husbands to the board, urging (and often obtaining) their induction and the monthly family allotment."[34] Three other categories stand out as more important, however: farmers, fathers and husbands, and students. In World War I, draft boards had to be directed by the Selective Service Headquarters to accept more agricultural deferments.[35] In World War II, special interest groups got legislation passed that made the farm "a much safer place than the factory for an American during the Second World War."[36] Exemptions for married men and fathers were justified on several grounds. In World War I, as noted, the argument made for exempting married men was to avoid a drain on the budget. In the Second World War, the argument was made that the drafting of fathers would make the home "a potential prey of the philanderers."[37] In all these cases, however, the draft boards were free to make their own judgments. Although responsive in the aggregate to changes in the central guidelines, individual boards could and did ignore them if they wanted to.

The deferment of students was not an issue in the First World War, and not an important one in the Second.[38] In the Korean and Vietnam wars, however, the practice of deferring college students was increasingly seen as controversial. Since the Vietnam War will be fresh in the memories of many readers, I limit myself to a brief account of some fascinating and surprising debates during the Korean War period.

In 1950 a committee chaired by M. H. Trytten recommended a system for student deferment that would take account both of absolute and of relative abilities. "To be deferred, an undergraduate student would have to (1) score high enough on a general aptitude test to place him in the upper sixth of the general population; and (2) maintain a class rank in his school, among those

---

[34] Ibid., p. 236.
[35] Ibid., pp. 189–190.
[36] Blum, "Soldier or Worker," p. 150.
[37] Ibid., p. 149.
[38] Chambers, *To Raise an Army*, p. 233; Blum, "Soldier or Worker," p. 149.

qualified under (1), above a level specified by the director of Selective Service."[39] General Lewis B. Hershey, head of the Selective Service from 1942 to 1969, then proposed to switch from a conjunctive to a disjunctive principle (see Chapter 3 for this distinction). On the revised principle, a student who stood near the bottom of his class could qualify for deferment by scoring well on the test; and one failing to pass the test could still gain deferment by maintaining a high enough class standing in his school. As Dr. Trytten made clear in his comment on these changes (which he accepted), they would favor highly selective institutions (since most of their students would pass the absolute threshold), while also offering something for the less selective schools (as some of their students would satisfy the relative criterion).[40] Among the many protests aroused by the plan, the strongest came from the presidents of Harvard, Princeton, and Yale—not because they feared for the fate of elite colleges, but because the plan violated "the democratic principle of equality of sacrifice" and amounted to an "almost blanket deferment of college students." In the end, the plan was accepted, but with an amendment that for all practical purposes made it void of any practical significance. Although the President was authorized to establish deferment programs, the standards for deferments would be guidelines only, to be followed or not at the discretion of the local boards and the appeals system.

In later chapters I shall take a closer look at the various allocative principles used (or proposed) in choosing young men for military service. Here, however, I would like to mention that doing military service can be an independent as well as a dependent variable in issues of local justice, to explain who gets to be a citizen and who gets to vote. Non-citizens who fight in American wars

[39] Gerhardt, *The Draft and Public Policy*, p. 158. The following draws heavily on this exposition.

[40] The exact distribution of winners and losers, compared to the original proposal, would of course depend on the thresholds chosen. By establishing a very high absolute threshold and a low relative one, approximate equality for all schools could be achieved. By lowering the absolute threshold and raising the relative one (keeping in mind the need to meet a given target of inductions), elite schools would be favored, unless the absolute threshold was lowered so much that most students at non-elite schools would pass it.

have been rewarded with American citizenship.[41] At the Federal Convention in 1787, Benjamin Franklin "observed that in time of war a country owed much to the lower class of citizens. Our late war was an instance of what they could suffer and perform. If denied the right of suffrage it would debase their spirit and detach them from the interest of the country."[42] After 1865, "the war record of black soldiers bolstered the Republican argument that the Federal government must protect certain rights of citizens, such as the right to vote."[43] Historically, there are close connections between being a citizen, paying taxes, doing military service, and doing jury duty. Athenian citizens, for instance, were disenfranchised for cowardice in war and for unpaid debts to the state.[44] These connections were exploited during the Civil War, when "draft authorities had used the same jury wheels that were used to choose prospective jurors, thus symbolically joining these two obligations of citizenship,"[45] and then again in the First World War, when the head of the Selective Service System "decided to use the voter registration machinery to register the 10 million young men between the ages of 21 and 30, [to create] a symbolic demonstration of the connection between the right to vote and the obligation of military service."[46] There is a cluster of goods and burdens here that mutually support and explain each other.

Getting out of the army. Once you are in the army, it can matter when you get out. When a war is over, soldiers are eager to get back to civilian life. Yet for all sorts of reasons, it may not be possible to release everybody simultaneously. Who, then, should be allowed to leave the army first? The American army in World War II took this problem sufficiently seriously to design and implement a complicated point system.[47] Both the scheme and the method by which it was determined are of considerable interest.

A proposal to retain the combat fighting teams and to discharge

---

[41] Chambers, *To Raise an Army*, p. 231.
[42] Farrand (ed.), *The Records of the Federal Convention*, vol. II, p. 210.
[43] Ibid., p. 65.
[44] MacDowell, *The Law in Classical Athens*, pp. 160, 165.
[45] Chambers, *To Raise an Army*, p. 184.
[46] Ibid., p. 181.
[47] The following draws on Stouffer et al., *The American Soldier*, vol. II, ch. 11.

the service troops and the untrained soldiers was discarded in favor of an individualized system. To implement this idea, the army considered and then discarded a "first in, first out" system, preferring a scheme that took account of several factors. The scheme that was finally chosen accorded 1 point per month in the army, 1 point per month in overseas service, 5 points per campaign star or combat decoration, and 12 points per child under eighteen, up to three children.

To determine the variables and their weights, the army conducted large-scale surveys among the enlisted men. In one survey, the criteria were held up against each other in pairwise comparisons. In another, the respondents were asked to name the category of soldiers to be released first and the category to be released last. In a third survey they were given thumbnail descriptions of three soldiers, and asked who should be released first. The individual rankings showed a clear self-serving bias. For instance, the percentage saying that married men with children should be let out first was 60 among married men with children, 37 for married men without children, and 24 for single men. Self-interest was not the exclusive consideration, however: 24 percent among single men thought that preference should be given to married men with children.

The rankings showed some collective inconsistency. Thus, 55 percent thought that a married man with two children who had not seen combat should be released before a single man with two campaigns of combat; 52 percent rated 18 months overseas as more important than two children; and 60 percent rated two campaigns as worth more than 18 months overseas. Apropos this finding, the authors of *The American Soldier* wrote that "a high degree of internal consistency on such intricate hypothetical choices was hardly to be expected," thus suggesting that the problem was one of individually inconsistent rankings. If the majorities had added up to more than 200 percent, this suggestion would have been justified. As they add up only to 167 percent, it is quite possible that the rankings were individually consistent, and yet gave rise to a collective intransitivity, in the manner of the Condorcet paradox or Arrow's impossibility theorem (see Chapter 6 for further discussion).

Allocating kidneys. In the United States today, point systems are extensively used in allocating scarce organs for transplantation. I shall focus on the allocation of kidneys, but note that somewhat similar systems regulate the allocation of hearts and livers. Unlike problems concerning the latter organs, the allocation of kidneys is not a life-and-death issue, since patients denied transplantation can use dialysis as a fallback. Currently, about 120,000 Americans with end-stage renal disease (ESRD) are on dialysis. Of these, 18,000 are on the waiting list for transplantation. This figure is not, however, a good indicator of the real need for transplantation, partly because dialysis is mostly done in for-profit centers which have an incentive to keep patients on treatment and partly because many patients fail to understand the benefits of transplantation.[48] Each year, about 9,000 transplantations take place.

The allocation of kidneys, that is, the matching of an available kidney with a patient on the waiting list, is made under a number of medical constraints. First, the donor and the recipient must be of compatible blood types.[49] Second, the recipient must not have cytotoxic antibody formation against the donor kidney. This constraint can be severe, as some candidates for transplants have antibody formation against most kidneys in the population at large. These patients are referred to as "sensitized." Third, the recipient should be well matched to the donor, in the sense of having as many as possible of six antigens in common. Unlike the first two constraints, this is not an absolute one, but is a determi-

---

[48] Among the many reasons that patients on dialysis are reluctant to get on the waiting list for transplantation, the following stands out. When a transplantation fails, the patient usually goes back to the dialysis center where he or she was treated before the operation. Other patients at this center will tend to form an impression that transplantation has high failure rates, as they do not observe any successes. They fall victim, in other words, to the "availability heuristic" identified in Tversky and Kahneman, "Judgment under Uncertainty."

[49] In practice, this is interpreted as a requirement that they have the same blood type. Kidneys from blood type O donors can be used for recipients with any blood type, but blood type O recipients can use only kidneys from blood type O donors. Earlier, this led to blood type O patients receiving fewer kidneys. Recently, however, UNOS has laid down that kidneys from blood type O donors should go only to blood type O patients. This policy is based on equity considerations, not on medical reasons.

nant of the probability of success.[50] Last, donor and recipient should not be too far from the transplantation center, as organs deteriorate rapidly with time. This constraint is negligible, however, and will be ignored in the following.

Currently, the allocation of kidneys is regulated by the United Network for Organ Sharing (UNOS).[51] It is based on a scheme for allocating points to potential recipients of a donated kidney and then selecting the patient with the largest number of points. I shall describe only the parts of the scheme that are relevant for my concerns here.

First, patients receive points for their time on the waiting list. The candidate with the longest waiting time gets one point, while those with shorter tenure receive proportional fractions of a point. For each additional year beyond one year of waiting time 0.5 points will be awarded. This part of the scheme reflects the idea that all should have a chance of getting transplanted.

Second, they receive points—from 0 to 10—corresponding to the number of antigen matches (or, rather, of nonobserved mismatches). This part of the scheme embodies efficiency considerations.

Third, they receive 4 points for high "panel reactive antibody formation." As explained earlier, many patients have preformed antibodies that make them strictly unsuitable as recipients for particular kidneys. By medical necessity, antibody formation retains its exclusionary function in matching individual recipients with individual kidneys. In addition, however, the point allocation just described ensures that a low chance of ever finding a suitable kidney can offset low antigen matching when a suitable kidney is finally found. By giving extra weight to the patients who have the bad luck to be incompatible with most donated kidneys, it embodies considerations of equity. The same patients also tend to accumulate points from being on the waiting list. As they usually get some points from antigen matching as well,[52] their selection is

---

[50] Although the medical literature is divided, this statement appears to remain true even after the introduction of cyclosporin. See notably Opelz, "Allocation of Cadaver Kidneys for Transplantation."

[51] For a fuller description, see "UNOS Policy Regarding Utilization of the Point System for Cadaveric Kidney Allocation."

[52] Antibody formation and antigen matching do not vary independently

virtually ensured *if* a suitable kidney becomes available. (Note, however, that the more points they get from antibody formation, the bigger the if.)

This system, introduced in 1989, replaced one in which patients received up to 12 points for matching, up to 10 points for time on the waiting list, and up to 10 points for preformed antibody formation (depending on the percentage of kidneys in the overall population with which their antibodies make them incompatible). The import of the changes is described as follows: "The initial UNOS point system emphasized queuing whereas the proposed modifications stress good [antigen] matching ordered by queuing."[53] A better summary might be to say that, whereas the early system involved trade-offs between matching and waiting, the new system uses time on the waiting list as a tiebreaker.[54] Since ties are frequent, time on the list retains considerable importance.

The system—old or new—provides insurance against two forms of bad medical luck. One, just mentioned, is that of having a high panel antibody formation. This handicap is offset both by the waiting list and by explicitly awarding points for the antibodies. The other is that of having an unusual antigen pattern that makes it unlikely that one will ever achieve a good antigen match. If efficiency, that is, the number of antigen matches, was all that counted, patients with such patterns would stand a low chance. Adding points for time on the waiting list partially offsets that handicap. This compensation mechanism is especially important for black patients. For cultural and genetic reasons, blacks are overrepresented in the population of patients. For cultural reasons, blacks are underrepresented in the population of donors. Also, their antigen patterns are markedly different from those of

---

of each other. "Widely reacting cytotoxic antibodies often have specificity against the class 1 antigens of the A and B histocompatibility loci; because of this, the demonstration of a negative cytotoxic cross match for a highly sensitized patient should predict a good antigen match. Thus, the antibody and antigen credits tend to be reinforcing" (Starzl et al., "A Multifactorial System for Equitable Selection of Cadaver Kidney Recipients," p. 3075).

[53] "UNOS Policy Regarding Utilization," p. 31.

[54] Strictly speaking, however, the system is not lexicographic. Time on the waiting list can make a tie as well as break one. In practice, this happens infrequently.

the white population. Any scheme in which the number of anti-gen matches is the major determinant of selection would therefore work against them (see Chapter 4 for more details).

The point systems are used at three levels: national, regional, and local. A national waiting list is used to ascertain whether there is a patient that has perfect (six-antigen) matching with a kidney that becomes available. If there is one, that patient automatically gets the kidney, even if it has to be flown from Seattle to Miami. For less than perfect matches, a regional waiting list is used. Sometimes, however, the transplantation team that actually ex-tracts the kidneys can keep one of them for patients on its local waiting list. The use of local lists can affect efficiency, both posi-tively (by creating incentives for organ procurement) and nega-tively (by making it less likely that a good matching is found). Local lists can also have a negative impact on equity, by adding "geographical bad luck" to the medical bad luck that I mentioned earlier.

In later chapters I shall return to other aspects of the schemes for allocating kidneys and other organs, notably hearts and livers. With respect to the latter organs, the main tension does not seem to be between efficiency and equity. Rather, it arises between efficiency and a norm of medical ethic that I shall refer to as the "norm of compassion." What detracts from the most efficient use of these organs is not the principle that all those who need an organ should have a reasonable chance of getting one, but the natural inclination of doctors to give an organ to the patients most urgently in need of it.

Layoffs. Jobs are among the most basic goods. They are central sources of income, self-respect, and self-realization.[55] Allocation of jobs or, equivalently, selection of workers to fill slots takes place in three contexts: hiring, promotion, and layoffs. Of these, hiring and layoffs are the most important, since they can determine whether one shall hold a job at all. In private firms, hiring is marginal as an issue of local justice. Although private firms can be subject to discrimination constraints, they are under no obliga-

---

[55] For further discussion, see my "Is There (or Should There Be) a Right to Work?" and "Self-realization in Work and Politics."

tion to take account of the applicants' need, desert, or "seniority" (which in this case would be length of unemployment).

Layoffs are a different matter, as a job one actually holds differs in a number of respects from a job to which one merely aspires. There is a general "endowment effect" that makes people value an object in their possession more highly than the same object when not in their possession.[56] Closely related to this effect, there is a tendency for any status quo to harden into a property right.[57] More importantly, the objects are in fact different: a job that one actually occupies goes together with job-specific skills, relationship with colleagues, and other attributes that add to its value.

Substantial numbers of firms and workers are affected by layoffs, as indicated in the following data from the United States. During the period of 1981–1985, 5.1 million workers with three years or more of tenure on the job were displaced—2.8 million due to plant closings, 2.3 million due to layoff from continuing operations.[58] A survey conducted by the American Management Association found that 34.9 percent of the companies surveyed engaged in some form of work force reduction in 1988, with half of these downsizings affecting more than 10 percent of the company's work force.[59]

In unionized firms, layoffs are regulated by collective bargaining agreements. To some extent, nonunionized firms mimic the practices of unionized firms, in order to avoid unionization, maintain worker morale so that short-term efficiency is not impaired, and preserve the firm's reputation as a fair employer.[60] Collective bargaining agreements usually specify seniority and ability as the main factors in determining who is to be laid off. There are two basic types of clauses. In one, it is specified that seniority shall govern as long as the senior person slated to be

---

[56] Thaler, "Towards a Positive Theory of Consumer Choice." See also Houseman, "Allocating the Costs of Economic Change."

[57] Zajac, "Perceived Economic Justice."

[58] Hammermesh, "What Do We Know about Worker Displacement in the U.S.?"

[59] Greenberg, "Downsizing and Worker Assistance."

[60] Abraham and Medoff, "Length of Service and Layoffs in Union and Nonunion Work Groups."

retained possesses sufficient ability to do the job.[61] The second type states that seniority governs only when the people being considered for retention are relatively equal in ability. Conflicts arise because the union tends to interpret "ability" and "sufficient ability" so as to maximize the importance of seniority in the layoff decision, whereas the firm is mainly concerned with productivity. Here is a representative example:

> The Union disputed the manner in which the Company evaluates skill and ability. In particular, the Company viewed the junior employee as having the greatest ability simply because he worked the fastest—he was the most productive. Here, the "skill" is not knowledge of complicated electrical machinery or the ability to perform an intricate procedure. It is simply "how fast you screw the bolts on," so to speak. The Union, in disputing this, highlighted a contract clause which forbids "piece work," their opinion being that this system of evaluation was tantamount to a piecework system. The Company pointed to a contract clause which reserved to itself the right to evaluate "ability." The arbitrator agreed with the Company and denied the grievance.[62]

Almost all firms are subject to federal legislation, notably Title VII of the Civil Rights Act of 1964, which offers protection for women and ethnic minorities, and the Age Discrimination in Employment Act. Title VII explicitly protects bona fide seniority systems formulated without intent to discriminate from being called into question under the Act. However, this left unsettled the issue of how to characterize a bona fide system and how to establish intent to discriminate. Over time, the conservative trend in the courts has established a strong protection for seniority systems. One early case involved a departmental seniority system that perpetuated the effects of a previously segregated work force by giving blacks little opportunity to be promoted out of their less desir-

---

[61] One would expect that the senior person would of necessity possess sufficient ability to perform his current job. However, during a restructuring of the workplace, many positions are being eliminated, and those retained may be moved into new positions.

[62] Leach Manufacturing, Inc., and International Brotherhood of Boilermakers, Iron Ship Builders, Blacksmiths, Forgers, and Helpers Local 583 (79 LA 1251). I quote from the summary in Romm, "Local Justice and Layoffs."

able jobs.[63] In this case, the judge ruled that perpetuation of prior intentional discrimination was sufficient to establish a violation of Title VII. However, in today's more conservative legal climate courts will not accept the argument that the disparate impact of a facially neutral system perpetuates prior discrimination committed by others.[64]

The "disparate impact" theory, under which an employment practice violates Title VII if it has a differential effect on a protected group and has no valid business justification, was generalized and legitimized by the Supreme Court in 1971 in *Griggs* v. *Duke Power Co.*[65] Subsequent to *Griggs*, some lower courts applied the disparate impact theory to seniority systems in ruling that they violated Title VII, while other lower courts emphasized the protection given to seniority systems under Title VII. In general, plantwide seniority in cases involving layoffs was more likely to be found to be protected than departmental seniority systems in cases involving promotions.[66] In 1977, the Supreme Court resolved this issue in *Teamsters* v. *U.S.* by in effect immunizing seniority systems from disparate impact claims.[67] Currently, to show that a seniority system violates the Act, one must show that it is not bona fide, that is, establish intent to discriminate. Complex departmental systems are more likely to be set aside, as intent can be inferred from the construction of a patchwork system that serves no ratio-

---

[63] *Local 189 United Papermakers and Paperworkers* v. *United States,* decided by the Fifth Circuit in 1969 (416 F.2d 980).

[64] See, for example, the Fifth Circuit's 1984 decision in *Salinas* v. *Roadway Express,* 35 FEP Cases 533, or the Eleventh Circuit's 1983 decision in *Freeman* v. *Motor Convoy,* 31 FEP Cases 517.

[65] 401 U.S. 424.

[66] Circuit Courts of Appeal in the immediate post-*Griggs* period tended to view plantwide last-hired, first-fired systems as protected. See, for example, *Jersey Central Power and Light* v. *Electrical Workers Local 327 et al.* (508 F.2d 687; 3rd Circuit, 1975) and *Watkins* v. *Steelworkers Local 2369* (516 F.2d 41; 5th Circuit, 1975). However, on the District Court level one can find liberal decisions based on the disparate impact/perpetuation of prior discrimination argument with respect to plantwide systems. See, for example, *Schaefer* v. *Tannian* (394 F.Supp. 1136) and *Delay* v. *Carling Brewing Co.* (10 FEP Cases 164). However, departmental seniority systems were in general not viewed favorably by courts on either level.

[67] 431 U.S. 324.

nal business purpose.[68] Segregation of black and white employees into two separate progressions can also result in a finding that the system is not bona fide.[69] Failure to grant female or minority employees the same seniority benefits as white males of equal tenure constitutes the clearest violation, but such practices do not call into question the seniority system itself, only the actions of those who administer it.[70]

In a layoff situation, the firm's preference does not simply reduce to a desire to retain the most productive workers. It also has an incentive to get rid of the more expensive—that is, more highly paid—employees. Sometimes, higher pay results simply from seniority, which is correlated with age. Therefore, some older employees singled out for layoffs have claimed protection under the Age Discrimination in Employment Act. The legal situation is not settled, but it seems that courts are more likely to find against the firm if the older employee is replaced by a young one doing the same job, than if the position is eliminated altogether. In fact, interviews with labor relations specialists indicate that firms often will use a layoff situation to redesign their operation, so that they can get rid of inefficient or highly paid employees by eliminating their positions.

In later chapters I shall return to the seniority principle in layoff situations to suggest that its widespread use may be due to the fact that it is preferred by employers (at least in unionized companies) no less than by workers. In most Western societies seniority has a central position.[71] Many, however, also accord great importance to a principle that has no explicit standing in the American context, namely, to retain the employees who have the largest *need* for the job, as measured by number of family dependents.[72]

[68] See, for example, the Tenth Circuit's 1981 decision in Sears v. Atchinson, 645 F.2d 1365.
[69] See, for example, the 1981 decision of a Georgia District Court in Miller v. Continental Can Co., 544 F.Supp. 210.
[70] See, for example, the 1981 decision of a Wisconsin District Court in Wattleton v. Ladish Co., 520 F.Supp. 1329.
[71] Italy, however, seems to be an exception. See Golden, "A Comparative Inquiry into Systems for Allocating Job Loss."
[72] The disregard for need in the American context is a recent phenomenon. In the 1934 White House Settlement issued by a conference called by President Roosevelt to avoid a strike in the automobile industry, it is said that "the

The procedural principle of seniority is often tempered by the substantive principle of ability, but it can also, as in many European countries, be modified by the substantive principle of need. By contrast, race, sex, and age matter only negatively, in that employers are *not* allowed to use them when selecting workers to be laid off.

Access to higher education. In all countries, some institutions of higher education are based on selective admission. When admission is open rather than selective, the explanation is usually one of the following facts. First, demand is at or below capacity (including the case where capacity is expanded to match demand). Second, students are admitted beyond what capacity justifies, creating in effect substandard education. Third, open admission is combined with selection at the end of the first year.[73] I have personal experience with the first two cases, as a student in Oslo in the 1960s and as a teacher at the Université de Paris VIII (better known as Vincennes) in the 1970s. The third case is observed, for instance, in French medical schools.

An intermediate case between open and selective admission arises when we are dealing with a system or network of institutions, which collectively ensures that all applicants will be accepted somewhere, but not necessarily at the place of their first choice. In Hofstee's terminology, we are then dealing with a placement system, which can give rise to problems of local justice if the available places vary in quality or, more generally, in desirability. In Germany, for instance, placement is used in certain

> non-selective subjects, in which the total number of university places that are available at the federal level, is sufficient to admit all applicants, although demand exceeds supply at *some* universities, due to fixed admissions contingents. If not all applicants can be admitted at the university of their choice, the Central Office for the Allocation of Places in Higher Education places some of them in another university. The criteria used in this (computerized) dis-

---

industry understands that in reduction or increases of force, such human relationships as married men with families shall come first and then seniority, individual skill and efficient service" (quoted after Gersuny and Kaufman, "Seniority and the Moral Economy of U.S. Automobile Workers," p. 463).

[73] For a discussion of this alternative to selective admissions, see Klitgaard, *Choosing Elites*, p. 58 ff.

tribution process are all non-academic. First disabled applicants are admitted, then those whose spouse or children already live at the locality in question, next the candidates who—due to health problems, social responsibilities or economic difficulties—can claim "a privileged consideration of their first preference," and finally students who choose to stay with their parents and who therefore want to study at the nearest university. After selection on the basis of this formula all other applicants to the university in question are considered for any remaining places. Applicants can list up to five additional universities, ranked in order of preference, to facilitate the placement process if their first preference cannot be met. If none of their stated preferences can be satisfied, the Central Office selects a university not explicitly mentioned in the application, using spatial distance to the most preferred university as the selection criterion. Subjects included in this placement procedure are geology, computer science, economics, and law.[74]

Admission to selective colleges in the United States would seem to fall into a very different pattern, as colleges have virtually full autonomy in deciding which applicants to accept. Indirectly and in the aggregate, however, some of the features of a placement system may obtain.[75] Most students apply to several colleges. I conjecture (there is no information on this topic) that the great majority of applicants to selective colleges are accepted by one of them. Because applicants know their own ability and, at least roughly, the ability requirements of the various colleges they consider, self-selection will ensure that most applicants get in somewhere.[76] Exceptions would be those who, because of unrealistic expectations, apply only to schools well above their ability level, including those whose ability is so low that they will not be accepted by any selective institution.[77]

[74] Adapted from Schmidt, "Local Justice in West Germany."
[75] Two valuable studies of student admissions in this perspective are Thresher, *College Admission and the Public Interest* and McPherson and Shapiro, *Selective Admission and the Public Interest.*
[76] As one director of admissions put it in his reply to a questionnaire I sent out: "Whereas each of the nation's selective colleges must, as a function of size, turn down more than they admit (the definition of 'selective'), the *pool* of candidates is well-served, in my experience."
[77] In this system, nobody is penalized (except for the admissions fee) for applying to schools above their ability, as long as they also apply to some schools within their ability range. In centralized placement systems, where

From the point of view of the institution, however, the question is perceived as one of selection—not as an admission or a placement problem. Each year, there are over 1.5 million applicants to all kinds of colleges in the United States. In 1987, 133 four-year doctoral-granting public institutions received on average 7,807 applicants, and accepted 66 percent. The 116 similar private institutions received on average somewhat fewer applications, and admitted a somewhat lower percentage. The 238 private liberal arts colleges received an average of 1,401 applications, and accepted 61 percent. About 10 percent of all four-year institutions accept less than 50 percent of their applicants; 33 percent accept between 50 and 75 percent; 53 percent accept between 75 and 99 percent, while only 4 percent practice open admission. The process as a whole, in other words, is selective but not severely so. At the most selective colleges, however, only 20 percent or less of the applicants are admitted. In other cases, strict eligibility criteria probably deter many from even applying. In general, the importance of self-selection cannot be stressed too much.

The admissions criteria for selective colleges vary too much to allow for a concise summary. Also, some admission operations are shrouded in considerable secrecy, and described to the public in what I assume to be deliberately vague terms. Nevertheless, some rough types can be identified. A first distinction is between colleges that consider only or mainly academic criteria of various kinds, and those that also consider other aspects of the applicants. In the former category, the main criteria are test scores, high school grades, and class rank in high school. To assign weights to these criteria, it is common to regress them against grades at the end of the first year and then use the regression coefficients as weights.

---

applicants have to rank schools according to their order of preference, a second-rate student who lists a first-rate school as his first preference may end up in a third-rate one, whereas he would have been accepted by a second-rate school had he listed it first. Formerly, applicants to high schools in Oslo and to the University of California campuses had to face this strategic problem, which still confronts applicants to the *classes préparatoires aux Grandes Ecoles* in France. Other examples of systems with this property are given in Roth, "The Evolution of the Labor Market for Medical Interns and Residents," pp. 1001–1002. See Chapter 4 for a more thorough discussion of these incentive effects.

Other schools also take account of nonacademic criteria, usually for the stated purpose of promoting "diversity" of some sort. Their practices fall into two sharply different categories. Stanford, for example, lists among their criteria for undergraduate admissions "personal achievements outside the classroom in a wide range of pursuits including academic activities, the creative and performing arts, community service and leadership, athletics and other extracurricular areas." Although these criteria are described as "secondary" compared to the "primary" criterion of academic excellence, they are clearly intended to serve as more than tie-breakers. There are, in other words, trade-offs between academic and nonacademic achievements. In larger schools extra-academic achievements are often rated and formally traded off against an index of academic achievements, whereas smaller schools tend to proceed in a more discretionary manner. Even when explicit trade-offs are made, however, admissions officers insist that they are used as an aid and guide to individualized judgment, not as a substitute for it.

In other schools, academic achievements are traded off against handicaps, membership in an underrepresented minority, and general economic disadvantage. Whereas Stanford may admit an applicant with a mediocre academic record (by Stanford applicant standards) if he or she has won national recognition as a violinist, the Univerity of California at Los Angeles might do the same if the applicant comes from a low-income family or is of black or Hispanic origin. Economic disadvantage is considered for several different reasons.[78] Admission officers believe that applicants should not be penalized for lack of resources and information that is effectively beyond their control. Also, they may believe that academic indicators lack predictive validity for applicants from a disadvantaged background, and that the ability to overcome hardship shows a strong motivation or other valuable traits.

With respect to minority applicants, many public institutions are caught between the decision of the Supreme Court in the Bakke case and affirmative action programs of their state legislatures. In the Bakke decision,[79] the Court decided that racial quotas

---

[78] See below, pp. 107–108, for a more formal discussion.
[79] 98 S. Ct. 2733 (1978).

were unconstitutional. Although membership of a minority might count as a "plus," it could not be allowed to be "decisive." Even after Bakke some institutions continued to admit every underrepresented minority student meeting minimal requirements. Other schools use "flexible targets," goals for the proportion of various ethnic groups in the overall freshman class. Still other schools use point systems in which minority membership *is* counted only as a plus. Unlike the two other systems, this procedure is at least consistent with the letter of Bakke. It does, however, raise the question whether the weights assigned to minority membership in the admissions process are chosen independently of the expected number of minority students that will be admitted using those weights. If they are truly independent, so that the chips are allowed to fall where they may, the spirit of Bakke is also inviolate. But if the weights assigned to minority membership (or to highly correlated variables such as economic disadvantage) are adjusted so as to yield a target number of minority students, we are in effect dealing with a disguised quota system.

Child-related allocation processes. Allocative decisions involving children have a special poignancy. Children are uniquely important to their parents, and uniquely worthy of protection in their own right. I shall briefly touch on four issues of local justice that involve children: the allocation of sperm for artificial insemination; the matching of children for adoption and parents seeking to adopt a child; the award of custody in divorce cases; and the admission of children to kindergarten.

The allocation of sperm in France[80] is organized by three different organizations, which follow somewhat different principles. Here, I limit myself to the largest and most restrictive, a network of 20 "Centres d'étude et de conservation de sperme." The organization imposes constraints on donors, on recipients, and on matches. Donors must be married; they must be fathers; and not be bearers of genetically inheritable diseases. In the spirit of the last condition one has decided that donors should not be paid, on the assumption that payment would create an incentive to hide

---

[80] The description of this system is taken from Herpin, "Le don de sperme."

any features that might lead to rejection.[81] Another argument is that paying donors might induce them to seek out several centers, with a subsequent risk of marriage between children from women who received sperm from the same donor. Recipients, too, must be married. Preferential treatment is accorded to women who can bring a donor along as well as to those who already have one child. (However, those who have two children are sometimes refused admission to the waiting list.) With these exceptions, women are treated in the order of inscription. Matches are constrained by ethnicity, blood type, and, more flexibly, by morphological features such as eye color.

Adoption is a more widespread and complex phenomenon. Around 1980, it was estimated that about 2 percent of the child population in the United States had been adopted.[82] Most of these were adopted by close relatives, and hence do not present problems of allocative justice. Among the rest—about one third of all adoptions, to judge by data from 1982[83]—two such issues arise. On the one hand, there is a group of infants—healthy white babies—who are in great demand, so that a severe screening of adoptive parents is needed. It has been estimated that there are forty white couples waiting for every available healthy, white infant. The eligibility criteria adopted by adoption agencies (which may be private or public) vary, but typically tend to exclude people above the age of forty, single parents, low-income families, and couples where the woman intends to go on working after placement.[84] In addition, social workers make discretionary judg-

---

[81] A similar argument has been made with regard to blood donation. For a discussion, see Arrow, "Gifts and Exchanges."

[82] Wingard, "Trends and Characteristics of California Adoptions: 1964–1982," p. 303.

[83] National Committee on Adoption, *Adoption Factbook*, p. 110 ff.

[84] There are many exceptions to these statements. In California, for instance, 10 percent of the 1,501 adoptions mediated by public agencies in 1981–1982 were to single parents. The difference between this practice and the exclusion of single women as recipients of sperm is easily understood. Once a child is born, it may be better off with a single parent than in a foster home, assuming that an adoptive couple is not forthcoming. But when it is a question of deciding about children yet unborn, the scarcity of sperm, together with a general presumption that children are better off with two parents than with only one, justifies restriction of sperm to couples. Were sperm abundant, this restriction could be justified only on the implausible

ments about various emotional and personality characteristics. On the other hand, handicapped infants and nonwhite infants are in excess supply, and often do not find adoptive parents. The latter problem is exacerbated by use of the same stringent demands that are used to screen families seeking healthy white children. As many children would be better off with above-forty parents or with a single parent than in a succession of foster homes, the best can become the enemy of the good.[85]

Two difficult issues are matching on grounds of religion and race. Some agencies (and some states) require the adoptive parents to be of the same religion as the biological mother. Also, some agencies are themselves religiously based and require applicants to share their faith. In the case of foundlings, some agencies formerly assigned a religion to the child, usually on a rotational basis.[86] Whether the agency insists on one particular religion, on respect for the religion of the mother, or simply on the need to match some arbitrarily chosen denomination, the result is to limit the number of adoptive parents and lengthen the process of adoption, to the detriment of the nonreligious interests of the child. For one thing, children become less "adoptable" as they grow older; for another, the period of waiting in a foster home is itself an undesirable situation. Matching on basis of race is even more controversial. Although the Supreme Court has decided that race cannot be the decisive factor in child placement, and some states (California and Montana) forbid racial matching as a basis for delay in adoption placements, there is still great resistance to transracial adoption. The National Association of Black Social Workers claims that "the placement of Black children in white homes [is]

---

assumption that it is better not to be born than to be the child of a single mother. Yet, as shown by Herpin ("Le don de sperme," p. 143), the reason French doctors limit sperm to couples is that they insist that artificial insemination is a medical act, intended to treat masculine sterility, rather than a personal choice unrelated to medical reasons. It would be interesting to see if this argument would survive were sperm to become abundant.

[85] See Fellner, "Recruiting Adoptive Applicants."

[86] Fellner, ibid., reports that in New York City this practice was in force until 1967. It can obviously not be justified by the needs of the child, since on those grounds one could have done better by simply requiring that the adoptive parents belong to some religious denomination. The only reason I can imagine is a desire to allocate children fairly among all denominations.

a hostile act against our community. It is a blatant form of race and cultural genocide."[87] There is, however, a surplus of black children not absorbed by the black community, due to the fact that black couples adopt infrequently, either because they view formal adoption as "institutionalized slavery" or because they are deterred by the lengthy and intrusive application process.[88]

Child custody award is not a case of local justice *stricto sensu*, being decided either by private bargaining or by the courts, rather than by administrative agencies. Here I focus on legal custody decisions.[89] These decisions stand, roughly speaking, in the same relation to adoption decisions as firing decisions stand to hiring decisions. To lose a job or to lose custody of a child is a more traumatic experience than to be refused a job or to be turned down for adoption. (However, the cumulative impact of a number of refusals may equal that of a single loss.)

Currently, child custody law in most Western societies stipulates that custody should follow the interest of the child. If it would be better for the child to be with the mother, she should have custody; if the child would be better off with the father, he should be the custodial parent. Other principles have included a presumption for paternal custody; a presumption for maternal custody; a presumption against the guilty party to the divorce, guilt being defined as adultery or desertion; and awarding custody to the parent who has had main responsibility for the child during marriage. It has also been proposed to decide custody by the toss of a coin and to let parental needs play some role in deciding custody.

As in adoption cases, the perfectionist search for an arrangement that is in the best interest of the child may work against the interest of the child. All allocative processes involve some costs, the minimization of which is one of many considerations that go into the choice of one procedure rather than another (Chapter 5). Usually, these are costs to be born by the administrative agency. Sometimes, however, different procedures impose different costs

[87] Merritt, Testimony to Senate Committee on Labor and Human Resources.

[88] In this paragraph I have drawn heavily on Toft, "Adoption as an Issue of Local Justice."

[89] The following draws on Chapter 3 of my *Solomonic Judgements*.

on the potential recipients or, more generally, potential beneficiaries. A doctor who has to choose which of many severely
wounded patients to treat first should not spend too much time
deciding on relative needs, lest they start dying on him before he
has even begun treatment. Similarly, protracted court proceedings
to decide which parent is more fit for custody may impose harm
and suffering on the child that more than offset the gains. One
lesson could be that a more robust principle, such as the maternal
presumption rule, is preferable to fine-tuning. "Simplicity is the
ultimate sophistication in deciding a child's placement."[90]

Adoption and child custody decisions involve the welfare of
parents no less than that of children, and are made in a constant
tension between these two considerations. This tension is also
manifest in the process of deciding which children should get a
place in kindergarten when such places are scarce. In Norway,[91]
the admission process to municipal kindergartens is largely decentralized. The ministry for consumer affairs has laid down a few
general principles, but the only hard constraint (and even that is
sometimes violated) is that handicapped children shall have priority. Some local variations are the following: (1) Some municipalities try to achieve universal but limited coverage by imposing
upper limits on the time that any one child can stay in kindergarten. (2) Some municipalities give priority to children of municipal
employees or, more specifically, to children of kindergarten teachers. (3) Some give priority to various categories of children whose
parents have special needs, such as children of low-income parents, children of single parents, children of students, and children
in families where both parents have to work. (4) Some give priority to various categories of children with special needs, including older children, children with few opportunities for play, and
children from homes that are disadvantaged in some respect.
(5) Sometimes, there are formal trade-offs between parental needs
and the needs of children. Thus, at the kindergarten of the Student Association in Oslo, admission is regulated by a point system
where both the age of the child and the number of years of study
of the parents are taken into account. (6) In some cases, children

---

[90]Goldstein, Freud, and Solnit, *Before the Best Interests of the Child*, p. 116.
[91]The following draws heavily on Rasch, "Barnas Beste?"

are admitted to create a balanced composition in the kindergarten as a whole, even if that child would not have been admitted on other criteria. A frequently cited consideration is the need to avoid too great a concentration of children of single parents, the argument being that children of that category will in fact benefit from the mix.

In these cases—adoption, custody, kindergarten admission—it is often hard to draw the line between parental interests, needs, and rights and those of children.[92] Children have an interest in the happiness (and in the income) of their parents, and parents in the happiness of their children. To the extent that these interests can be separated from each other (and they often can), decision makers find themselves in an uncomfortable situation. On the one hand, the law usually tells them to decide in the light of the interests of the child. On the other hand, the advocates of the various options tend to be the parents, and it would be unrealistic to disregard the tendency of their arguments to be shaped by their own interests. The situations invite dissembling, hypocrisy, and bitter jealousy.

Household tasks. The preceding remark applies even more strongly to the allocation of household tasks, such as taking care of children, maintaining and cleaning the house and other property, shopping, and preparing meals. The decision can be imposed unilaterally, by a selfish, malevolent, or benevolent family dictator. Or the parents may negotiate an agreement and impose it on the children. Or the allocation may be decided by negotiations involving parents as well as children, opening up the possibility of coalition formation. Since there is little hard information about the procedures by which such agreements are reached or about their content, the following comments are based largely on casual observation. They take the form of enumerating various arguments, objections, and dilemmas that arise even in the best of marriages, and can accelerate the breakdown of not-so-good marriages.

As far as possible, allocative solutions ought to combine equity

---

[92] I mention in passing that the same argument applies at the other extremity of life. Admission to a nursing home may be as good for the children as well as, or as much as, for the applicant.

and efficiency. In the present context, equity is most easily interpreted as equality of time spent on household tasks. Given the constraint of equality, efficiency is then most naturally interpreted as allocation of tasks according to each family member's comparative advantage. This combined proposal gives rise, however, to a number of problems.

Some tasks are less desirable than others. Cleaning the toilet bowl is less attractive than setting the table for breakfast. Mowing the lawn or clearing the road of snow takes more effort than sewing on a shirt button. Queuing in the supermarket is more boring than reading stories to the children. One obvious solution is to take turns, but this procedure may reduce efficiency by violating the principle of comparative advantage. Another solution is to weigh tasks according to their desirability, with negative weights being assigned to the activities that the person would rather do than not do (cooking often falls in this category). That proposal, however, immediately runs into some well-known difficulties (further discussed in Chapter 4). For one thing, it gives each family member an incentive to overstate the effort or pain involved in the task for which he or she has a comparative advantage, and to hide the fact that there are some household tasks that he or she actually enjoys doing. For another, and even if we assume that no preference revelation problems exist, the proposal presupposes the possibility of comparing the utility or disutility of different individuals, a notoriously difficult and controversial operation.

Preferences, in fact, enter doubly into this process. First, as just mentioned, family members have different preferences with respect to the household production process; secondly, their preferences can differ with respect to the product which results from the process. Assume that one spouse hates cleaning the house, but loves to have a clean house, while the other spouse has the opposite set of preferences. If they love each other, the second spouse will do the cleaning without complaining. If concerns for justice intrude into their love, he or she may well say to the other: "Since you're the one who insists on the house being impeccably clean, you cannot expect me to do all the work." Indeed, it may be sufficient if the second spouse can credibly express a lack of interest in a clean house, even if he or she secretly hates dirt.

Perhaps both spouses really would like a clean house, but neither dares to say so because of a fear that he or she will then be left to do the cleaning; as a result, both are worse off.[93] The truly asymmetric case combines the difficulties of this collective action problem with those of a bargaining problem.[94] Although there are many allocations of cleaning activities (with corresponding levels of cleanliness) that would make both spouses better off than if no cleaning was ever done, the fact that they rank them differently may prove an obstacle to agreement.

Also, some family members are better at some tasks than are other members, a fact that is reflected in the idea that tasks should be allocated according to comparative advantage. Sometimes, however, the differences may be so large that absolute advantage appears as a more reasonable criterion. If tasks are carried out by the members who are best at them, total time spent on household tasks in the family is minimized. Although this may lead to an unequal distribution of time (or utility-weighted time), the welfare of the family as a whole is enhanced. To the extent that family life is based on love rather than on a concern for justice, such unequal allocations may be forthcoming spontaneously. And because family life is supposed to be based on love, even when it is not, appeals to justice by the more competent person may be met by the argument that justice is a mean virtue that displays a calculating attitude which is out of place in the context of the family. Similarly, a person who claims household credits for reading stories to the children may be met with the argument that parents who really love their children would do so spontaneously rather than use the activity as a bargaining chip.

Furthermore, time, even utility-weighted time, may not be the right criterion at all. Opportunity costs also have to be considered. In families with small children and two parents working full-time, there can be large opportunity costs associated with staying home from work when a child is too sick to go to nursery school. Also, the weight of responsibility for planning the activities and finances of the household is not easily measured in hours and minutes, although it may represent much more of a burden than do routine household chores.

[93] I elaborate on this point in *The Cement of Society*, p. 127.
[94] For a discussion of such cases see Chapter 4 of *The Cement of Society*.

The relationship between work in the household and work out-side it also matters. The principle of equal time might be inter-preted as equal total time, including both job and home. A spouse who works a great deal of overtime may claim the right to do less in the house, at least if he or she can credibly present the job as inherently boring and unrewarding. A spouse that earns a high income as, say, a lawyer, may insist on using part of that income to buy household equipment and employ a cleaning person. He or she may even insist on getting credit from the whole reduction, arguing that "Since it is *my* income that enables us to employ a cleaning person, the time you save on scrubbing the floors should be used to take over my shopping duties," to which the other may reply that "You would never have gotten through law school if I had not taken a job to support us," or "I do not want our children to get used to the idea that there will always be others to clean up after them." If unhappy marriages include those in which justice has taken the place of love, the stratagems deployed to shift household work onto the other spouse serve to confirm a well-known dictum by Tolstoy: "All happy families resemble one another, each unhappy family is unhappy in its own way."

Allocation of prison space. The judiciary and penal systems create a number of local justice problems. First, there is a problem of allocating limited police attention. Since not all crimes that are reported can be investigated, at least not with equal thorough-ness, some priorities must be set.[95] Second, the limited capacity of the courts requires a conscious decision as to which cases are to be adjudicated first. Finally, limited prison capacity forces deci-sions about the allocation of prison space among sentenced crimi-nals. All three problems could, at least in theory, be resolved on a first-come, first-served basis. In practice, however, this is not a satisfactory solution. There is wide agreement that serious crimes should be treated differently from less serious ones. Yet what crimes *are* serious? And *how* should they be treated? Here I shall summarize some of the literature on the allocation of prison space, conceived as a scarce good.

In the United States, prison overcrowding has become a severe problem over the last few decades. On the one hand, many states

[95] See, for instance, "For Police, a Delicate Job of Reordering Priorities," *New York Times*, October 28, 1990.

passed laws to restrict parole discretion and to increase prison terms for certain offenders; in some states increased prosecutorial capacity also caused dramatic increases in incarceration rates. On the other hand, legislatures were unwilling to provide the funds needed to build new prisons,[96] and sometimes construction was obstructed by local reluctance to host a prison facility. With an expanding population of prisoners serving longer terms and a prison capacity that failed to keep up with demand, trouble was inevitable. In 1980, the Illinois Department of Correction "faced what seemed to be an endless barrage of over 1,000 lawsuits protesting every conceivable condition of confinement including the practice of double celling."[97] In 1984, thirty-three states were facing court intervention in at least one of their major penal institutions.[98] Although the Supreme Court had decided, in Justice Rehnquist's words, that there is no "'one man, one cell' principle lurking in the Due Process Clause,"[99] there were many avenues of litigation left to explore.[100] In addition, overcrowding was causing prison riots and untenable working conditions for the prison staff.

Under these circumstances many states were forced to introduce early release schemes. In Illinois between 1980 and 1982, offenders with good behavior in prison could receive up to 90 days' "good-time credits" *on any given day.* Prisoners who were approaching the end of their sentence received credits if many new arrivals were expected in the near future, but prisoners were also awarded credits at other times as part of long-term planning. Some offenders had their sentence reduced by more than 800 days; the average reduction was 105 days or, on average, 12.5 percent of the sentence.[101] Nearly two-thirds of the inmates benefited from this policy. The program was initially reserved for offenders with no prior record of violence, but was later extended to cover other categories as well. The overall profile of those re-

[96] This unwillingness is often portrayed as due to sheer myopia or irrationality; and perhaps it was. Some legislators, however, may have believed that the deterrence effect of harsher sentences would reduce the number of crimes so much that existing prisons would suffice.

[97] Austin, "Using Early Release to Relieve Prison Crowding," p. 405.

[98] Lane, "The Case for Early Release," pp. 400–401.

[99] 441 U.S. 520 (1979), p. 542.

[100] Angelos and Jacobs, "Prison Overcrowding and the Law."

[101] Details in Austin, "Using Early Release to Relieve Prison Crowding."

leased early differed nevertheless from the remaining third, in being disproportionately convicted of nonviolent crimes, being housed in minimum or medium security at release, and having no history of disciplinary segregation in prison. If we look at their behavior after release, they also commit fewer dangerous crimes.

Indirectly, therefore, the early release program allocated prison space according to the principle of selective incapacitation. In addition to the non-consequentialist principle of desert, sentencing has been justified by one of several consequentialist principles: rehabilitation (including individual deterrence), general deterrence, and selective incapacitation (protecting society from dangerous criminals by keeping them in prison).[102] In the face of increasing disillusionment over the first two, various proposals have been made to turn the last into the basic principle of sentencing. Models have been developed to predict likelihood of recidivism as a function of various properties of the criminal and the crime.[103] Even if such models predicted perfectly, their use in actual sentencing would offend our notions of justice: we would not want to let a murderer go free even if we were sure that he would never harm anyone again. And since the models actually predict far from perfectly, the risk of false positives—imposing a long sentence on someone who in fact would not have been a risk to society—poses an insuperable ethical obstacle to the proposal. We may, however, use selective incapacitation as a criterion for reducing the sentence. "In [this] scenario it also is the case that false positives will be punished more harshly than will those selected for release based on the selection device. The critical distinction is that they will not be punished more harshly than they would have been had the device—and prediction—not been used."[104] Like the laborers of the first hour, these false positives cannot complain if others obtain a good to which none can claim a right.[105]

Immigration. American immigration policy is complex, contro-

---

[102] Gottfredson and Gottfredson, "Selective Incapacitation?" p. 136.

[103] Details in Austin, "Using Early Release to Relieve Prison Crowding," p. 470 ff. and in Gottfredson and Gottfredson, "Selective Incapacitation?" p. 139 ff.

[104] Gottfredson and Gottfredson, "Selective Incapacitation?" p. 148.

[105] See also Feinberg, "Noncomparative Justice."

versial, and constantly changing.[106] The most recent revision of the system was enacted in November 1990. Before that, the system had undergone large overhauls in 1965, 1952, 1921, and 1882, as well as a steady stream of small and medium-sized revisions. The numbers involved are considerable. In 1980, the United States admitted about twice as many immigrants as the rest of the world combined.[107] The 1990 changes will raise annual immigration from about 490,000 a year to a projection of 700,000 during the first three years and 675,000 thereafter. Many more would like to be admitted. In 1986, 10,000 visas were provided on a first-come, first-served basis to countries that were disadvantaged by the 1965 reforms (see below). The offer generated more than 1 million applications. In 1987, 20,000 visas were provided for similar purposes by a computerized randomizing mechanism, generating 3.2 million applications.

Over time, American immigration policy has undergone two major changes. First, the reforms of the early 1920s transformed immigration from an admission-based system into a selection-based one. Prior to 1921, immigration policy was regulated by a number of pure and impure admissions procedures. Criminals, paupers, and bearers of various handicaps or diseases were excluded on the grounds that these would be undesirable citizens. (In the colonial period there had also been exclusion of Catholics, for similar reasons.) By contrast, head taxes and literacy tests were used largely to keep down the total number of immigrants and, especially, immigrants from Southern and Eastern Europe. In addition, there was a blanket ban on (almost all) immigration from China and by Chinese persons. Although most of these exclusionary principles were kept on after the reforms, they were now embedded within a system of quotas by national origin. In the final version, effective from 1929 onward, a total of 150,000 immigrant slots were to be allocated among countries (outside the Western Hemisphere) proportionally to their 1920 representation in the American population. No quotas were imposed for countries in the Western Hemisphere (Canada, South and Central

---

[106] For a comprehensive survey see Hutchinson, *Legislative History of American Immigration Policy*. In preparing this summary I have also been much assisted by Mackie, "U.S. Immigration Policy and Local Justice."

[107] Teitelbaum, "Right Versus Right," p. 23.

America) and the Far East, although the Chinese remained excluded.

The second major reform was the abolition in 1965 of the quota system, and a move toward kin-based admissions. Separate ceilings of 170,000 and 120,000 per year were set on immigration from the Eastern and Western Hemispheres respectively, with an annual limit of 20,000 for any one country. Within these constraints, first and second preference were given to spouses and unmarried adult children of U.S. citizens and permanent resident aliens; third preference to exceptionally able artists, scientists, and members of the professions; fourth and fifth preference to married children and siblings of U.S. residents; and sixth preference to workers in occupations for which labor was in short supply in the United States. The change was motivated by the inequitable character of the old system which, as President Kennedy said in 1963, "discriminates among applicants for admission into the United States on the basis of accident of birth." Yet the new system, too, had a built-in bias in favor of the relatives of the most recent members of American society. The extra visas allocated on a first-come, first-served basis and by lottery were a response to this imbalance. In the 1990 legislation, which maintains kinship as the main immigration criterion, annual lotteries (beginning October 1995) are planned to allocate visas for 55,000 "diversity immigrants" to benefit countries that currently experience little kin-based immigration.

Wartime rationing. More than anything else, rationing in wartime confirms what I said in the introduction about local justice being a messy business. The very emergency that makes rationing necessary also forces the authorities to proceed by improvisation, makeshift, patchwork, exceptions, and revocation of exceptions when they turn out to have unintended consequences.[108] By the time things work smoothly, the war may be over.

In 1942 the United States introduced gasoline rationing, partly as the result of transportation bottlenecks (oil tankers had been

---

[108]For a discussion in general terms, stressing practical difficulties, see Gettell, "Rationing." A case study illustration is Maxwell and Balcom, "Gasoline Rationing in the United States," Parts 1 and 2. I am indebted to Frederick Pryor for these references.

diverted to the national defense program or sunk by German submarines), partly and more durably as the only efficient means to implement rationing of tires. Initially, the rationing was carried out by reducing deliveries to retail dealers to two-thirds, and later to one half, of 1941 deliveries. The dealers then had the thankless task of allocating the gasoline among their customers. As one of several anomalies produced by this system, "those with leisure to shop around could secure gasoline by wasteful driving."[109] After another unsuccessful interim system, rationing based on coupon books in various categories was finally introduced. The administration of the books, together with the assessment of needs, was delegated to local boards, modelled on the Selective Service System. Although the rationing boards, like the draft boards, had considerable autonomy and discretion, they were constrained by government regulations that enumerated the following as eligible for "preferred mileage": (a) government officers and employees, (b) school teachers or officials, (c) transportation of groups of students or teachers, (d) transportation of mail, (e) delivery of newspapers, (f) nonportable equipment for making newsreels, (g) medical profession, (h) veterinarians, (i) interns, medical students, and public health nurses, (j) embalmers, (k) ministers, (l) religious practitioners, (m) farmers, (n) transporting certain workers, (o) workers in establishments essential to the war effort, (p) representatives of organized labor and management, (q) construction, maintenance, and repair services, (r) members of armed forces, (s) messenger service, and (t) scrap dealers.[110]

Some episodes from the history of this rationing scheme can be cited to show that such systems are vulnerable to unraveling.[111] (1) In the interim measure mentioned above, consumption was regulated by issuing cards to be punched by the dealer. Since punching did not leave the dealer with any evidence of the transaction, he had no incentive for doing so and, in fact, clear incentives to conspire with the customer not to do so. The plan oper-

[109] Maxwell and Balcom, "Gasoline Rationing in the United States," I, p. 562.
[110] Maxwell and Balcom, "Gasoline Rationing in the United States," II, pp. 129–130.
[111] For details see Maxwell and Balcom, *op. cit.*, Part 1, pp. 563, 573, 577 and Part 2, p. 136.

ated efficiently in the early weeks, but collapsed when dealers and consumers became aware of the loopholes. (2) The ban on pleasure driving led to protests that individuals' investments in their summer homes were being jeopardized. The Administration then ordered an amendment permitting one round-trip to a vacation resort. "This meant that the 'pleasure driving' ban was at an end. The ban depended very much upon public cooperation, and this now evaporated rapidly." (3) The attempt to distinguish between different categories of customers met with the following difficulty: "In the best of circumstances a differential system of rationing which attempts fairly precise measurements of individual needs (as contrasted with a system which simply counts each person as one) tends to slacken with the passage of time. When errors are made in the form of under-issuance, the applicants naturally demand and receive rectification. When errors are made in the form of over-issuance, these are in general detected only by closer Board scrutiny, and this is a laborious and difficult process." (4) As non-highway consumption of gasoline (in farming or construction) by and large did not use tires, the local boards tended to issue the amount the farmer or contractor said he needed. Not surprisingly, some of this gasoline spilled over into the black market. All attempts to block the loophole failed, mainly because the vagaries of the weather made it impossible for the farmers to estimate their needs with precision.

The reader will appreciate that these brief sketches are not intended as thumbnail summaries or condensed overviews of the various allocative issues. The descriptions are highly selective and often emphasize the telling detail more than the overall structure. The purpose behind the selection—both of issues and of their aspects—has been to provide the reader with the necessary reference points for the more analytical discussion in the following chapters.

3 / Principles of Local Justice

In this chapter I survey the main principles and procedures that have been used to allocate scarce goods and necessary burdens. The survey aims at being exhaustive, at least in the sense of covering all the major principles. It does not offer a natural typology, based on first principles that would generate exhaustive and mutually exclusive categories. I think it belongs to the nature of the case that no classification of this kind is possible. The best one can do is to survey as many cases of local justice as possible, enumerate and classify the principles used (or, in some cases, merely proposed) for solving them, and hope that nothing important has been missed.

CONCEPTUAL PRELIMINARIES

I shall use the term *principle* to designate any general conception of how the scarce good is to be allocated. Some principles refer to substantive properties of individuals, such as "to each according to his need" or "any close relative of a citizen is allowed to immigrate." I shall refer to these properties as *criteria*. Other principles are embodied in *mechanisms*, which do not require individualized knowledge about the potential recipients. Equal division, lotteries, and queuing are prime examples. I shall refer to *procedures* as the operational version of a principle.[1] Because a principle can always be implemented through several different procedures, it does not in itself fully determine who the recipients are to be. Thus the principle of academic merit in college admission can be implemented by using high school grades, high school class rank, test scores, or some combination of these. The principle that organs for transplantation should be given to those who can benefit most from them could be interpreted in the sense of maximizing graft-survival rates or in the sense of maximizing additional life years. Finally, I shall sometimes refer to an allocative *scheme* as the full set of procedures used to implement mixed principles. These distinctions are not sharp, and are intended for heuristic purposes only. Although the basic distinction between a general principle and its practical implementation is clear enough, many rules could equally well be classified as the one or the other, depending on the desired fineness of grain.

There are two basic types of procedures. Some procedures lay down explicit criteria that can be applied without any discretionary elements. The point system for allocating kidneys belongs to this variety, as did the scheme for demobilizing soldiers at the end of World War II. Others accept the need for discretionary interpretation of the basic principle, but lay down rules for selecting and (at least sometimes) controlling the decision makers. Local draft boards, rationing boards, college admission offices, and prison parole boards can have a great deal of latitude in interpreting the general guidelines they are to implement. The committee that allocated access to dialysis in Seattle in the early 1960s had virtually unlimited discretion, as further explained in Chapter 5.

As a broad generalization, the trend in most Western countries seems to be toward less discretionary decision making. Instead of using individualized criteria (e.g., medical need), one turns to mechanisms (e.g., queuing). To the extent that individualized cri-

---

[1] Cp. the distinction between "standards of comparisons" (principles) and "standards of distribution" (procedures) made by Selten, "The Equity Principle in Social Behavior."

teria are retained, they are implemented by the first rather than by the second kind of procedure. Many exceptions occur, however. Below I cite a decision from a German federal labor court that struck down a decision by a lower court, which had relied on a point system for selecting workers to be laid off, and ordered the selection to be made instead on a discretionary case-by-case basis. American college admission officers jealously guard their right to select students by the exercise of trained judgment, rather than by using standardized and mechanical formulas. I return to these issues in Chapter 5.

It might seem as if the subset of principles that I have called mechanisms need no further specification. Are not lotteries and queuing, for instance, themselves procedures? It turns out, however, that implementing a seniority system (closely related to queuing) or operating a lottery requires procedural decisions with considerable scope for choice. Sometimes, the seniority clock starts running some time after the worker is hired and has completed a probationary period. Sometimes, it starts running before he is hired, as when retroactive seniority is awarded in discrimination cases. After World War II, some veterans who had not held a job before induction received seniority credit for their service time once they were hired.[2] That two workers have equal seniority may mean that they are hired on the same day, in the same month, or in the same year. Similarly, the apparently clear notion of random selection harbors a number of problems.[3] Some attempts to select individuals at random have been flawed because they have been based on proxies that were not truly randomly distributed in the population. Thus the use of fifth-letter alphabetization to select jurors "meant that many people in the same panel would have the same fifth letter in their last name. This explained how some panels had large numbers of Jewish names (e.g., Wiseman, Feldman) or Italian names (e.g., Ferrarro, Dinardo)."[4]

[2] Gersuny and Kaufman, "Seniority and the Moral Economy of U.S. Automobile Workers," pp. 469–470.

[3] For a survey, see Chapter II.2 of *Solomonic Judgements*.

[4] Hans and Vidmar, *Judging the Jury*, p. 57. First names are no more reliable. "In the town of Mannheim, for example, statistics were compiled regarding the number of children in each family. The sample comprised the families whose names had the initial letters A, B, and M. It turned out,

Sometimes, one principle is used as a proxy, or second-best approximation, for another. Age may be used as a proxy for deciding whether a patient is a medically suitable candidate for a transplantation. Time spent queuing for a good may be seen as a proxy for need. The cost of using proxies is that type 1 and type 2 errors may occur: some of the people who should get the good don't get it, and some get it who shouldn't. The benefit is that proxies allow one to economize on the costs of decision making. The relation between a principle and its proxy is not the same as that between a principle and its procedural implementation. Consider again the problem of eliminating medically unsuitable candidates for transplantation. For patients under a certain age, the principle is implemented by going through a checklist of medical counterindications. For patients above that age, the probability that one of these counterindications will in fact be present is so high that age is used instead as a proxy.[5]

Most of the principles I shall discuss aim at selecting *individuals.* Once selected, they form a group with various group-level properties, such as "having 5 percent minority membership" or "having an average age of 45." Sometimes, these properties obtain accidentally, in the sense of being the result of interaction between independently chosen properties of individuals and the distribution of these properties in the population. In other cases, the individual properties, while facially neutral, are chosen with a view to create certain properties of the ensuing group. Examples are given in the next chapter. In still other cases, the group-level property is a direct consequence of the selection procedure, as when quotas are used to ensure the representation of minorities.

---

however, that names with these initials were especially numerous among Jewish families, and as the children of Jewish families were particularly numerous, the enquiry gave a misleading result" (Jensen, "The Representative Method in Practice," pp. 429–430).

[5]"What about the sixty-year-old patient without any evidence of cancer, or of vascular or other systemic disease, who now develops chronic renal failure? If he is in full possession of his faculties and productive at his work, what reason can be found to refuse him treatment? Many such patients are under treatment in the United States, but few in Britain. An English consultant in a large community hospital had a ready answer. Everyone over fifty-five, he said, is 'a bit crumbly' and therefore not really a suitable candidate for therapy." (Aaron and Schwartz, *The Painful Prescription,* p. 35.)

In all these cases selection operates by choosing individuals one at a time.

Sometimes, however, selection operates directly on groups. In the presence of externalities among the successful applicants or recipients, it may not be enough to consider each individual on his merits. In addition, one must take account of the impact he can make on others. The emphasis in most selective colleges on the value of diversity is usually justified by such interaction effects. Even assuming that the sole value of the college is the promotion of intellectual excellence, that goal may not be best advanced by selecting students on the basis of intellectual excellence.[6] A mix of students from many backgrounds and with many skills, academic and nonacademic, may provide the best environment for overall academic success. This argument makes good sense for the humanities and social sciences, whose subject matter *is* human diversity, but is less plausible for the natural sciences. A similar argument might also apply to the latter, however, if one assumes that college should educate good leaders and not just good scholars. In such cases, the admission of minority applicants is justified by their impact *on the majority*, not by concern for their own life chances. An extreme case—a parody, really—of this line of reasoning is the "search for the happy bottom quarter" undertaken by a former dean of admissions to Harvard college, on the basis of the following argument:

> Inevitably . . . 25 percent of the entering students would end up in the bottom quarter of the class. If they were former academic stars, they would be unhappy—perhaps they would even be broken by the experience. So, intentionally admitting less academically able students as "the bottom quarter," who were strong in sports or social life or the arts and would therefore not care so much about their academic standing, would make everyone's educational experience happier.[7]

Diversity may be achieved by selecting at the individual level,

---

[6]To this argument from interaction we may add an argument from self-selection: "The most academically able students might not want to join a college that selected on purely academic criteria" (Klitgaard, *Choosing Elites*, p. 25).

[7]Reported in ibid., p. 26.

using disjunctive selection procedures (see below) which evaluate applicants by their greatest talents rather than by their average scores. Colleges also, however, strive directly for diversity by composing a student body with the desired variety of talent. As mentioned in Chapter 2, a similar practice is found in admitting children to kindergarten in Norway. Although children from single-parent families and disadvantaged homes are given priority, other categories of children may also be admitted to create the right age-gender mix. Projects of public housing have used quotas to ensure the presence of white tenants, but for the purpose of benefiting blacks rather than whites.[8]

A CLASSIFICATION OF PRINCIPLES

In the following, the main allocative principles are grouped together under six main headings, including one covering the "mixed principles" that are almost invariably found in actual cases. Since the pure principles can be combined and mixed in innumerable ways, this is one area where I do not pretend to be exhaustive. By contrast, my enumeration of the pure principles is, as I said, intended to be complete. The main exception to this claim concerns principles of allocation according to status. Over and over again, I have thought that my list of status principles relevant for allocative justice was essentially complete, only to find a new case based on a variety that had escaped me. It would be too much to hope that the enumeration offered below will prove more robust.

In addition to presenting the principles and mentioning some important applications, I shall try to identify the features that make them seem attractive—be it on grounds of efficiency or equity—to allocators, recipients, authorities, or the general public. A general observation, which will prove important in Chapter 5, is that a given principle or procedure can be attractive on several grounds.[9] When different groups are attracted to the same princi-

---

[8]Firms might also seek diversity, although for very different reasons: an ethnically heterogeneous work force will display more internal hostility and hence be less likely to organize. See my *Making Sense of Marx*, p. 371 ff.

[9]Basically the same point is made by Hofstee, "Allocation by Lot," when he refers to the overdetermination of mechanisms by principles.

ple, for different reasons, the task of political coalition-building is obviously easier.

The principles fall into two major groups: those that do not make any reference to properties of the potential recipients and those that do. Among the former, egalitarian principles form one major category. Another consists of time-related principles, such as seniority or queuing. Among the latter, the main distinction is between properties based on status and other individual properties. The four categories just mentioned presuppose that the good or burden in question is allocated by a single institution in a unified and coordinated manner. Allocations that emerge as the result of decentralized, uncoordinated decisions—the market being the paradigm case—have no place in the present classification. The one exception is when an institution deliberately creates a market for goods that are not normally traded in the market. These administered markets form a separate category. The final category consists of mixed schemes, based on various combinations of the pure principles included in the other categories.

Individualized criteria can also be organized around a dichotomy. On the one hand, there are principles that focus exclusively on (nonrelational) *properties* of the individuals. Although allocation is made by comparing the extent to which different applicants possess these properties, the properties themselves do not make any reference to other people. On the other hand, there are principles that essentially invoke the *relations* of the potential recipient to other individuals. Some of these principles have the form: If individual X has the good, that is a reason for also giving it to individual Y who stands in some special relation to X. Kin-based immigration and preferential admission to children of alumni are examples. Others have the form: If the good is provided by individual X, that is a reason for allocating it to individual Y, who has certain relevant properties in common with X. Allocation of organs, of children for adoption, and of sperm for artificial insemination are examples.

A further classification of principles will prove useful when, in Chapter 5, we consider the problem why a specific principle is used to allocate some specific good. Properties of individuals can be classified along two dimensions. On the one hand, there is a distinction between properties that are easily and objectively observable, and those that cannot be ascertained without some discretionary assessment. On the other hand, there is a distinction between properties that can be manipulated by the individual or, more generally, affected by individual behavior, and those that are given and, if not unchangeable, at least do not depend on actions taken by the individual. (Age is changeable, but not manipulable.) By crossing these two distinctions with each other, the following table is obtained:

TABLE 3.1 /

	Need Discretionary Assessment	Do not Need Discretionary Assessment
Depend on Actions Taken by the Individual	Need, desert, social usefulness, acquired skills	Weight, lifestyle-related illnesses, citizenship, marital status, religion, literacy, other status criteria, wealth
Do not Depend on Actions Taken by the Individual	Pain, inborn skills, intensity of preference	Age, gender, race, genetically based illnesses

The choice of examples in the cells should not be taken too literally. It is easy to think of exceptions and ambiguous cases. Yet the distinctions themselves are robust and important. Institutions that are concerned with information and incentive problems (Chapter 5) will have to think very carefully whether a first-best criterion in the upper left-hand cell may not have to be abandoned in favor of one in the lower right-hand cell.

A final comment may be in order, to underscore the pragmatic and heuristic purposes of the enumeration. In other lists of allocative principles, the categories are logically on a par with each other. In one trichotomic scheme, Morton Deutsch distinguishes between equity, equality, and need.[10] In another, Michael Walzer enumerates free exchange, desert, and need as three major catego-

---

[10] Deutsch, "Equity, Equality and Need."

ries.[11] These classifications are not exhaustive, but at least the categories are (1) mutually exclusive and (2) at comparable levels of generality. This is not the case for the classification proposed here. For instance, allocation by desert and allocation by citizenship are obviously not at the same level of generality. Moreover, the two principles are not mutually exclusive. Often the latter is based on the former, as when it is argued that because foreign nationals have not paid taxes, they do not deserve to receive scarce medical services.[12] However, citizenship may also be seen as an autonomous criterion, in societies that believe in their inherent superiority to others.[13] Such ambiguities—and there are a great many of them—constitute one of the reasons why the study of local justice is endlessly fascinating. They also, however, make it difficult, or pointless, to construct neat and logical taxonomies.

Egalitarian Principles

Absolute equality. As further discussed in Chapter 6, most political philosophers view equality as the baseline for distribution. In the absence of reasons to the contrary (in Chapter 6 several such reasons are spelled out), goods ought to be divided equally among everybody. Even when there is no consensus that equality is inherently fair, it is often the only focal point for the resolution of conflicts.[14] The debate over the suffrage illustrates this proposition. Given the competing claims to superiority of various social groups (the rich, the educated, the well-born, the old, the male, and so on), universal (and equal) suffrage was the only outcome that could command stable agreement.[15] Also, egalitarian principles can be sustained by utilitarianism: If the recipients have equal utility functions with respect to the good (and it has decreasing marginal utility), total utility is maximized by dividing it equally.

---

[11] Walzer, *Spheres of Justice*, p. 21 ff.

[12] For a survey of such arguments, see Kilner, *Who Lives? Who Dies*, Chapter 4.

[13] In Qing, China, for example, a foreigner could be sent to prison because he had had the presumption to learn Chinese (Spence, *The Search for Modern China*, p. 121).

[14] For this idea see Schelling, *The Strategy of Conflict*, Chapter 2.

[15] Barry, "Is Democracy Special?" p. 195.

Equal and universal allocation often requires dilution of the good. The French principle of universal admission to nursery school would be impossibly costly if these schools were required to conform to Norwegian standards for the ratios of teachers and cubic feet to children. (The reason officially given for these high standards is that anything less good would be unacceptably bad. The real explanation is that they are upheld by a coalition of nursery school teachers and those parents who have already ensured a place for their children.) Similarly, work-sharing, as, for instance, the three day week, is sometimes chosen in preference to layoffs.

When a good is indivisible, so that it cannot be divided equally without being destroyed or losing its value, the principle of absolute equality dictates that it should not be given to anyone. This conclusion is advocated, for instance, in the part of Jewish ethics that regulates the allocation of life-saving resources.[16] The state of Oregon some years ago declared a moratorium on organ transplantation, on similar all-or-none grounds. "Pointing to federal Medicaid statutes requiring equal treatment for similarly situated patients, the [Division of Adult and Family Services in Oregon] stressed that there was no way the state could limit its funding to a prescribed number of transplant patients."[17] The grounds for refusing to all what not all can get vary. In Jewish ethics, the argument is grounded in a refusal to condemn anyone to death. Thus if the Jews are beleaguered and the enemy says, "Give up one among yourselves to be killed and we shall lift the siege; otherwise you will all be killed," the Talmud tells them to refuse. If, however, the enemy says to them, "Give us Paul," they do nothing wrong in handing him over.[18] According to Tocqueville, "the democratic sentiment of envy" explained the nonselective military service in the United States. "It is the inequality of a burden, not its weight, which usually provokes resistance."[19] In Oregon, fear of litigation may have played a role.

---

[16] Cahn, *The Moral Decision*, p. 61 ff.; Jakobovits, *Jewish Medical Ethics*, p. 98; Rosner, *Modern Medicine and Jewish Ethics*.

[17] Welch and Larson, "Dealing with Limited Resources," p. 171.

[18] Leiman, "Therapeutic Homicide."

[19] De Tocqueville, *Democracy in America*, pp. 651–652. For a further discussion of envy, see my "Envy in Social Life."

Lotteries. Goods that cannot be divided without great loss of value are often allocated by a lottery which gives all applicants an equal chance of getting them.[20] Lotteries respect the spirit of equality, while avoiding the conclusion that a good must be wasted if it cannot be given to everyone. Also, lotteries are attractive as a focal point solution, if indeterminacy or conflict prevents the application of a substantive principle. A further reason for using lotteries is that it may be useful to create uncertainty when certainty would lead to corruption. To prevent jurors or politicians from being bribed one may select them randomly and have them serve for a short period. For the same reason, judges are often assigned randomly to cases.

The main use of lotteries in contemporary societies is in selecting citizens for jury service[21] and for military service.[22] Their use has been advocated in a vast range of cases, including child custody, layoffs, and admission to higher education. As noted in Chapter 2, American immigration will from October 1995 onward admit about 8 percent of the applicants by lot. In the past, lotteries have been used for an amazing number of allocative purposes, including the distribution of land,[23] the selection of seamen to be eaten by the others when a ship was lost at sea,[24] and the division of the garments of Jesus (Saint John 19:23–24).

Equal deviation from a baseline. Many problems of local justice arise from the need to reduce the total production of some good or bad from a preexisting level (the "baseline"). Many Western countries today allocate milk quotas among farmers to avoid overproduction, often by allowing all to produce a certain percentage of the pre-quota volume. Gasoline rationing in the United States during World War II initially took the form of a proportionate reduction in deliveries to all dealers. In the Minnesota prison system, the early release program has taken the form of reducing

---

[20] For an extensive survey of the use of lotteries to allocate resources, see Chapter II of my *Solomonic Judgements.*

[21] For details, see Hans and Vidmar, *Judging the Jury.*

[22] For details about the American draft lotteries see Fienberg, "Randomization and Social Choice." For the French case, see Choisel, "Du tirage au sort au service universel."

[23] See, for instance, Dale, "Oklahoma's Great Land Lottery."

[24] Simpson, *Cannibalism and the Common Law.*

everyone's sentence by the same proportional factor. Similarly, proposals to reduce emission of CO_2 and other gases usually impose the same percentage cut for all countries. I conjecture that in such cases equality is adopted because it is the obvious focal point for agreement rather than because of its fairness properties. Note, however, that the principle of equal deviation or equal sacrifice could also be achieved by imposing equal *absolute* reductions on all parties.[25] To some, other allocative principles, such as allocating production or emission proportionately to land or to population, might appear equally obvious and natural. As Howard Raiffa observes, "one person's symmetry is frequently another person's asymmetry."[26] The principle of equal deviation has a particularly strong appeal, however, since it allows one to combine equality with respect for established rights.

Rotation. Tasks, burdens, and goods are sometimes allocated by having everyone take turns, according to a predetermined order. Communally organized enterprises often have everybody take turns to operate the switchboard or wash the floors. As mentioned in Chapter 2, rotation may also be used for the distribution of household tasks. The same effect may be approximated by using lotteries without replacement, as in the allocation of political offices in Athens or in the allocation of religious offices in ancient Israel. Under the Qing dynasty, the thankless task of serving as "headman" for tax collection under a system of communal responsibility was allocated by a rotating system.[27] When divorced parents have joint custody of the children, they often stay every other week with each parent. Some firms use rotation to assign the most-sought-after holiday periods.

Time-related Principles

Queuing. Often, scarce goods are distributed on a first-come, first-served basis. Queues require that one actually waste time standing in line, whereas waiting lists (see below) only involve

[25] In wage determination both principles are found (see my book, *The Cement of Society*, p. 219).
[26] Raiffa, *The Art and Science of Negotiation*, p. 54.
[27] Spence, *The Search for Modern China*, p. 125.

mailing-in or depositing a claim. Examples of queues include standing in line for consumer goods and queuing for higher education (every year French television brings pictures of students and their parents sleeping in queues outside university registration offices). Although a highly inefficient allocation mechanism (see Chapter 4), queuing is often ranked highly on grounds of fairness.[28] There are several reasons for this preference. First, the sacrifice involved in standing in line is widely seen as generating *desert*. Second, the willingness to stand in line can be seen as a measure of the *need* for the good. Third, the use of queuing can be seen as a valuable counterweight to the pervasive use of money in allocating scarce goods. To prevent the rich from getting everything, let some goods be allocated by a mechanism that puts them at a disadvantage, because of their greater opportunity costs of queuing.[29] Finally, queuing offers the advantages of an impersonal mechanism that does not lend itself to accusations of bribery or favoritism.

Waiting lists. Examples of goods allocated by place on the waiting lists include operations for hernia, varicose veins, hip displacement, and heart bypass surgery in Norway; sperm for artificial insemination in France; public housing in the formerly Communist countries; the serving of prison sentences for some categories of crime in Norway; and places in nursery school in Italy. Access to a medical specialist often involves getting on a waiting list, whereas access to general practitioners frequently requires queuing. Some countries have had waiting lists for immigration, others for emigration. As we saw in the previous chapter, time on the waiting list generates points in the allocation of kidneys.

As with queuing, the use of waiting lists can be justified in several ways. With some medical goods, time spent on the waiting list is a proxy for medical need, since a patient's condition often deteriorates over time. A list, like a queue, is a self-sorting device that does not require controversial and costly discretionary decisions.

Seniority also gives major importance to the sheer passing of

---

[28] See Kahneman, Knetsch, and Thaler, "Fairness as a Constraint on Profit-seeking."

[29] Calabresi and Bobbit, *Tragic Choices*, p. 93.

time. This principle differs from queuing and waiting lists in that seniority accumulates as a by-product of some other activity, such as working in an enterprise, whereas standing in line has no other end besides that of accumulating priority. Seniority is a central— although rarely the unique—criterion in the allocation of many work-related goods and burdens, such as promotions and lay-offs.[30] It is also a part-determinant of other allocations, such as the American demobilization scheme mentioned initially.

The use of seniority in layoff contexts can be defended on many grounds.[31] Workers, in particular, have a number of reasons for preferring seniority. First, a majority of organized workers want seniority out of self-interest. As long as workers feel confident that the firm will never lay off more than half the work force, the senior 51 percent of the workers will always prefer seniority over any other layoff principle. Second, seniority, like queuing, reflects the ethics of desert. Workers feel they ought to be rewarded for having devoted the best years of their lives to the firm.[32] Third, the jobs become more valuable to them the longer they have worked in the firm, because of job-specific skills and the like. Fourth, seniority, being a mechanical principle, protects workers from arbitrary managerial decision making. Historically, this was probably the main reason for the introduction of the seniority system.[33] Finally, seniority can be seen as protecting older and more vulnerable workers, and thus being to some extent a proxy for need.

Managers, too, have multiple reasons for preferring seniority. By encouraging workers to stay in the firm, the seniority principle reduces turnover costs. Also, because workers like seniority, using another system could be bad for morale and productivity. In

---

[30] For a survey see E. Yemin (ed.), *Workforce Reductions in Undertakings.*

[31] The following draws on discussions with Stuart Romm and on helpful suggestions by Miriam Golden.

[32] In my opinion, this is a spurious argument. To devote one's life to a task is meritorious only when it involves forgoing other activities that would have been more satisfying personally. But most workers do not have any such alternatives. A fortiori this spuriousness applies to the argument that the elderly deserve to take priority because of what they have contributed to those who are now in the work force. (Parents may deserve reward for what they do for their children, but that is another matter.) Whether spurious or not, the argument is effective.

[33] Gersuny, "Origins of Seniority Provisions in Collective Bargaining."

particular, arbitrary foreman behavior is costly for the firm if it causes work stoppages and discontent among the workers.[34] Moreover, as seniority rights ensure that the workers have more to lose from being fired, they also enhance the efficacy of the firing threat as a worker discipline device.[35] In a crisis, of course, managers would always like to be free to retain the most productive workers. Although the ensuing problem of credibility can be solved by having unions to enforce the seniority principle, this solution obviously has other costs that, in the eyes of managers, may well offset the benefits. American studies indicate, in fact, that unionized firms are more productive and less profitable than nonunionized ones.[36]

Principles Defined by Status

This category consists, roughly speaking, of principles based on observable biophysical properties or on social and legal features that are a matter of public record. For the present purposes, the category is best defined through its extension, that is, by the various subcategories listed below.

Age. Queues, waiting lists, and seniority allocate goods by time as accumulated from a moment which is related to the good to be allocated, such as onset of an illness or entry in a firm. Allocation by age counts time from birth. A lower bound on age, serving as a proxy for other qualities highly correlated with age, constrains acceptance in a number of contexts: entering elementary education, voting, serving as an adoptive parent,[37] doing military service. An upper bound constrains a few of the same activities, plus some others: being admitted to medical school, serving as an adoptive parent, receiving artificial insemination, doing military service. In all these cases, the age constraint is relatively (but far

---

[34] Goldberg, "Bridges over Contested Terrain," p. 256.

[35] Golden, "A Comparative Inquiry into the Allocation of Job Loss."

[36] For the impact of unions on turnover and productivity, see Freeman and Medoff, *What Do Unions Do?* pp. 107, 174. For the impact on profits, see ibid., Chapter 11.

[37] Age enters doubly into the process of adoption, since older children are harder to place than others. "It is estimated that between 100,000 and maybe as high as 250,000 older children are currently waiting for families to adopt them" (Martin, *Beating the Adoption Game,* p. 190).

from wholly) uncontroversial. A more contestable role of age is as a proxy for medical suitability, as when British doctors deny dialysis to patients over fifty-five,[38] or as a proxy for mental and physical agility, as when workers are forced to retire at sixty, sixty-five, or seventy. In all cases, we can ask whether the benefits of more discretionary, individualized assessments of fitness would exceed the costs of carrying them out; or we can accept the need for some cutoff point but argue that it should be set higher or lower. In some cases one can also argue against discretionary assessments on the grounds that the self-respect of those *not* deemed fit would suffer less if they, along with everybody else of their age, were automatically excluded.

Age can also be used as a positive or negative criterion in its own right. On the one hand, the elderly are often thought to deserve high priority in the allocation of life-saving medical resources because of what they have given to society. In an especially poignant way, the argument takes the following form: "The efforts of the previous generation enable us to enjoy a much higher standard of living than they did. The least we can do to pay them back is to ensure that they get priority in the competition for scarce resources." On the other hand, it is argued that old people should have a low priority because more life years are saved if these scarce resources are given to the young, partly because treatment is less likely to succeed, given the medical problems correlated with age, and partly because even if it does work the old have fewer years left to live.[39]

In the United States, the use of age as an allocative criterion could violate federal civil rights. For this reason, adoption agencies are reluctant to state an explicit upper bound on age for the adoptive parents.[40] The problem is most acute in employment, however, following the passage in 1967 of the Age Discrimination in Employment Act, to which reference has already been made in Chapter 2. The following example shows how, in such cases, age and seniority may interact:

[38] Aaron and Schwartz, *The Painful Prescription*, pp. 34–35.
[39] For a survey of such arguments, see Kilner, *Who Lives? Who Dies*, Chapter 7.
[40] Martin, *Beating the Adoption Game*, p. 36.

In *Hodgson* v. *Greyhound,* the court noted that although bus drivers between ages fifty and fifty-five had safer driving records than younger drivers, this may have been in part because of the seniority system that allowed older drivers to choose safer, less strenuous routes. Old applicants without seniority would have been subjected to the strenuous routes. That the "essence" of Greyhound's business was safe transportation justified age as a qualification.[41]

Gender. Gender has often been used to allocate goods and burdens. Consider, for specificity, differential treatment of women in Western societies. Goods have included exemption from military service, priority in disaster situations ("women and children first"), and—more ambiguously, as I mentioned in the previous chapter—child custody under the maternal presumption rule. Burdens have included the denial of the right to vote, child custody under the paternal presumption rule, exclusion from certain jobs (for example, firefighters), and a disproportionately large share of household tasks. Today, these forms of explicit discrimination have largely disappeared in most Western countries. Of the old benefits, exemption from military service still survives. Some new benefits have been created, through quota systems and other forms of affirmative action.

Formal discrimination by gender must be distinguished from other gender-related phenomena: informal discrimination of women, self-selection and self-exclusion by women, and the disparate impact (which may or may not be intended) of gender-neutral principles on women.[42] When the selection principle contains a discretionary element, discrimination of women still occurs, probably to a larger extent than can be documented by hard evidence. However, as discretion becomes less important, discriminatory practices also become less frequent. Self-exclusion of women is probably one of the reasons why fewer female ESRD patients get transplanted. For various reasons, fewer women ask

[41] Esposito, *The Obsolete Self,* p. 168. The case is cited as 449 F.2d 244 (1976).
[42] Rational discrimination and rational self-exclusion may interact in a vicious circle. If employers discriminate against women on the grounds that they are more likely to drop out of the work force to have children, women may in fact prefer to drop out rather than pursue an uncertain and unsatisfactory career. (Sunstein, "Three Civil Rights Fallacies" and "Why Markets Won't Stop Discrimination.")

to get on the waiting list for transplantation. But disparate impact also enters into the explanation of why fewer women are transplanted, since they tend to be more highly sensitized than men.

Sexual orientation. This serves to exclude applicants in various contexts. If you are homosexual, you cannot get into the American army. Adoption agencies do not knowingly place children for adoption in homes of homosexuals.[43] Both in the United States[44] and in Great Britain,[45] custody has been denied to lesbian mothers. The 1965 Immigration Act added "sexual deviation" to grounds for exclusion.

Ethnic status. This has often been used to allocate goods and burdens. Because of their race, Jews, blacks, and other minorities have been denied the right to vote; they have been denied the right (or exempted from the duty) to do military service; and they have been kept out of universities and certain professions. The comments just made on gender transfer immediately to ethnicity. There is no longer much formal discrimination, the main exceptions arising in child-related cases where donors and recipients are matched on the basis of race. Informal discrimination, though probably widespread, is elusive. The remaining differences are mainly caused by a combination of self-selection and disparate impact. In the United States, the reason why there are few black students in college is partly that fewer apply, partly that fewer of those who do apply meet academic requirements for admission. The reasons why fewer black ESRD patients are transplanted are more complex. As explained in Chapter 2, and discussed in more detail in Chapter 4, schemes that select for good antigen matching have a disparate impact on blacks. In addition, there is an element of self-exclusion, since blacks more frequently than whites prefer to remain on dialysis. In all these cases, one should note that what appears as self-selection at one stage may be the result of discrimination at an earlier stage in the life cycle.

Other physical features. Height is a requirement in various professions. Eye color has been used as one of several matching criteria in the allocation of sperm for artificial insemination. Obesity

[43] Martin, *Beating the Adoption Game*, p. 222.
[44] Ibid., pp. 223–224.
[45] Maidment, *Child Custody and Divorce*, p. 181.

has been used as a criterion for excluding couples as adoptive parents. In the United States, there have been several contested cases of overweight nurses being turned down for jobs. Formerly, several elite institutions of higher education in California used to ask applicants about their height and weight. Although the purpose of gathering this information was not to eliminate the anorexic and the obese, one reason for discontinuing the practice was self-suspicion by admissions officers that they might be subconsciously influenced by such knowledge. For the same reason, colleges no longer ask applicants to send in photographs of themselves together with the application. Many airlines no longer require stewardesses to conform to traditional standards of feminine beauty, although they still may not constitute a random sample of the population in this respect. Physical handicaps serve as exclusionary criteria in a number of contexts, beyond the obvious ones related to occupational requirements. The blind are excluded from airplane seats near the emergency exits.[46] In a few contexts, notably access to higher education, the physically handicapped are given preferential treatment.[47]

Mental features. The severely mentally handicapped do not have a right to procreate. Here, a lower bound on mental capacity serves as a constraint. In admitting children for special education programs, an upper bound is used: in some states, eligibility requires an IQ below 70.[48]

Freedom. Whenever formal slavery has existed, allocation and selection mechanisms have distinguished between slaves and freemen. Like women, slaves have often lacked the right to vote and been exempt from military service. It was only in the last months of the Civil War that the South drafted slaves, in return, however, for a promise of manumission.

---

[46] The president of the National Federation of the Blind called this policy a "classic discriminatory position" ("Who Can Sit by Plane Exit?" *New York Times,* April 16, 1989). See also "Prejudice Against the Blind Claimed in Arrest on Plane," *Chicago Sun-Times,* April 2, 1989. I owe these references to Michael Dennis.

[47] In general, tall and beautiful people earn more than others. Is this fact a deplorable one? Can it be remedied? Should it be remedied? Is it due to employer discrimination or to the fact that tall and beautiful people have more self-confidence and therefore perform better?

[48] Handler, *The Conditions of Discretion,* p. 46 ff.

Nobility. In many premodern societies nobles were treated differently from commoners. The French nobles of the *ancien régime* were legally prohibited from entering the retail trade. They also, of course, had numerous rights and privileges. The Roman empire had a "dual-penalty" system that distinguished between nobles and commoners.

Caste. The Indian caste system regulates innumerable parts of social life. From the present perspective, the most important aspect is the strict regulation of entry into the various professions.

Civil status. Citizens and aliens are often treated differently, and not just with respect to inherently citizen-related goods such as the right to vote and the duty to do jury service and military service. In the early 1980s, many American transplantation centers adopted upper limits on the percentage of kidneys that could go to aliens. In Britain, admission to college does not differentiate between citizens and aliens, but the latter pay much higher tuition fees.

Family status.[49] In immigration decisions, relatives of citizens or residents are standardly given priority, as explained in Chapter 2 with respect to American immigration law. Married patients are sometimes given preference for transplantation, on the grounds that a spouse is needed to provide follow-up care.[50] In the French system for allocating sperm for artificial insemination, unmarried women are excluded. By contrast, single mothers are given preferential access to kindergarten in Norway; in Germany, single mothers keep their jobs when married women are laid off. In China in the mid 1950s, sons without brothers were exempt from military

[49] This criterion and the two following ones differ from the other status criteria in that they depend wholly on voluntary acts by the individual, except for the countries (such as China) that do not allow free choice of occupation and residence. They form an exception, therefore, to the general proposition that status criteria are immune to incentive effects. People do sometimes marry only for the purpose of being allowed to immigrate; or move to another state solely for the purpose of obtaining scarce medical goods available on better terms for residents of that state; or join a religious order for the purpose of becoming exempt from military service. Even race can be manipulated if, say, one grandparent suffices for membership.

[50] Kilner, *Who Lives? Who Dies?*, p. 105. Note the difference between this argument and the claim that married patients should take precedence to save spouses from suffering.

service. In the United States, there is a long history (and controversy) of exempting married men, or married men with children, from service. These groups were also given preferential status in the American demobilization scheme after World War II. Patients with family dependents have regularly been favored in the allocation of dialysis (in times and places of scarcity) and of organs for transplantation.[51] Although nepotism is largely eliminated (or hidden), it lingers on in some institutions as an official policy. Most colleges will give some kind of preferential treatment to applications from children of alumni, staff, or faculty. The relative importance of these categories can be gleaned from the Stanford Admissions brochure. Children of eligible Stanford staff and faculty "receive favorable consideration, . . . provided they meet basic requirements." (A similar phrase is used to describe applications from members of underrepresented minorities.) Children of Stanford graduates have to meet higher standards: they "receive preference in choices among applicants of approximately equal qualifications."

Residence status. Place of residence within a country is sometimes used as a criterion for allocative purposes. In the United States, state universities give priority to students residing in the state. In Chapter 2 we saw that in the placement system that allocates students among German universities, spatial distance to the most preferred university was used as the selection criterion. In the 1920s, Yale College professed to strive for a geographical balance among its students, as an indirect strategy to reduce the number of Jews admitted (see Chapter 4 for some details). Although kidney sharing in the United States is organized as a national network, remaining elements of local allocation create some measure of "geographical bad luck."

Residence (i.e., distance from the donor) matters more in the allocation of hearts, which deteriorate much faster than kidneys. Hence the allocation of organs for heart and heart-lung transplantation incorporates both medical urgency and distance from donor. Urgent patients are classified as Status 1 patients, less urgent ones as Status 2. Having the donor hospital as the center, two concentric circles are drawn, with radii of 500 and 1,000 miles.

---

[51] Kilner, *Who Lives? Who Dies?* Chapter 6.

Zone A includes the area within 500 miles of the donor; Zone B the area 500 to 1,000 miles from the center; Zone C is defined as beyond 1,000 miles. Unless allocated locally, organs are distributed by the following UNOS priority scheme:

1. Status 1, heart only patients in Zone A
2. Combined heart and lung recipients in Zone A
3. Status 1, heart only recipients in Zone B
4. Combined heart and lung recipients in all zones outside Zone A
5. Status 2, heart only recipients in Zone A
6. Status 2, heart only recipients in Zone B
7. Status 1, heart only recipients in Zone C
8. Status 2, heart only recipients in Zone C.

Occupational status. In wartime, workers in vital industries are often exempted from military service and receive larger gasoline rations. In many Norwegian municipalities, children of nursery school teachers are preferentially admitted to nursery school. In Oslo, children of all municipal employees take preference over everybody else, even before the physically handicapped children that are the only group explicitly accorded priority in the law. Whether this criterion is motivated by efficiency concerns or simply reflects the successful play of self-interest, its overt form is that of a status principle. Workers in occupations for which labor is in short supply are often given priority for immigration.

Religion. As mentioned in Chapter 2, Catholics were not allowed to immigrate to America in the colonial period. In Norway, the 1814 constitution prohibited the entry of Jews and Jesuits to the kingdom. The first clause was abolished in 1851; the second as recently as 1956. Religion as basis for matching adoptive parents was mentioned in Chapter 2. Exemption from military service is regularly granted to those who invoke their religious beliefs as grounds for not serving, and sometimes to those who have entered orders. Note the difference between these practices and that of excluding some citizens from military service on grounds of their religion. In eighteenth century France, for instance, the exclusion of Jews from the army was justified on the grounds that their refusal to fight on the Sabbath made them bad soldiers.

This exclusion, in turn, was used as a reason to deny them full citizenship.[52]

Literacy. The right to vote and the permission to immigrate have often required a literacy test. In the United States, the literacy test for immigration has been the ability to read and understand a statement of thirty or forty words in any language chosen by the immigrant. Mainly intended to exclude "alien races,"[53] the test could, however, cut both ways. Thus in 1896, Senator Gibson (Maryland) argued that the literacy test would exclude manual workers whose strength is needed, but would let in "the communists and socialists, and loud-mouthed and filthy anarchists . . . because they are able to read."[54] As a criterion for restricting the suffrage, literacy was officially justified by the need for competent citizens and secretly on the grounds that it would allow the exclusion of Catholics, blacks, or workers.[55] (To my knowledge, nobody has objected to the test on the grounds that it gave the suffrage to Communists, Socialists, and anarchists.) In immigration, those fleeing from religious persecution have been exempt from the literacy test. Property owners have often been exempt from taking the literacy test for voting.

Principles Defined by Other Properties

Individual levels of welfare. Often, recipients of scarce resources are chosen through interpersonal comparisons of welfare, as assessed by some observable proxy (e.g., one of the status properties listed above). I shall distinguish between two welfare-based principles. On the one hand the good may be allocated to people at low *levels* of welfare. On the other hand, it may go to those in whom it would produce the greatest *increment* of welfare.

Need. The concept of *need* can be interpreted according to the level criterion of welfare. When public housing is allocated to

---

[52] For diametrically opposed views on this topic, see the interventions by Clermont-Tonnerre and Maury in the French Assemblée Constituante of 1789–1791 (*Archives Parlementaires,* vol. X, p. 754 ff.).

[53] See Higham, *Strangers in the Land,* p. 101 ff, as well as discussions in Chapters 4 and 5 in this volume.

[54] Hutchinson, *Legislative History of American Immigration Policy,* p. 117.

[55] Creppell, "Democracy and Literacy."

those with the lowest present housing standards, it is natural to say that it is allocated to those who need it most. At the University of Oslo, office parking space is allocated according to distance from home. Medical goods are often accorded in priority to those who are at low levels of health and, in that sense, need them most. (See below for an elaboration of this important theme.) In layoff situations, as mentioned above, married women are sometimes laid off before single women, presumably on grounds of need. For similar reasons, male workers with dependents took precedence in the United States before the war, as they do in many European countries today. In designing rationing schemes in wartime, individual need competes with contributions to the war effort. Admission to kindergarten in Norway follows, ambiguously, the need of parents as well as that of children. In immigration, the principle is present in the decision to allow priority to victims of political or religious persecution. Although many of the kin-based preferences in immigration may reflect considerations of need, the preference for siblings is more plausibly understood on incremental grounds: immigrants adjust and adapt more easily when they can stay with their family.

By contrast, the need of the parents for a child is *not* supposed to be a determinant in adoption or child custody decisions. Although parental need would seem a more legitimate consideration in the allocation of sperm (as the interests of the child cannot take precedence in this case), the French centers have chosen to use a simple waiting list. Nor is need supposed to be a relevant consideration in allocating places in higher education (but see below for some important modifications of this claim). In the United States today, need has largely disappeared as a determinant of layoff decisions.

Individual increments of welfare. One may also decide to allocate the scarce good to those in whom it will produce the greatest *increment* in welfare (or produce the smallest loss in welfare).[56]

---

[56] This criterion, too, might be seen to reflect the idea of need. Although G. A. Cohen has argued persuasively (in discussion) that need should be defined in terms of level of welfare rather than increment of welfare, the following passage suggests that usage is not always consistent with his recommendation: "When asked what criteria should determine who receives a transplant . . . , two American surgeons answered, medical need. One,

Since the distinction between these two ways of taking account of individual welfare is fundamental, I shall dwell on it at some length. It is superficially similar to the distinction between theories of justice that advocate the welfare of the worst-off as the maximand for social policy and theories that propose instead to maximize total welfare. For a further discussion of these two theories the reader is referred to Chapter 6. Here I only want to point out why the correspondence between the two conceptions of justice and the level-increment distinction is really quite imperfect. It is not always the case that social welfare is maximized by giving a good to a person who can derive the greatest individual increase in welfare from it. To maximize social welfare one may sometimes have to give the good to the person who, by using it, can most benefit others. The criterion of maximizing welfare increments in the recipients does not correspond to any of the major theories of justice. From the abstract philosophical point of view, it represents an unstable halfway house between the principle of maximizing the welfare level of the worst-off individual and the principle of maximizing the welfare increment of society. Yet since the welfare-increment criterion is usually easier to implement than the general principle of utilitarianism, it offers itself naturally to the consideration of efficiency-minded administrators.

The initial level of welfare and the increment over that level must be sharply distinguished from the end-state level as a criterion. On this principle one should give a unit of the scarce good to X rather than to Y if it would bring him to a higher level of welfare than that which would be achieved by Y if he were given the good. One survey article of scarce medical resources writes that "It is an almost universally accepted standard for selection that the patient whose chances of survival will be most greatly increased by a resource will be preferred over others." This is a clear statement of the increment principle. In a footnote the authors then refer to interviews with doctors which show that "The shift from the 'most critical' to the 'most salvageable' standard in

---

however, took this to mean selecting the 'individual who has the best chance of survival' . . . , whereas the other constructed it as choosing the patient whose life would be most endangered if denied the transplant" (Halper, *The Misfortunes of Others*, p. 110).

the allocation of intensive care ward space can have a dramatic effect. Under the former standard the Los Angeles County–University of Southern California Hospital Intensive Care Unit had a mortality rate of 80 percent. By shifting to the latter standard the rate has been reduced to 20 percent. . . . The corresponding figures of the Jackson Memorial Hospital Surgical Intensive Care Unit are 25–30 percent with critical admissions and 4–5 percent with salvageable admissions."[57] These figures, however, refer to end-state levels, not to increments. Clearly, mortality rates can always be reduced by concentrating on less severe cases, but it would defeat the purpose of medical treatment to use this as a criterion of admission.[58]

In the previous paragraphs, I have in effect considered three possible welfare-related criteria, defined in terms of pre-allocative levels, post-allocative levels (i.e., the level at which a recipient would be if selected for the good or burden in question), and the difference between the two levels. This trichotomy may be crossed with the dichotomy between goods and burdens, yielding six cases in all.

Table 3.2 enables us to clarify further what we mean by allocation according to need. If we are allocating goods, they should go to individuals at the lowest pre-allocative welfare level. If we are allocating burdens according to need, they should go to those at the highest post-allocative level. Or, equivalently, the good of being spared the burden should go to those at the lowest post-allocative levels. Although I have just described an instance in which goods are given to those at the highest post-allocative level, I believe such allocations are rare and usually objectionable. The converse idea—allocating burdens to those at the highest pre-

[57] "Scarce Medical Resources," p. 655, n.188.
[58] For-profit hospitals sometimes concentrate on the easy cases, leaving the hard ones for the public sector. There is also some evidence that there is "substantial waste in the provision of mental health services—that large numbers of highly trained provider groups are being well paid mostly to talk about personal matters to people with mild emotional problems" (Knesper, Pagnucco, and Wheeler, "Similarities and Differences Across Mental Health Services Providers and Practice Settings in the United States," p. 1367). A more legitimate reason for preferring the easy cases arises in warfare, where the overriding consideration is to get soldiers combat ready and not to cure them (Winslow, *Triage and Justice*, Chapter 1).

TABLE 3.2 /

	Pre-allocative Level	Post-allocative Level	Increment
Goods	Public housing Medical goods (treat most critical cases first)	Medical goods (minimize mortality rates)	Education (value-added approach) Medical goods (treat those who benefit most)
Burdens	?	Job loss Loss of child custody (needs-based criterion)	Loss of custody (utilitarian criterion)

allocative level—seems even more strange. Assume that a child would be equally well off with each of the two parents, and that we want to base the custody decision on arguments from parental welfare. One could argue, on utilitarian grounds, that the custody loss should be suffered by the parent who would have the smallest loss from not getting custody. Or one could argue that the loss should be suffered by the parent who would be at the highest welfare level if denied custody: this is the needs-based argument. But I cannot imagine what argument one would use for imposing the loss on the parent who is at the highest pre-allocative level. Nor do I think such practices are common.

For many purposes, it does not matter whether we choose the level criterion or the increment criterion. When X and Y are reasonably similar individuals and consumption of the scarce good has decreasing marginal utility, a person at a lower level will always derive a larger increment than a person at a higher level. This corresponds to the relation between individuals II and III in Figure 3.1. Here, each vertical line represents a person. The line begins at the welfare level of the person before allocation of the scarce good and ends at the level that he would reach if allocated one unit of the good.

The criteria diverge in two cases. First, the good may produce *increasing* marginal utility over some range. A person who already

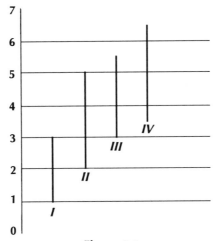

Figure 3.1

has four units might benefit more from an additional one than a person who has three, even assuming that the two have the same skills and preferences. This corresponds to the relation between III and IV in Figure 3.1. This argument was made by Leibniz, initially with respect to all sorts of goods,[59] later with respect only to "useful" goods, as distinct from "necessary" goods.[60] For some goods, the argument is not palpably absurd. If X and Y are identical except that X is at a higher level of education and hence of welfare than Y, X may benefit more from an additional unit of education because he possesses more prior information with which the new information can be combined. A little learning need not be a dangerous thing, but it can be somewhat pointless. By and large, however, the assumption of decreasing marginal utility is more plausible, and in most cases overwhelmingly more plausible.[61]

The other case in which the two criteria point in different directions is more interesting. Some people might be inherently less efficient in converting goods into welfare. This corresponds to the relation between I and II in Figure 3.1. We may suppose that I suffers a handicap that causes him both to be at a lower level of

[59] Leibniz, *Philosophische Schriften*, vol. I, p. 74.
[60] G. Mollat, *Mittheilungen aus Leibnizens ungedruckten Schriften*, p. 85.
[61] For an argument that *necessary* goods have increasing marginal utility see Karellis, "Distributive Justice and the Public Good."

welfare, for instance because he earns less, and to derive less welfare from an additional unit of the good. In such cases, those who make allocative decisions face a dilemma. Should schools, for instance, allocate extra resources—smaller classes or additional equipment—to the least gifted or to the most gifted children? Should agencies for the mentally retarded give priority to those who are so severely retarded that they are unlikely to enjoy life much under any circumstances, or to those who can benefit substantially from supportive measures? Should agencies for rehabilitation of prisoners give priority to recalcitrant high-risk or to more promising low-risk cases? If a judge is allowed to take account of the circumstances of persons to be sentenced, should he emphasize their current level of welfare or the drop in welfare they would experience if severely sentenced? Should he reason that "This person has already suffered enough," or "This person would suffer excessively if imprisoned"?

In many cases of this kind we are not really trying to compare people's welfare. The principal of a school looks at levels and increments of knowledge, not of welfare. The rehabilitation officer considers risks of recidivism with or without assistance, not welfare. To be sure, we usually assume that knowledge and recidivism are correlated with welfare. And presumably that correlation is a major reason for caring about such things as knowledge and recidivism. Individual welfare is not the only reason, however; social welfare also matters. When an individual acquires more knowledge or keeps away from crime more of the time, other people can benefit in amounts that are not linearly related to the benefit of the individual. A slight reduction in the risk of recidivism for a murderer might provide greater social benefits than a large reduction for a check forger. The benefits to society from offering special education to very gifted children might exceed those of offering the same benefits to less gifted children, although the latter might derive more personal benefits from them.

To overcome this problem I now focus on cases in which such possible contributions to society are explicitly ignored, namely, the allocation of scarce life-saving medical resources such as admission to intensive care units, access to dialysis, or organ transplantation. In contemporary Western societies, the outcome of these treatments is evaluated solely by its impact on the patient (and on the patient's family), not also by the impact on society.

With respect to lifesaving resources, the distinction between level and increment can be spelled out in two main ways. On the one hand, welfare may be operationalized as number of life years.[62] The level criterion then takes the simple form of age, suggesting that younger patients should be given priority over older patients. The increment criterion takes the form of additional life expectancy, suggesting that the scarce good should be directed where it would produce more extra life years. On the other hand, welfare may be understood as the probability of eliminating the specific medical problem that calls for intervention, regardless of life chances in general. The level criterion then tells us to give more to the person whose chances of spontaneous remission are the smallest, that is, the person in the most critical condition. The increment criterion tells us to give the resources to the person for whom the chance of eliminating the relevant condition would be most increased by the intervention.

I shall mainly consider the second interpretation, in which the tension between the level and increment criteria appears most clearly. Giving an organ to a young person will usually produce more additional life years than giving it to an older person, so that the two criteria point in the same direction. There may be exceptions, which may make for hard choices, but the systematic tendency is for the two criteria to converge rather than diverge.[63]

[62] I shall not discuss the notion of "quality-adjusted" life years, except for the following remarks. What must be meant by quality in this context is *not* subjective level of well-being. Assume, namely, that we had constructed the perfect hedonometer so that people's cardinal levels of welfare could be measured and compared with precision. Nobody, I am sure, would propose that in allocating organs for transplantation one should prefer people with a sunny disposition over people with a morose temperament. The only relevant quality-of-life aspects are those that stem directly from the medical condition itself, such as pain and the ability to function. Moreover, for reasons set out in Chapter 6, I do not think one can construct valid trade-offs between quantity and quality thus defined, or, within quality, between pain and functioning.

[63] In the hard choices, what should we do? I shall not take a stand on this issue, but simply make an observation. It might seem obvious that the value of adding x years to the life of a person of y years is a decreasing function of y. Other things being equal, we should rather give ten extra years to a five-year-old child than to a sixty-year-old person: the older person, after all, has had a full life. (We might still prefer the older person, but on grounds of desert rather than on outcome-oriented considerations.) I believe, however, that very young children have less of a claim on us than adolescents

I believe, however, that under the second interpretation the level and increment criteria tend systematically to diverge.[64] From the inception of medical triage, it has been recognized that patients fall into three categories.[65] At one extreme, some patients are too ill to benefit from treatment: they will die in any case. At the other extreme, some patients do not need treatment: they will recover by themselves without it. In between are the patients who can benefit substantially from treatment and to whom, therefore, it should preferentially be given. The relation between severity of illness and efficacy of treatment can thus be summarized as follows:

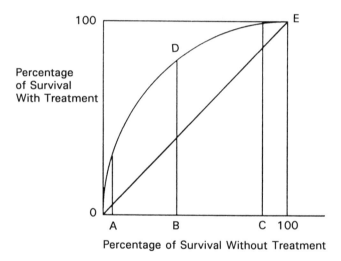

Figure 3.2

---

and young adults have (although a larger claim than older people have). To cut short a life in midair is more tragic than to cut off a life that has not really yet begun as an autonomous enterprise. Also, the value of x matters. The argument I just made has less force if the extra time given to the patient is too short (and perhaps too filled with illness) to allow much flowering and development.

[64] The statement that "sometimes there is a tension between urgency of need and probability of success" (Childress, "Some Moral Connections Between Organ Procurement and Organ Distribution," p. 99) is, therefore, too weak.

[65] Winslow, *Triage and Justice*, p. 1.

The increment criterion tells us to concentrate on patients around B. The level criterion would have us prefer patients around A. The criterion of enhancing end-stage level, to which reference was made earlier, focuses on patients around C.[66] I believe this relation obtains quite frequently, not just for medical treatment. Among the cases cited earlier, education, support to the mentally retarded, and rehabilitation of prisoners are probably subject to similar constraints. Roughly speaking, efficiency dictates concentration on intermediate cases, compassion on the hard ones, and laziness on the easy ones.

A first illustration of this dilemma concerns the admission of patients to intensive care units:

> The dominant strategy that physicians used to cope with decreased bed availability in the ICU was to restrict its use for monitoring purposes. Although this strategy may be intuitively appealing, it is worth noting that it is not necessarily the optimal use of the ICU. There are patients with manifest critical illness who are

---

[66]I am assuming here that treatment never makes things worse. Sometimes, this assumption is false. For instance, "selection of patients who are not sick enough [for a heart transplantation] may result in the premature death of a 'successful' recipient" (Copeland et al., "Selection of Patients for Cardiac Transplantation," *Circulation*, p. 1). In such cases the relation between severity of illness and efficacy of treatment can be summarized as follows:

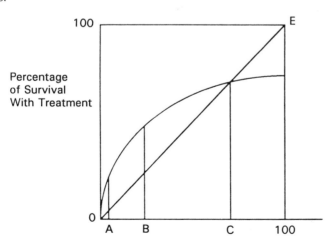

Percentage of Survival Without Treatment

admitted to the ICUs whose outcomes are not affected by intensive care. Conversely, there are patients who are admitted solely for monitoring in whom complications develop that are reversed only because they are in an ICU. The problem is that physicians cannot feel certain about the marginal benefit of ICU care for any individual patient. As a result, they appear to ration ICU beds on the basis of immediate need rather than of ultimate benefit. This approach appears to extend to care of the dying patient. Among patients admitted to the ICU who subsequently die, there are some whose fate seems unavoidable well before their actual death. . . . Physicians appeared to be reluctant to conserve resources by withdrawing care from acutely ill patients even when the anticipated benefit of that care was vanishingly small.[67]

In Chapter 5, I offer some conjectures about the psychological mechanisms supporting the norm of compassion. Here, I only want to emphasize the focal-point quality of a "clear and present danger," as distinct from more uncertain—although possibly greater—later benefits.

Kidney transplantation in the United States does not offer clear examples of the choice between level and increment criteria. Since dialysis is universally available as a fallback solution, urgency of need is rarely a major consideration. Diabetic ESRD patients may provide an exception. Renal disease caused by diabetes has more complications than that caused by hypertension, yet patients with diabetic renal disease have higher transplant rates. According to one author, "This may be due to the thought that these patients' conditions do particularly badly while receiving dialysis."[68] Even if correct, this observation does not show that the level criterion is being used. Perhaps the compassion of doctors leads them to prefer patients who are suffering more—but perhaps efficiency considerations lead them to prefer patients whose conditions can be improved more. Although the outcome is less good in absolute terms for diabetic patients than for others, the improvement in relative terms is larger since they start out being worse off.

In Great Britain, where dialysis is far from universally available,

---

[67] Singer et al., "Rationing Intensive Care—Physician Response to a Resource Shortage," p. 1159.

[68] Kjellstrand, "Age, Sex, and Race Inequality in Renal Transplantation," p. 1308.

urgency of need is a real issue. "One physician, for instance, might favor a transplant for the healthier patient, in order to maximize the likely benefit from the organ. Meanwhile, the second physician might argue for a transplant for the sicker patient, emphasizing that his need is more urgent."[69] My impression, for what it is worth, is that the utilitarian ethic of the National Health Service in Britain would lead most doctors there to favor the healthier patient, whereas more American doctors would favor the sicker one. Although all doctors probably are attracted by both criteria, there may be national differences with respect to which has the stronger pull.

Liver and heart transplantations offer many illustrations of the level-increment dilemma. Liver transplantations in the United States are caught in a tragic situation. There is a long waiting list for such operations. As people wait, their medical situation deteriorates to the point where death is certain unless they receive a new liver immediately. Doctors understandably feel compelled to give priority to these urgent cases. The very medical deterioration that creates the need for transplantation also, however, reduces the chances of graft survival. More people could benefit and survive if they were transplanted before their situation reached that urgent stage.

Concerning heart transplantations, I shall quote at some length a passage that makes the point with exemplary clarity:

> A major conflict with the efficient or "best" use criteria for use of a heart arises once patients have been selected as candidates for transplant. . . . The current selection system gives priority to those candidates on the list whose cases are most urgent, including those who have rejected a transplant and those who have received a temporary artificial heart as a bridge to transplant. A strict concern with efficacious use of donated hearts might argue against such an allocation, for the most urgent cases are less likely to do as well as healthier candidates. Yet it is not clear that decisions in favor of these candidates are ethically unacceptable. While efficiency is important, a strong equity consideration is to avoid abandonment of critically ill patients. Once on a candidate list one could argue that there is a special need not to abandon those in greatest need. . . . Retransplantation after rejection of a heart also appears

---

[69] Halper, *The Misfortunes of Others*, p. 115.

to conflict with efficiency by allocating a second heart to a patient who does not have as good a chance of surviving as a healthier candidate. Yet aggressive efforts on behalf of a recipient in acute rejection are viewed by some physicians as essential to demonstrate commitment and to avoid abandonment. Such a choice is not unreasonable, and could justify a second transplant even if some patients receive two hearts and still die and others receive none.[70]

Efficiency. Often the good is allocated to promote some other end than the welfare of the recipient. One person may derive greater personal benefits from a good than another, yet the latter may use it more productively, with greater benefits for the allocating institution or for some socially defined end. A firm will rather hire an efficient worker with no dependents than a less productive worker who has a family to support. The father may get custody because he is more fit to promote the child's welfare, although he does not derive the same personal benefits from custody as the mother would. In disaster situations, priority might follow the principle "Doctors, women, and children first." Eugenic proposals would reserve the right to procreate to those with good genes. In China during the Civil War, there was a fierce debate whether land should be allocated on a per capita basis or proportionately to labor power, the argument for the latter being that it would lead to more efficient land utilization.[71] It has been proposed that life-saving medical resources should be allocated on the basis of the recipients' expected contribution to society in the future. In choosing among applicants to college, one might use "social value added" as a criterion.[72] Young men are inducted into military service on the basis of their fighting efficiency or, more generally, on the basis of where they can do most for the war effort. In Norway, children of health care personnel get priority in nursery schools, because of the scarcity of health workers. The proposal

[70] Robertson, "Supply and Distribution of Hearts for Transplantation: Legal, Ethical, and Policy Issues," p. 82. See also Kamm, "The Report of the U.S. Task Force on Organ Transplantation: Criticisms and Alternatives," especially p. 214 ff.

[71] Dequn, "Criteria for Land Distribution During the Second Revolutionary Civil War Period (1927–1937)."

[72] Klitgaard, *Choosing Elites,* pp. 61–71, has a good discussion of this criterion and the objections to it.

has also been made in Norway that those who are active in the work force should be allowed to jump the health queues. Prisoners are selected for early release on criteria that are correlated with the likelihood of recidivism. Examples could be multiplied indefinitely.

There is a spectrum of such outcome-oriented principles. At one end, the maximand that guides the allocation is the increment in welfare of the individual recipient (including perhaps that of his family). At the other end, the maximand is social welfare. Intermediate principles include maximizing the financial health of the institution (e.g., firms or universities); maximizing the welfare of a subset of the class of nonrecipients (e.g., children, or victims of crime); and maximizing a social aggregate (e.g., military capacity, or gross national product) that may or may not also be a part of the arrangement that maximizes social welfare. In a broader sense of the term, all these outcome-oriented concerns might be grouped together under the heading of efficiency. The effort to maximize a social aggregate such as GNP or total welfare reflects a concern for global or overall efficiency. The more restricted outcome-oriented principles embody a concern for what we may call *local efficiency*. Further discussions of consequentialism and utilitarianism are found in Chapter 6.

The efficiency criterion is often justified by the claim that the gains achieved by adopting it will enable the authorities to offer the good to those who claim it on other grounds. By saving doctors first, one can save more women and children than if these had taken priority. By allowing active workers to go to the head of the health queues, extra resources are generated that can be channeled back to the health sector and allow everybody to be treated without waiting any longer than they would have done had the priority rule not existed. In the terminology of Calabresi and Bobbit, second-order allocative decisions can have a favorable influence on the first-order decisions that determine supply. They can, but they need not do so. Even improvements that might benefit everybody are not always realized. The government might well decide to use the extra resources generated from the larger work force for some other purpose, such as building schools or waging war. Part of the reason why second-order decision makers insist on their locally just criteria is probably a suspicion that any efficiency gains realized by adopting different criteria might be diverted to other purposes.

Contribution. Sometimes, goods are allocated according to earlier contributions to some socially valued goal. In the World War II demobilization scheme, contribution to the war effort was an important criterion. (In another example from the same war, efficiency took precedence over contribution, when scarce penicillin was used to treat soldiers with venereal disease to get them combat ready rather than to treat the severely wounded.)[73] Veterans, quite generally, take priority in many cases, ranging from the special seats for *gueules cassées* in the Parisian Métro to extra tickets in land lotteries[74] and preferential access to civil service employment. The proposal to give custody to the parent who has had main responsibility in raising the child is an instance of similar backward-looking reasoning. The seniority principle in layoffs can, as mentioned earlier, be seen as a special case of the contribution principle. Contributions to good works or to holy wars have been thought to be decisive for the allocation of grace and salvation.

Often the goal toward which a contribution has been made is related to the good to be allocated: one might award custody to a mother because she has taken care of her child, but not on the grounds that she has cared for an old aunt. In the American demobilization scheme, only contribution to the war effort counted. Sometimes, however, there may be no relation whatsoever, as when veterans take priority in the job queue.[75] Although some actions tend to create merit across the board, as it were, most do not extend beyond their own sphere. I return to this question in the next chapter.

Sometimes, the relevant contribution is defined as an abstention. In China, an exception to the policy of one child per family was made if two only children married: they were allowed to

---

[73] Beecher, "Scarce Medical Resources and Medical Advancement."

[74] Dale, "Oklahoma's Great Land Lottery of 1832."

[75] It is presumably because of this lack of relation that Walzer argues (*Spheres of Justice*, p. 154 n.) that "offices are surely the wrong currency to pay" debts to veterans. The U.S. Veterans Administration provides extensive care for service-related medical problems, but less extensively for non-service-related problems (Kilner, *Who Lives? Who Dies?* pp. 42–43).

have two children. Whereas in some countries (e.g., Israel) public housing is preferentially given to families with many children, India has had the policy of giving priority to families with fewer than three children.[76] The same effect is obtained when denial of a scarce good is used as a punishment for undesirable behavior. In many countries, it used to be the case that the adulterous party in a divorce was automatically denied custody. A criminal record (except for convictions for political offenses) has standardly provided grounds for denying applications for immigration.

The contribution principle is backward-looking, whereas principles that seek to maximize efficiency or individual increments in welfare are forward-looking. Yet this contrast is to some extent misleading, since many schemes based on contribution are set up because of their good effects on incentives. Recipients are told at time t_1 that allocation at time t_3 will be made on the basis of their behavior at time t_2. This is the generic form of an incentive system.

We may distinguish, perhaps, between three varieties of contribution-based systems. At one extreme, there are the *pure desert systems* in which the individual did not know, at the time he performed the meritorious action, that it would generate access to the scarce good in question. At the other extreme, there are the *pure incentive systems,* in which the institution tries to encourage a certain kind of behavior by telling the actors that it will not go unrewarded. In between, there is a set of cases in which the individual is told ahead of time that meritorious actions will be rewarded, but only on the condition that they be not performed for the sake of the reward. In the Christian doctrines that hold up good works as a path to salvation, it is a central idea that the works have to be motivated by the love of God, not by the desire for salvation. In Maoist China, activists were to be rewarded in the form of access to scarce goods, but only if their activism was truly based on ideological loyalty. In practice, such purity of mind could be proved only by refusing the goods to which it entitled them.[77]

Character. Contribution systems reward or punish people for

---

[76] Calabresi and Bobbit, *Tragic Choices,* p. 216.
[77] See Walder, *Communist Neo-Traditionalism.* Other Catch 22 effects are cited in Chapter 4.

what they do. Character-based systems reward or punish them for what they are. Although assessment of character must be based on observation of behavior (except for God, who can see directly into hearts and minds), there is a difference between using specific forms of behavior to allocate a good related to that behavior and using behavior across the board as a guide to character which, in turn, serves as a principle of allocation. Thus in their search for people who could form the basis for a new political order, the Chinese Communists excluded not only "those who stole crops, worked as prostitutes, had ties to bandits or opium smugglers, frequented Japanese-occupied areas, were prominent members of secret societies, or had once served in puppet forces," but also those who "had a 'mysterious past,' committed adultery, had bad tempers, failed to attend political meetings, smoked opium, or had roving wives."[78] Clearly, the purpose here was to assess character and reliability as a whole.

The selection of adoptive or custodial parents also involves assessment of character in this overall sense. In theory, one can be a good person without being a very good parent. In practice, many will find the distinction a tenuous one. Those who are rejected for lack of parental fitness certainly do not seem able to make it.

MECHANISMS BASED ON POWER

Purchasing power. Often, scarce goods—other than goods routinely provided through the market, like consumer goods—are given to those who pay (or pay most) for them. It is easier to get into some Oxford colleges if your father is a large benefactor. The absolution of sins conditionally on gifts or bequests to the church was widely practiced before the Reformation. Employees might be allowed to bid for the best offices.[79] Under conditions of unemployment, one might allow people to bid for jobs (and perhaps use the proceeds to subsidize the unemployed).[80] Under conditions of

---

[78] Spence, *The Search for Modern China*, p. 481.
[79] Boyes and Happel, "Auctions as an Allocation Mechanism in Academia."
[80] This proposal is from P. van Parijs (unpublished work).

overpopulation, one might have families bid for a limited number of procreation rights.

We can distinguish between several roles of purchasing power in local justice contexts. First, wealthy individuals can bribe the allocators. This practice does not classify as a principle, being an explicit violation of the official principle adopted by the institution. Second, if the rich cannot get the good through regular channels, they can buy it from those who do. If this practice is illegal, the same comment applies. If post-allocation trade is legal, it belongs to the mixed principles further discussed below. Third, the institution that allocates the good may decide to do so through an administered market, such as an auction or a voucher scheme. Broadcasting licenses, procreation rights, taxi licenses, and school places could be allocated in this way. Finally, an ordinary market might be created through a process of deregulation. Today all Western countries, with the exception of the Netherlands, have laws forbidding the sale of human organs for transplantation purposes. Although there appears to be wide political agreement on this policy, academics frequently advocate the creation of a market in organs.[81]

Money can matter for allocation even when it is not to be spent on obtaining the good. Among the criteria used by the Seattle committee that regulated access to dialysis (Chapter 5) were income and net worth. Here financial status was used not to show that the patient was able to pay for the treatment, but as a proxy for social worth—the higher the income, the greater the worth (or so I assume). In finding adoptive parents or choosing the custodial parent, income is also used as a criterion—not, however, as one that can be traded off against other criteria, but only as a floor constraint. Immigration to the United States has traditionally been regulated by imposing quality standards on the ships that brought the immigrants from Europe, thereby eliminating those who could not afford to pay for the more expensive trips. The requirement that immigrants must have some financial resources so as not to be a burden on the country also served to regulate immigration. The head tax on immigrants was originally introduced to generate

---

[81] H. Hansman, "The Economics and Ethics of Markets for Human Organs."

revenue, but later proposals to raise it were often justified as a screening device. The restriction of voting rights and eligibility by property has been justified both as "a crude measure of the best and wisest" and on the grounds that property was an interest in its own right: "The House of Representatives is intended as the Representatives of the Persons, and the Senate of the property of the Common Wealth."[82]

Influence. Sometimes, people get access to scarce goods because of their formal political power or informal connections. In China, *guanxi*, or "instrumental friendship," is an important mechanism in the allocation of scarce consumer goods, certificates of illness, and the like.[83] Children of alumni, staff, and professors are preferentially admitted to many American colleges, as are (or were) children of party bosses in Communist countries. In the United States, preferential access to college is sometimes given to children of local politicians who have it in their power to raise taxes for the university,[84] and to children of firemen whose cooperation is vital for the institution's interest. People who know doctors often manage to jump the queue for scarce medical resources. Others achieve the same end by capitalizing on their nuisance value, for instance, by camping on the doctor's doorstep or bypassing his gatekeepers.[85]

Many of these practices are akin to bribery or blackmail, and so must be thought of as negations of principles rather than as principles in their own right. Sometimes, however, the operation of influence almost amounts to an explicit principle. *Guanxi* in China and *blat* in the former Soviet Union are in many ways indispensable for the functioning of the economic system. Preferential ad-

[82] Wood, *The Creation of the American Republic*, p. 218.
[83] Walder, *Communist Neo-Traditionalism*.
[84] Oren, *Joining the Club*, p. 58.
[85] Aaron and Schwartz, *The Painful Prescription*, p. 107, report a British doctor as saying that "the key to turning down the patient 'is not to get eyeball to eyeball with him because if you do that there is no way you can actually say no.'" Similarly, Calabresi and Bobbit, *Tragic Choices*, p. 229, report an Italian doctor as saying that "I can say 'no room' on the telephone, but not in person." The strategy of getting access to scarce medical resources by turning up in person and refusing to leave has also been observed in French transplantation units (Paterson, *Enquête sur la justice locale: La transplantation rénale*, p. 131).

mission to college for children of alumni, staff, and faculty in the United States is not an underground practice. In the United States the majority of immigration measures taken in Congress result from "private bills" that promote the cause of an individual who has been unable to gain admission. Between 1937 and 1973, about 55,000 such bills were introduced, of which approximately 6,300 were approved, corresponding to less than 1 percent of total immigration.

MIXED SYSTEMS

The principles discussed so far constitute, as it were, *the elementary building blocks of local justice.* Actual allocative systems can virtually never be reduced to a single principle. Instead, they rely on several criteria or mechanisms, combined in some way or other. I shall discuss a number of such mixed systems, subsuming them under three main categories. In the first kind of mixed systems, several criteria are considered simultaneously and aggregated to yield an overall score for each applicant or potential recipient. These systems include point systems, disjunctive models, conjunctive models, lexicographic models, and more intuitive trade-offs. In the second kind, several principles are applied in succession, either to reduce the number of recipients to match the available goods or to improve the match. These systems include selection from a pool of eligibles and post-allocation trade. In the third kind, impersonal mechanisms and individualized criteria are fused into one overall system. These systems include weighted lotteries and multiple queues.

Linear point systems. Often formal schemes are constructed that take account of several, differently weighted, criteria. The point systems used for allocating kidneys in the United States (especially in its first version) and for deciding on the order of demobilization from the American Army in World War II are outstanding examples. Some institutions of higher education also use explicit, mechanical point systems to choose among applicants. Admission to the nursery school run by the Student's Union at the University of Oslo is run on a point system, in which points are awarded for properties of the children (need and age) as well as of the parents (years of study). Canada and Australia use point systems for immigration, with most of the criteria being assessed on a subjective basis.[86]

Layoffs are sometimes decided by the use of point systems. It is reported that a British firm "incorporated many individual criteria into one overall point system in selecting employees for dismissal," with points allocated for "length of service, age, marital status, dependents, quality of performance, and versatility."[87] The State Labor Court of North Rhine-Westphalia developed a similar point system for layoffs in 1981, giving up to five points for age, four points for each year of seniority, four points for each child, and ten points for any severe handicap, with ten points deducted for a working spouse. This scheme was declared invalid by the Federal Labor Court in 1983, on the grounds that it suppressed relevant individual differences.[88] For instance, if a worker has a child with a speech defect that requires attendance at a special school, he should not have to move. Or a worker might have a handicap that does not in fact affect his labor power or his labor market opportunities.

The normative weights used in point systems must be distinguished from the implicit, descriptive weights that can be reconstructed from actual or hypothetical decisions made on discretionary grounds.[89] Assuming additive relations among the relevant variables, one can use regression analysis to assign weights to the various criteria. The assumption of additivity is often questionable, however. In the German layoff case just cited, it amounts to saying that the difference between no seniority and five years seniority is the same as that between twenty-five and thirty years of seniority; and the difference between no child and one child the same as the difference between five and six children. It implies,

---

[86] Briggs, *Immigration Policy and the American Labor Force*, p. 94.

[87] J. Gennard, "Great Britain," pp. 129–130.

[88] *Entscheidungen des Bundesarbeitsgerichts*, p. 151 ff.

[89] Two studies of implicit weights are Bazerman, "Norms of Distributive Justice in Interest Arbitration" and Taylor et al., "Individual Differences in Selecting Patients for Regular Hemodialysis." The former of these studies also compares the implicit weights of the various criteria with the explicit weights assigned to them by the decision makers when asked to identify the criteria that were most important in their decisions. We must distinguish, then, between institutionally imposed weights (point systems), revealed weights (found in regression analysis), and self-reported weights.

moreover, that the child-seniority trade-off is the same for all levels of seniority and all numbers of children. Actual decision makers who incorporate these criteria in a discretionary way would surely want to make finer distinctions here. By the same token, explicit point systems will often be quite crude and occasionally inadequate. Whenever possible, one should try, therefore, to construct the trade-offs that specify how the marginal importance of one variable depends on the values taken by all variables.[90]

The previous paragraphs have identified two weaknesses of point systems as a method for allocating scarce goods. First, they are restricted to a limited, usually small, number of variables. Because two individuals could be identical in all these respects and yet differ in other, morally relevant ways, point systems can easily produce morally undesirable results.[91] Second, point systems are very rigid because of their linear, additive form. A system that gives equal importance to the first child and to the twenty-fifth year of seniority is quite obviously inadequate. A further objection arises out of a problem that we encountered in the American demobilization scheme. If the weights are to represent a social consensus, the procedure for aggregating individual opinions into socially optimal weights can yield an inconsistent result. Against these various drawbacks one must cite the advantage that point systems are easy to operate and not vulnerable to charges of abuse or corruption. For many practical purposes, they may do as well as any other procedure.

Conjunctive and disjunctive systems.[92] Point systems allow for low scores on one dimension to be compensated by high scores on

---

[90] This is a central concern in Keeney and Raiffa, *Decisions with Multiple Objectives.*

[91] In *The Critique of the Gotha Program*, Marx claimed that all systems of justice suffer from this defect. To the extent that they have to be fully stated in written codes of law, without any scope for discretionary assessment on a case-by-case basis, he was right. The problem may be alleviated by including a large number of individual criteria, and eliminated by adding an element of discretionary judgment.

[92] The following draws on Dawes, "Social Selection Based on Multidimensional Criteria" and Einhorn, "The Use of Nonlinear, Noncompensatory Models in Decision Making." Mellers and Hartka, "Fair Selection Decisions," show that conjunctive and disjunctive models are special cases of a more generally defined selection procedure.

another. In noncompensatory systems this is not the case. Conjunctive systems evaluate applicants by their weakest feature, whereas disjunctive systems evaluate an applicant by the criterion on which he scores highest. In the former, an applicant has to be a jack of all trades; in the latter, it is sufficient to be a master of one. In college admissions, for instance, conjunctive selection procedures will lead to a body of well-rounded students, whereas disjunctive systems will lead to a well-rounded body of students, given sufficient diversity among the applicants.[93]

Lexicographic principles. Sometimes, a secondary criterion is used to break ties. Thus in selecting workers to be laid off, some firms use ability as the main criterion, with seniority as a tiebreaker. At the University of Oslo, female applicants for academic jobs are chosen over men when judged equal in ability. In the American scheme for allocating hearts for transplantation, length of time waiting is used to break ties among patients whose need is deemed equally urgent. Under the most recent system for kidney allocation, time on the waiting list also serves as a tiebreaker among ESRD patients with the same number of antigen matches.

The importance of the secondary criterion depends on the precision with which the primary criterion is applied. Urgency of need for heart transplantation has only two degrees: urgent and less urgent. Hence the secondary criterion is regularly invoked. In appointment to academic positions, small differences in recognized ability are often cited to justify the appointment of one applicant rather than another. In such cases, the secondary criterion is idling and serves mainly a symbolic purpose. In layoff contexts, equality of ability can be interpreted narrowly, so as to give little scope for seniority, or so broadly that seniority—the secondary criterion—de facto becomes the primary one.

Selecting from a pool of eligibles. Sometimes, one criterion or mechanism is used to form a pool of eligibles and another to select from within the pool.[94] In Norway, jurors are chosen randomly from a larger set established by the municipality. (Actually, they are chosen from two pools, since the law requires the jury to

[93] J. C. Kemeny, as cited in Dawes, *op. cit.*

[94] Formally, this amounts to using a lexicographic procedure with a dichotomous primary criterion.

have an equal number of men and women.) In the United States, prosecutors and defense lawyers can exclude jurors from a pool selected at random from the population at large. When sailors had to choose one among themselves by lot to be eaten, married men were sometimes taken out of the pool.[95] In the allocation of scarce medical resources, the first step usually is to admit patients to a waiting list on the basis of their need for treatment and some minimal ability to benefit from it. In selecting from the waiting list, ability to benefit from treatment might again be used as a criterion, but other criteria—time spent waiting, or medical bad luck such as having an unusual antigen pattern—can also serve.

Intuitive trade-offs. In allocative situations with multiple objectives and some scope for discretion, decision makers often proceed more informally, by intuitively trading off against each other the strengths and weaknesses of the applicants. Assuming that they have an interest in efficiency as well as in equity, two different trade-off maps may be required. To illustrate this idea, consider the widespread practice of preferential admission of disadvantaged students to elite colleges.

At the entry level, students can be characterized in the two-dimensional space in Figure 3.3. At the exit level, one can measure their performance (e.g., by fourth-year college grades). In principle, it should be possible to establish the shape of the iso-performance curves. If these curves are vertical, earlier disadvantage is irreversible: students who have had few opportunities in the past do not, for equal grade levels, perform better when they are admitted to an elite institution.[96] If they are not vertical, some of the earlier disadvantage can be offset. An efficiency-oriented institution would have indifference curves that coincided with the iso-performance curves. An institution that was also oriented toward compensatory justice would have indifference curves less steep than the iso-performance curves, as in the diagram. When interviewing admissions officers in institutions that practice such preferential admission, it has been remarkably hard to get them

[95] Simpson, *Cannibalism and the Common Law*, p. 131.
[96] This language is somewhat inaccurate. Instead of referring to vertical iso-performance lines, I should say that academic indicators are equally good predictors of performance for students from all economic and cultural backgrounds. But I suppose for simplicity that everything is deterministic.

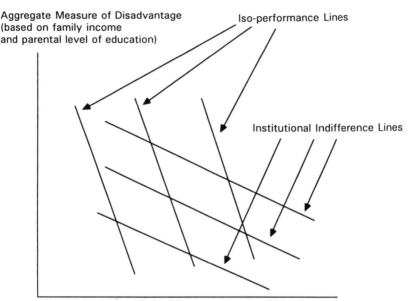

Aggregate Measure of Disadvantage
(based on family income
and parental level of education)

Iso-performance Lines

Institutional Indifference Lines

Aggregate Measure of Academic Achievements
(based on high school grade and rank, test scores, etc.)

Figure 3.3

to assess the slope of these curves or, what should be easier, the difference between their slopes. They knew that they wanted to favor "students who have been deprived of good educational opportunities in the past," to use a phrase I often heard, but they could not explain why they had this preference.

Post-allocation trade. Sometimes, goods are allocated institutionally, with the possibility (which may or may not be legal) of private post-allocation trade. To allocate milk quotas among farmers, the government often uses a mixed system to decide who gets to produce how much at guaranteed sale prices. In Norway, for instance, quotas are mainly allocated as a percentage of pre-quota levels of production, with exceptions in favor of small producers and producers in Northern Norway.[97] In the European Community and in Canada, a variety of quota schemes are in use.[98] In most of these countries, the sale of quotas is forbidden. In Canada and France, however, black markets in quotas have emerged; and

[97] I am indebted to A. Moxness Jervell for information about this system, as well as for guidance in the literature on milk quotas.
[98] See Burrell (ed.), *Milk Quotas in the European Community* and Perraud et al., *Quotas Laitiers.*

in Great Britain sales of quotas are legal and substantial. The debate over the right to sell quotas reflects a conflict between the goal of promoting economic efficiency and that of ensuring a decent income for all groups and regions. Along similar lines, the proposal has been made (and quite widely embraced) to create a market in emission rights to ensure global reductions of CO_2.

Other examples include the Norwegian practice of allowing students who have been admitted to medical school in Oslo and Bergen to swap places. As might be expected, this practice has created a gray market in which the current price for a place in Oslo is about $4,000 (on top of a place in Bergen). The selection by lot for military service, combined with the possibility to buy a substitute, was widely practiced in nineteenth century France.[99] In the United States, selection on substantive grounds, combined with substitution and commutation (exemption from service against payment of a fee to the state, which then used it to pay volunteers) was widespread before the twentieth century.[100] At the Federal Convention in Philadelphia, Gouverneur Morris argued against extension of the suffrage on the assumption that votes could and would be sold: "Give the votes to the people who have no property, and they will sell them to the rich who will be able to buy them."[101] In Graham Greene's novel, *The Tenth Man,* one of the people chosen at random by the Germans to be shot in retaliation was able to persuade another to take his place, against the payment of a large sum of money to the latter's family.

Allowing post-allocation trade need not make everybody better off, even assuming ideal conditions.[102] It can encourage wasteful investments in entitlements by individuals who do not really need the good, but can benefit from selling it. A bright high school student who really intends to become an engineer might apply to medical school in Oslo just to be able to sell his place to a student from Bergen, and then drop out of medical school in Bergen as soon as he got there. Under non-ideal conditions, post-allocation

[99] de Bohigas, "Some Opinions on Exemption from Military Service in Nineteenth-century Europe."

[100] Chambers, *To Raise an Army,* index under "substitution" and "commutation."

[101] Farrand (ed.), *Records of the Federal Convention,* vol. 2, p. 202.

[102] Sah, "Queues, Rations, and Market: Comparisons of Outcomes for the Poor and the Rich."

trade could be even more objectionable. Myopia, weakness of will, collective action problems, or poor information might induce a disadvantaged person to accept a big sum of money for taking another's place in the army or to sell his vote or his quota. I return to these issues in Chapter 6.

Weighted lotteries. Sometimes equality and substantive criteria can be combined by using weighted lotteries in which the weights depend on the substantive criteria. Thus in the Netherlands all applicants to medical school have a chance of getting in, but those with higher grades have a larger chance than others.[103] In Georgia's land lottery of 1832 "each citizen was entitled to one chance, unless he belonged to a favoured group—orphans, Revolutionary War veterans, head of a family, and the like—in which case he was given two chances."[104] It has been proposed that scarce organs for transplantation be allocated in the same way.[105]

Weighted lotteries are a normative principle. As in the case of point systems, they have a descriptive (and predictive) analogue. Thus consider the following two diagrams. The first describes the Dutch system of weighted lottery on admitting students to medical school, with grades ranging from 5.5 to 8.5 determining the chances of admission.

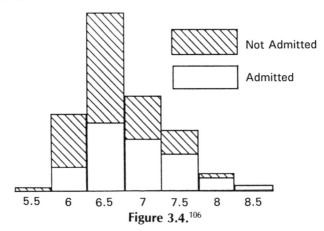

Figure 3.4.[106]

[103] Hofstee, "The Case for Compromise in Educational Selection and Grading."

[104] Wilms, "Georgia's Land Lottery of 1832."

[105] Brock, "Ethical Issues in Recipient Selection for Organ Transplantation."

[106] After Hofstee, "The Case for Compromise in Educational Selection and Grading."

The next diagram describes the chances of admission to Harvard Law School as a function of test scores and quality-adjusted college grades, combined into an overall admissions index.

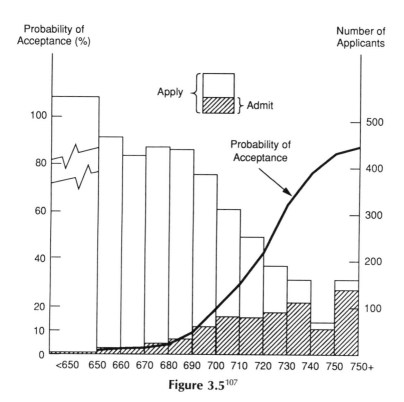

Figure 3.5[107]

Although Figure 3.4 is formally similar to Figure 3.5, the interpretation is quite different. Figure 3.5 describes an empirical correlation between scores on the admission index and actual admission. The reason the correlation is imperfect is that admission committees consider a number of other variables in addition to the index. In the selection system described in Figure 3.4 no other variables than grades are considered. Although grades are all that matters, the element of chance ensures that they do not form a perfect predictor of admission.

[107] After Klitgaard, *Choosing Elites*, p. 36.

Multiple queues. In a closely related arrangement, one may have separate queues for different categories of recipients, with specific proportions of the good being made available in each queue. Thus, in Poland, pregnant women and old people can shortcut the main queues in shops by taking their place in queues with shorter waiting time.[108] At Oslo airport, taxis queue for passengers in two separate lines, one being made up of taxis registered in the city of Oslo and the other of taxis registered in the municipality of Bærum where the airport is located. Every other passenger is directed to the Oslo taxi queue and every other to the Bærum queue. (Since there is never any scarcity of taxis, this amounts to a scheme for allocating passengers to taxis, not for allocating taxis to passengers.) The allocation of police attention to different categories of crimes may, for practical purposes, be very similar to a system of multiple queues (or weighted lotteries): all offenders run a risk of being investigated, but the risk is higher for the more serious offenders. The proposal has also been made to allocate scarce medical resources by using multiple queues, in which older patients would be more rarely selected.[109]

At the end of this catalogue, it may be useful to remind ourselves that not all scarce goods are allocated through principles. I do not have in mind the widespread phenomenon that principles can be violated, but the equally pervasive fact that allocation can be made on a discretionary basis without any guidelines or principles whatsoever. In pre-modern societies, many scarce goods were allocated by whim or favor by the powerful, and nobody thought it could be or should be otherwise. Even today, such practices are not uncommon. Small family firms can hire whomever they want without having to provide a reason or appeal to a principle.[110] The Internal Revenue Service has unbounded discretion in selecting individuals for tax audits. These examples also point to the limits of discretion in modern societies. Beyond what is justified by the right to privacy or the need for secrecy, modern institutions are held accountable for their practices.

[108] Cwartosz, "On Queuing."
[109] "Scarce Medical Resources," p. 665.
[110] Walzer, *Spheres of Justice*, p. 161.

4 / Consequences of Local Justice

In this chapter I discuss how a scheme for allocating a good or a burden can have consequences over and above the consequences embedded in the scheme itself. Assume that the scheme offers the good to all and only the members of X, as defined by one of the principles discussed in Chapter 3. I shall refer to this fact as the *primary consequence* of the scheme. It may also be the case, however, that members of X (or at least those members who actually end up with the good) are also, or disproportionately, members of Y. This consequence of the scheme, that it offers the good selectively to members of Y, I shall refer to as a *secondary effect*. Literacy tests for immigration exclude those who cannot read. The American literacy tests, when introduced in 1917, also had the effect of excluding large numbers of immigrants from Southern and Eastern Europe.

Suppose now that there is a group Z, whose members would not normally be eligible for the good. Knowing that membership in X brings access to the good, members of Z may engage in a variety of actions so as to obtain such membership. Such behavior I shall refer to as *incentive effects* of the scheme. When military service is compulsory for able-bodied young men, most will have to serve. They can, however, achieve exemption (but risk prison) by cutting off a finger.

A third and more subtle set of effects is broadly analogous to the Prisoner's Dilemma, in which the aggregate effect of individually rational actions is collective irrationality.[1] Similarly, the overall effect of many locally just decisions may be the production of global injustice. Institutions rarely compensate for the bad luck of being turned down by other institutions: someone who by sheer bad luck is laid off from the job is not for that reason given preferential access to college.

In the following chapter I shall consider various explanations for the adoption by institutions of specific principles. Secondary effects or incentive effects are often cited as elements of such explanations, in one of two ways. In some cases, it is claimed that such effects are anticipated by the rule makers, and the rules chosen precisely because they have these consequences. This is a straightforward case of intentional explanation. In other cases, it is alleged that these effects can explain the rule even though no explicit intention was at work. This is a more dubious kind of functionalist explanation—usually, although not necessarily, unsupported by a specific mechanism.[2] In the present chapter, I shall consider secondary effects and incentive effects that obviously have no explanatory role, as well as those that have clear or possible explanatory import. To some extent, therefore, the two chapters overlap.

SECONDARY EFFECTS

The only system that is not susceptible of having secondary effects is a true (unbiased) lottery. Queuing works in favor of those who can afford to spend time standing in line. Waiting lists work against individuals subject to myopia, who find it hard to imagine that their turn will eventually come. Calabresi and Bobbit also argue that first-come, first-serve "may be deeply inegalitarian

---

[1] See Barry and Hardin (eds.), *Rational Man, Irrational Society.*
[2] For more about intentional and functionalist explanations, see Chapters 2 and 3 of my *Explaining Technical Change.*

if usable knowledge of the availability of the resource is unevenly distributed, particularly if the uneven distribution is linked to social or economic attributes."[3] Although correct, the observation is somewhat misleading, as it applies to *all* systems (even lotteries) in which people have to apply for the good in order to be considered as candidates. When recipients are selected without application (as in the draft, early release from prison, layoffs, or admission to intensive care units), no such knowledge-based bias can arise. The same holds true for another, probably more important bias, further discussed in Chapter 5: not all applicants have the resources to go through the bureaucratic procedures which are required before they can get what is rightfully theirs. This remark, too, is anticipated by Calabresi and Bobbit: "Imposing a complicated procedure functions as a system for allocation."[4] Characteristically, they also suggest that the complications are chosen by "society" to hide the fact of scarcity. I return to this aspect of their analysis in Chapter 5.

I shall consider in more detail four instances, all from the United States, of hotly debated secondary effects: transplantation of kidneys to blacks; admission of Jews to Yale; the doctrine of disparate impact in labor law; and finally, literacy tests and quota systems in immigration law. It is no accident that all cases involve ethnicity.[5] Although—to take an example from another arena— one does occasionally come across objections to student deferment for military service on the grounds that it favors sons of the wealthy, the argument is much more frequently made that it favors whites over ethnic minorities. The study of local justice should have a sobering effect on those who believe that social conflicts revolve around class rather than race or, more generally, status.[6]

Blacks and kidney transplantation. There is no overt discrimination against black candidates for transplantation, yet they are transplanted at significantly lower rates than whites. Black pa-

---

[3] *Tragic Choices*, p. 43.
[4] Ibid., p. 96.
[5] See also Conley et al., "The Use of Race as a Criterion in the Allocation of Scarce Resources."
[6] For some comments on this issue, see my *Making Sense of Marx*, p. 331 ff. and especially p. 390 ff.

tients on dialysis are transplanted half as frequently as whites, a fact that can be explained partly but not wholly by self-selection. Three facts conspire to bring it about.

First, blacks are highly overrepresented in the population of patients with end-stage renal disease (the incidence is about four times that of whites), partly for cultural and partly for genetic reasons. Hypertension, a main cause of renal disease, is much more frequent in the black population, a fact that may be due to "psychosocial stress caused by darker skin color" in lower socioeconomic groups.[7]

Second, blacks are underrepresented among organ donors.[8] The low rate of donation is due mainly to the reluctance of relatives to give their permission to recover an organ that could be used for transplantation. The reluctance has several causes, one of them being a belief that the organs are mainly going to white patients (as of course has to be the case, given that blacks form a small proportion of the population as a whole).

Third, blacks (as well as other minority groups) have unusual antigen patterns.[9] In an allocation system in which antigen matching plays a major role, this fact, in conjunction with the two others, is certain to ensure that blacks will get fewer transplantations.

[7] Klag et al., "The Association of Skin Color with Blood Pressure." The authors mention, however, that another interpretation is also possible: the hypertension might be due to an interaction between some environmental factor (stress or diet) caused by socioeconomic disadvantage (shared by blacks and low-income whites) and a gene that has higher prevalence among blacks with darker skin color. On both hypotheses, being a *disadvantaged black* explains the hypertension, but only on the first is the explanation in terms of stress caused by this double disadvantage.

[8] In the only systematic study of minority organ donation, Perez, Matas and Tellis, "Organ Donation in Three Major U.S. Cities by Race/Ethnicity," p. 815, found in their 40-month survey that black and Hispanic family refusal rates were 45 and 43 percent, respectively, while for the white population it was 17 percent in New York, Los Angeles, and Miami between January 1984 and April 1987.

[9] See Milford, Ratner, and Yunis, "Will Transplant Immunogenetics Lead to Better Graft Survival in Blacks?" p. 37, for a table comparing antigen frequencies by race. A second table demonstrates that blacks are more likely to have "blanks," that is, antigens which have yet to be designated by tissue-typing experts. Under the new UNOS system (see Chapter 2), the latter fact no longer works to the disadvantage of blacks, as it did under the old system. The new system gives points for the absence of observed mismatches, whereas the old was based on the number of observed matches.

This is especially so under the new point system. Under the old system, blacks could hope that if they waited long enough, they would eventually accumulate enough points to offset their lower matching score. Under the new UNOS point system, waiting time mainly serves to break ties in matching. Because of the fact cited above, however, blacks are unlikely to achieve parity of matching.

Consequently, doctors in areas with a heavy proportion of black patients have acted as a pressure group to change the point system. Last year, for instance, one regional organ bank decided, in a four to three vote, to increase the number of points allocated for time on the waiting list, in the expectation that more blacks would be transplanted. (As mentioned in the Introduction, the central UNOS system is subject to local variations.) Since the change would also benefit other groups with unusual antigen patterns, it could well be defended on neutral grounds of fairness and equity. The actual argument and intent, however, were not neutral. The secondary effects of the original system may or may not have been unintended and unforeseen; those of the modified system certainly were not.

In the design of any point system, two decisions are crucial. First, one has to decide on the properties that are to go into the system. Secondly, one has to decide how much they are to be weighted. The weights can be chosen because of their perceived fairness, or because they can be expected to bring about some desirable final allocation.[10] In the latter case, we may ask ourselves why that final allocation could not be produced by more direct means, such as quotas. One answer is that a point system may be easier to administer than a direct quota system. Another is that quotas, especially racial quotas, might well be illegal or otherwise unacceptable. I return to this point below.

Jews at Yale. Dan Oren's account of the admission of Jewish students to Yale University turns largely on the problem of secondary effects.[11] Officially, Yale never had quotas for Jews. Yale administrators wanted to avoid the public outcry that met Harvard's attempt in 1923 to impose explicit quotas (see Chapter 5).

---

[10] The same applies to the choice of properties. Formally, however, the choice of properties may be subsumed under the choice of weights, by assigning zero weight to properties that are not used in the scheme.

[11] The following draws on Oren, *Joining the Club.*

Also, they were concerned that the politically influential Jews in New Haven might retaliate by raising taxes. Yale's public position was that students were evaluated on the basis of scholastic merit and leadership abilities. Over the years, Yale admission officers, with the more or less explicit approval of the president and the deans, nevertheless used a number of subterfuges with the effect and usually the intent of reducing the number of Jews admitted. They introduced obligatory English examinations; gave preference to applicants from prep schools; rejected scholastically borderline Jews on the grounds that they would not contribute to the social life of the college and scholastically qualified Jews on the grounds that they were "book-grinds" and not leadership material; argued that many Jews wanted their children to go to Yale precisely because there were not many Jews there; and fudged the statistics of acceptance by counting as Jews everyone with a German-sounding last name.

In addition, Yale adopted a policy of geographical diversity, ostensibly as a goal in its own right, but in reality a measure taken to reduce the number of enrollments from the predominantly Jewish pool of applicants from New York City. The beauty of this last strategy, from the point of view of publicity-conscious admissions officers, was that it could be presented as unbiased. "Though many individual Jews (concentrated in the northeast region from which Yale received most of its applications) would be affected by this principle, it was not an innately anti-Jewish principle. A geographical policy applied without regard to religion that would help an individual Milwaukee Jew or Duluth Catholic as much as it would hurt a New York atheist or Hoboken Protestant could not appropriately be termed religiously biased."[12]

The facts, however, pointed toward discrimination. In 1952, the Jewish proportion of Yale College students remained at the traditional 10 percent level, whereas Jewish enrollment at the liberal arts colleges of Harvard and Cornell was approaching 25 percent. Also, the near-constant rate of 10 percent was seen as evidence of an informal quota system. The university replied that "The number of candidates qualifying for admissions in *all* of the so-called minority groups strike so nearly the same average year

[12] Ibid., p. 198.

after year that the results give the impression that quota systems are used. The same consistency of average probably obtains among *fat boys* and *harelips*—but we have never been accused of discrimination in these categories."[13] Oren adds that this "position was well taken. To claim that annual constancies of any group at Yale was evidence of a quota was a form of *post hoc, ergo propter hoc* reasoning." This argument is invalid, however, for small-number phenomena like the Yale admissions process. If the process had been truly random, one should expect substantial fluctuations around the average. If proportions close to the average are realized year in, year out, it is a sign of an intentional mixing.[14]

These two examples suggest a few generalizations. Institutions are often constrained by law or public opinion to use facially neutral criteria of selection. Although a given institution might like to favor or exclude applicants on the basis of race, gender, or age, a direct principle to this effect would violate the condition of facial neutrality. To get around the problem, allocators often adopt a plausible-looking facially neutral criterion that has a large extensional overlap with the prohibited category. To set a quota for blacks in kidney transplantation would probably be illegal. A change in the point system that assigns more points for time on the waiting list can, however, be defended in neutral terms of equity and fairness. Although it does benefit blacks, other patients with unusual antigen patterns also benefit. Similarly, although the Yale principle of geographical diversity did have an adverse impact on Jews, it also had an adverse impact on other groups that were overrepresented in the large states. A college that wants to ensure a minimum representation of blacks, but is prevented from using racial quotas, can achieve the same end by favoring economically and culturally disadvantaged applicants more gener-

---

[13] Cited after Oren, ibid., p. 193.

[14] The fallacy is similar to that instantiated in the following story (after Feller, *An Introduction to Probability Theory and Its Applications*, vol. 1, p. 161). During the Second World War, Londoners were persuaded that the Germans systematically concentrated their bombing in certain parts of their city, because the bombs fell in clusters. This inference reflected a lack of understanding of the statistical principle that random processes tend to generate clustering. If the German bombs had been evenly spaced, the evidence for non-random distribution would have been stronger.

ally.[15] If the extensional overlap approaches extensional equiva-
lence, the newly adopted system will be deemed unacceptable,
but if the secondary effects are sufficiently diluted among other
groups it has greater chances of being accepted.[16] The trick, for
the would-be discriminatory institution, is to find the minimal
level of dilution that keeps the system legal.[17]

Disparate impact and disparate intent. In the law, secondary effects are referred to as "disparate impact." When the effects are
also intended (or no other plausible explanation can be found),
they amount to "disparate intent." Various employer or union
practices have been successfully challenged on the grounds that
they have a disparate impact on blacks or women. The use of an
IQ test to select employees for hiring or promotion would, for this
reason, be regarded as a violation in the majority of circumstances.[18] As mentioned in Chapter 2, seniority systems can also
have a disparate impact, by locking women or minority members
into inferior positions. However, the fact that intent is specifically
referred to in the section of the Civil Rights Act dealing with
seniority systems affords them much stronger protection than
other practices. Although some early decisions found some bona
fide seniority systems with disparate impact unlawful, recent
courts have been reluctant to accept this argument, unless intent
to discriminate could also be proved. The turning point was a

---

[15]This seems actually to be the trend in American admission policies. It
may be due partly to the problem discussed in the text, partly to a perception
that minority students with mediocre grades and an upper-class background
have no special claim to admission.

[16]Thus at Yale, "Without specifically discriminating against Jews, the
board adopted policies that would, seemingly impartially, discriminate
against population groups that were largely, but not wholly, Jewish." (Oren,
Joining the Club, p. 54.)

[17]The illegality of quotas may also be overcome in a different way. Instead
of using different criteria for members of, say, minority groups, one may
give them extra resources to qualify for admission on the same criteria as
everybody else, as when minority students receive compensatory education
to qualify for college. I discuss this option in Chapter 6.

[18]Such tests have an adverse impact on blacks. In the absence of any
demonstrable relationship between the test and performance on the job, or
in the presence of an equally effective alternative means, its use would be
prohibited.

Supreme Court decision in 1977, laying down that a system can be a bona fide system even if it perpetuates the effects of discrimination that occurred before the Civil Rights Act.[19]

Secondary effects of immigration law. In the 1920s, a series of immigration bills were passed that allocated quotas by national origin. The 1921 Act adopted country-quota limits on European immigration based on 3 percent of the number of natives of the given country enumerated in the 1910 census. The 1924 Act settled on 2 percent of the 1890 proportions, while the 1929 Act changed the baseline to 1920. Clearly, the choice of baseline year would greatly affect the composition of the immigrant stream. Equally clearly, it was hard to argue from first principles for any particular year. Inevitably, the various proposals came to be judged by their secondary effects. The shift from 1910 to 1890 as a baseline was directly motivated by a desire to reduce the number of immigrants from Central, Southern, and Eastern Europe who had dominated immigration in the years after 1890:

> If immigration from southern and eastern Europe may enter the United States on a basis of substantial equality with that admitted from the older sources of supply, it is clear that if any appreciable number of immigrants are to be allowed to land on our shores the balance of racial preponderance must in time pass to those elements of the population who reproduce more rapidly on a lower standard of living than those possessing other ideals.[20]

The nature of the argument used to buttress the shift to the 1890 baseline is worth looking into. Albert Johnson, chairman of the House Immigration Committee, was strongly in favor of this shift, which would reduce the Italian quota from 42,000 to about

---

[19] *Teamsters* v. *U.S.* (431 U.S. 324). To be bona fide, a seniority system must be "rational and consistent," it must apply equally to all race and ethnic groups, it must not have had its genesis in racial discrimination, and it must have been negotiated and maintained free from any illegal discriminatory purpose. For an effort to show how statistical data concerning the impact of a seniority system might be used to establish that a system is not bona fide, see Kelley, "Discrimination in Seniority Systems."

[20] House of Representatives Committee on Immigration and Naturalization, cited after Hutchinson, *Legislative History of American Immigration Policy*, p. 484.

4,000, the Polish quota from 31,000 to 6,000 and the Greek from 3,000 to 100.[21] Yet he faced a problem:

> Was it not unfair and disciminatory to shift to an antique census base in order to favor the old immigration at the expense of the new? Johnson knew that his bill would face this charge, and it worried him. His concern at this point was significant. Despite the committee's actual determination to discriminate against southeastern Europe, it could not admit to any but equitable intentions. Despite the prevalence of racial nativism, Johnson could not openly justify his bill on grounds of Nordic superiority. The use of the 1890 census would have to be rationalized as a way of treating all Europeans by a principle of true equality. That much tribute, at least, America's democratic creed demanded.[22]

One of Johnson's advisors provided a solution, by arguing that

> quotas based on the number of foreign-born of various nationalities in the United States in 1910 did *not* reflect the racial status quo: by 1910 northwestern Europeans had lost the preponderant position among the foreign-born which their descendants still retained among the native-born. By a racial yardstick, the existing law could be charged with actually discriminating against the *old stock,* because it gave northwestern Europeans a smaller share in the annual quota immigration than they had in the total American population. *Thus the use of the 1910 census really favored southeastern Europeans.* Congress should base quotas on an earlier census, when the old immigration furnished the vast majority of America's foreign born, to do justice to everybody's ancestors.[23]

Various other proposals or bills were motivated by similar secondary effects. A literacy test was repeatedly proposed from 1897 onward (it was finally passed in 1917), on the grounds that it would not only "separate the ignorant, vicious, and the lazy from the intelligent and industrious," but also favor Northern and Western Europeans.[24] In Chapter 3, I cited fears that were expressed that the test might keep the wrong people out, by admitting anarchists and excluding honest workers. In his annual mes-

---

[21] Higham, *Strangers in the Land*, p. 319.
[22] Ibid., p. 319.
[23] Ibid., p. 320. Italics in original.
[24] Ibid., p. 466.

sage to the nation in 1901, President Roosevelt also commented on the fact that a literacy test "would not keep out all anarchists, for many of them belong to the intelligent criminal class."[25] However, he went on to say, "it would do what is also in point, that is, tend to decrease the sum of ignorance, so potent in producing the envy, suspicion, malignant passion, and the hatred of order, out of which anarchistic sentiments inevitably spring." Although the test would not exclude the anarchists, it would draw their fangs by depriving them of their raw material.

Another indirect method for keeping Southeastern Europeans out was by imposing a head tax. Originally introduced to generate revenue, the tax was soon seized upon as a possible policy instrument. When in 1906 a majority in the House Committee proposed to raise the tax from two to five dollars, the minority objected that the tax, although "obviously intended to keep out Southern Italians, Hungarians, Poles, and Slovaks," would in fact also "penalize the Germans, Scandinavians, English, and others who come with large families."[26]

These examples from immigration law—and they could have been multiplied indefinitely—suggest two general remarks about the problem of teasing out the relation between ends and means in local justice contexts. First, when the secondary effect of a principle is in fact the one for the sake of which it has been adopted, we may sometimes view it as a proxy for a more general principle. One overarching idea behind immigration law has always been to keep out certain classes of undesirables. Rather than leaving the implementation of this ideal to immigration inspectors, Congress adopted the head tax and the literacy test as easily enforceable, nondiscretionary proxies.[27] Similar arguments, however, do not apply to the indirect measures taken to increase the number of blacks transplanted or to reduce the number of Jews admitted to Yale. These, or at least the latter, were subterfuges rather than proxies.

Second, we observe that the relation between principle and proxy can be many-many rather than one-one. The goal of exclud-

[25] Ibid., p. 128.
[26] Ibid., p. 139 (I quote from Hutchinson's summary).
[27] Ibid., pp. 439, 463.

ing Southeastern Europeans could be achieved by quotas, literacy tests, or head taxes. Conversely, Roosevelt's remarks show that the literacy test could serve other purposes than that of shaping the ethnic composition of immigrants. This remark applies in other contexts, too. Thus in Chapter 3, I observed that giving priority for transplantation to patients with dependents could be justified either on grounds of need (to save dependents from suffering) or on grounds of efficiency (since dependents can provide support in the post-transplantation period). Conversely, the goal of efficiency can also be implemented by using age as a proxy. (And some would advocate the use of age as a criterion in its own right.) When the relation between principles and proxies is many-one, the task of coalition-building (Chapter 5) is facilitated. When the relation is one-many, conflict may ensue over the most efficient or desirable means to a shared end. When it is many-many, as in the cases I have mentioned, more complex patterns of cooperation and conflict arise.

INCENTIVE EFFECTS

Many failures of allocation schemes arise because allocators *naively assume that applicants for the scarce good are naive*, that is, that applicants will act as if they were ignorant of the rules that govern the allocation of these resources. Conversely, when the sophistication of allocators matches that of the applicants, allocative schemes may be designed with incentive effects in mind.

For such effects to arise two conditions must be fulfilled. First, the scheme must be known to the potential recipients. In most of the examples I have been discussing, this condition is satisfied. Possible exceptions include the allocation of police effort to different types of crime and the selection of tax payers for auditing by the Internal Revenue Service. College admission is also surrounded by some degree of uncertainty. Thus "[Harvard] Law School publishes a table for prospective applicants . . . that shows the probability of being admitted, given various grades and test scores. Some admissions committees keep this information secret, even from faculty members."[28] Second, and more crucially, the princi-

---

[28] Klitgaard, *Choosing Elites*, p. 18. As explained in Chapter 3, these probabilities do not form part of an admission scheme, although it reflects the way the system works.

ples must be based on individual properties that are capable of being modified by behavior. Thus lotteries and many status criteria have no incentive effects. As we shall see in Chapter 5, this feature of these principles often provides a main reason for adopting them.

When assessed from a social or institutional point of view, incentive effects may be desirable or undesirable, positive or negative. Three main forms of negative incentive effects are moral hazard, wasteful investment in entitlements, and misrepresentation of preferences and other private facts. Wasteful investment in entitlements has an obvious positive analogue, namely, when the effort to make oneself eligible for some scarce resource is socially useful. Although there can be no direct positive form of moral hazard, I shall draw attention in the next chapter to a partial and potentially important analogue.

Moral hazard. This phenomenon arises when an individual's knowledge that he will receive compensation or treatment in the case of an accident or other unforeseen event influences behavior so as to make that event more likely to occur. Fire insurance, for instance, makes fires more likely because the knowledge that they will be compensated makes house owners behave more recklessly. A plausible instance in local justice contexts is seniority.[29] If layoffs are made strictly by seniority, or with only minimal qualification requirements, workers may be less diligent in acquiring skills than if they know that firms will use ability as the main criterion.[30] Furthermore, if less-qualified senior employees are retained in a layoff, then the profits of the firm may be negatively affected, thus creating a need for more workers to be laid off than would otherwise have been the case. Against this we must cite the fact that the use of seniority creates an incentive for workers to stay in the firm, thus reducing turnover and increasing productivity (Chapter 3). This is a general feature of many reward schemes: they may have good as well as bad incentive effects, with the net effect often being uncertain.

A more controversial question concerns the role of moral hazard in the allocation of medical resources, and the possibility of

[29] I am indebted to Stuart Romm for the following observation.
[30] This is a variation on the theme that firms may benefit if workers run some risk of unemployment (see Shapiro and Stiglitz, "Equilibrium Unemployment as a Worker Discipline Device").

improving the provision of health services—making it more efficient as well as more fair—by refusing free treatment to those who have only themselves to blame for their illness. A utilitarian argument is that "an assignment of responsibility to the individual for self-caused illness may have a useful deterrent effect."[31] The following amounts to some skeptical comments on this claim. The policy issues are further discussed in Chapters 5 and 6.

Suppose that scarce life-saving medical goods were allocated by lottery, queuing, age, or some other principle that is insensitive to the past behavior of the applicants. In that case, the incentive to behave prudently would be smaller than if access to treatment had been linked to demonstrably prudent behavior in the past. Possible examples include transplantations of hearts to heavy smokers, of livers to alcoholics, and of kidneys to hypertensive patients with ESRD due to drug abuse or to neglect of the medicative regime. It is not clear, however, that these are true cases of moral hazard. The probability that a heavy smoker will one day need *and get* a heart transplant is so small even under the present, nondiscriminating system that a further reduction based on discrimination against smokers would hardly have much motivating power. The incentives may be so weak that even rational individuals would not be swayed by them. Even if I knew that I would not be treated for cancer of the pancreas if the cause could be shown to be excessive intakes of coffee, the chances of getting the illness *and* being successfully treated for it are so small, and the importance of coffee in my life so large, that I would be willing (rationally, I believe) to take the risk. If one wants to modify behavior, a higher tax on cigarettes is probably vastly more efficient.

Furthermore, even strong incentives may not reach individuals who are subject to myopia, weakness of will, self-deception, and other irrational propensities.[32] Impulse control is a complicated

---

[31] Wikler, "Personal Responsibility for Illness," p. 338.

[32] The fact that not all treatment succeeds reduces the force of the incentive effect argument. Assume that for a given individual the risk of dying from heart disease is 10 percent if he is a nonsmoker, 30 percent if he is a smoker who is refused treatment because of his smoking habits, and 20 percent if he is a smoker who is given the full treatment. If he can be reached by an incentive scheme, it is superfluous, assuming that the increase in risk from 10 percent to 20 percent does more to deter him than a further increase from

matter.[33] It can require great material and social resources, as well as considerable stability in the environment. Those who are deprived of these resources may not be swayed by schemes that rely on their ability to defer gratification and to believe things they don't want to believe.

Investment in entitlements. Such investments are wasteful when individuals modify their behavior, in ways they would not otherwise have chosen and that do not benefit anyone else either, to become eligible for the scarce good. It is a pervasive problem in local justice situations. When applicants to medical school are given extra points for work experience,[34] some waste years of their life to little purpose. In Israel, public housing is allocated on the basis of, among other things, number of children and present living conditions. In consequence, people have (and act on) an incentive to have many children and to move into slum dwellings. The first effect may or may not be welcome, the second is surely not.

Stratagems to get exemption or deferment from military service have included the following: joining religious orders, bungling a burglary to get into jail, joining the National Guard, cutting off a finger or toe, going on a severe diet, blinding an eye, taking drugs, growing an ulcer, getting married.[35] In the wars fought by the United States in this century, occupational deferment or exemption has not created an incentive to enter specific occupations because, as was noted in Chapter 2, virtually no blanket occupa-

---

20 percent to 30 percent. Although the numbers are rigged to prove my point, it remains to be shown that there are many cases in which the prospect of getting ill, being treated, and yet dying fails to deter, whereas the incremental risk created by removing the possibility of treatment provides a sufficient deterrent.

[33] See Ainslie, *Picoeconomics.*

[34] See Lorentzen, "Admission to Medical Schools in Norway 1970–1988."

[35] This list draws on Ibsen, *Peer Gynt;* Badeau, *Le village sous l'ancien régime,* pp. 289–296; Chambers, *To Raise an Army,* pp. 185, 215; Gerhardt, *The Draft and Public Policy;* and "Death Toll Spurring Increase in Spanish Draft Resistance," *New York Times,* October 5, 1989. Not all these effects are unambiguously negative. In 1956, for instance, the deferment of fathers was defended on the grounds that it "fosters the family life of the Nation," not simply by protecting existing marriages, but by stimulating them. As evidence was cited the growth in the group of I-A fathers from 151,000 to 370,000 in that single fiscal year (Gerhardt, *The Draft and Public Policy,* p. 233).

tional deferments were given. Student deferments, by contrast, have set up a clear incentive for strategic behavior. Most obviously, young men who would not otherwise have gone to college now had a reason to do so. More subtly, the choice of college might also be influenced by the deferment rules. Under the disjunctive system decribed in Chapter 2, for instance, a second-rank student had a clear incentive to apply to third-rank colleges, to ensure that he would be in the upper portion of his class. I do not know how often such incentives were acted on. Deferment of students was always unpopular, but mainly, or so it appears from my selective reading of the literature, because the public saw it as instantiating the Matthew effect: to him that hath, shall be given. Why should wealthy, white young men be given a further advantage? This is an objection to deferment of those who would have gone to college in any case—not to deferment of those who go there only in order to be deferred.

Queuing is an eminently wasteful way of allocating scarce goods. When all desire the scarce good equally strongly, the expected value of queuing is zero in equilibrium—the expected loss from standing in line being exactly equal to the expected gains. If some desire it more keenly than others, they can derive a net expected benefit from queuing, although the waste can still be substantial.[36] To stand in line is like paying a price[37]—except that there is nobody to collect the price and benefit from it.

In general, waiting lists do not induce wasteful behavior, since one can do other things while being on the list. If people behave less than rationally, however, a somewhat similar effect arises. In Norway, cooperative housing was formerly allocated by waiting lists. Young people often had the choice between staying on the list and hoping that a good apartment would come up, and entering the high-price private housing market. If they had been on the list for a few years, they sometimes remained there even if their hopes were constantly frustrated and any reasonable calculation would tell them to enter the private market, since to go off the list would mean that their sacrifices had been for nothing. (This "sunk-cost fallacy" also arises in queuing.)

---

[36] Johansen, "Queues (and 'Rent-seeking') as Non-cooperative Games."
[37] This analogy is explored in Holt and Sherman, "Waiting-Line Auctions."

A more complex example suggests that the use of waiting lists for hospital admission can have perverse incentive effects.[38] By varying the strictness of the criteria for being admitted to the waiting list, hospitals can determine the expected waiting time for patients. If it is very short, there will be excess capacity some of the time.[39] If it is very long, the cost of administering the list will, for a given budget, reduce the number of patients that can be admitted. In between, there is an expected waiting time that maximizes the hospital's objective function, which is assumed to depend positively on the number of patients treated and negatively on expected waiting time. If, however, the government uses expected waiting time as a measure of the demand for health services and hence as a criterion for allocating funds to the hospital, the hospital has an incentive to use a low threshold for admission to the waiting list, with the result that fewer patients are treated with a longer waiting time than is optimal.

A more ambiguous incentive is set up by the clause in American immigration laws that opens for admission of people in occupations in short supply in the United States. As observed by one student of the problem, "In a world in which hundreds of millions live in conditions of desperate poverty, immigrant visas to Western high-income countries clearly are scarce and valued goods. Any given visa allocation scheme, or any changes in such schemes, should be expected over time to evoke behavioral responses designed to improve access to the scarce good."[40] Admitting that this hypothesis is difficult to test, he goes on to point to a few "natural experiments" such as "the development and expansion of educational training institutions, designed for production of exportable skilled manpower (e.g., doctors, nurses). Such institutions produce graduates in numbers acknowledged to be well in excess of domestic demand; they have developed in countries as diverse as Jordan, Sri Lanka, the Philippines, and

---

[38] The following draws on Iversen, "A Simple Model of Waiting List Generating Incentives."

[39] This follows from the fact that getting ill and needing treatment are events governed by a stochastic process.

[40] Teitelbaum, "Skeptical Noises about the Immigration Multiplier," p. 893.

Barbados."[41] In the absence of more information, it is hard to judge the welfare effects of this practice. The analysis would involve a number of counterfactuals that can probably not be decided with much confidence.

Some principles create incentives for useful investments in entitlements. An example is the principle of awarding custody to the primary caretaker, which is currently practiced in several American states. By and large, it is good that parents spend much time with their children in order to have a good chance of being awarded custody. (One might wonder, however, whether behavior during marriage will in fact be guided by concerns about divorce and, if it is, whether it might not make divorce more likely.)[42] A more obvious example is the fact that when students work hard in high school to get into college, society as a whole benefits from their investment. In Israel, the incentive to have many children created by the system for allocating public housing is probably seen as a desirable one. These examples have two noteworthy features. First, if all invest in entitlements, nobody gets the immediate benefits they hoped for. They may, however, gain indirectly, since society as a whole benefits from their activities. Second, in the cited cases the principles are not selected for the purpose of modifying recipient behavior. The purpose of using time spent with the child as a criterion for allocating custody is either to reward parental contribution or to ensure that the child will be better off after the divorce, not to make the parents behave differently during the marriage. The purpose of selecting by grades is to ensure that one gets the best students, not to make students work harder. I return to this issue in the next chapter.

Misrepresentation. An intriguing instance of such behavior has been observed in the labor market for medical interns and residents. In the United States, interns are currently assigned to hospitals by the National Resident Matching Program.[43] In Great Brit-

---

[41] Ibid., p. 894.

[42] See my *Solomonic Judgements*, p. 157.

[43] For a description, see Roth, "The Evolution of the Labor Market for Medical Interns and Residents." The first elucidation of this matching problem is due to Gale and Shapley, "College Admissions and the Stability of Marriages."

ain, similar programs have been used on the regional level.[44] In both cases, the assignment[45] of residents to hospitals is organized centrally, on the basis of preferences expressed by students and hospitals. Students rank hospitals in their order of preference, and hospitals likewise rank students. The matching algorithm used in the United States and in most of the surviving British programs is *stable:* under the chosen assignment, it can never happen that some student and hospital who are not matched to one another would both rather be matched together than stay with their assigned matches. Such stability is clearly desirable. In its absence, the ill-matched student and hospital would have an incentive to seek each other out and come to a private arrangement. Since a student and a hospital who have each other as their first choices are always matched together by the algorithm, the ill-matched pair could improve their position by submitting preference rankings in which they both rank each other at the top.[46]

In the United States, this stable algorithm was introduced in 1952, when the chaos and waste created by private, decentralized matching had become intolerable. Similar problems led to the introduction of centralized clearing systems (at the regional level) in Great Britain in the late 1960s. Alvin Roth reports that among these systems, "There are eight matching algorithms for which I have been able to obtain sufficiently precise descriptions to determine whether they produce stable matchings. . . . Two of these always produce stable matchings, and both of these have . . . survived to the present. The six remaining schemes are based on algorithms that may frequently produce instabilities. Only two of these have survived (and these are in the smallest two markets); the other four have been abandoned."[47] By detailed analysis of

[44] For a description and a comparison with the American program, see Roth, "New Physicians."

[45] As there are more would-be residents than there are places, these are selection systems, not placement systems.

[46] I should add that the stable algorithm is also vulnerable to strategic misrepresentation of preferences. For this to be a serious problem, however, agents have to know more about the preferences of other agents than it is plausible to assume in the case under discussion. For a full discussion of these and other technical issues, see Roth and Sotomayor, *Two-sided Matching.*

[47] Roth, "New Physicians," p. 1526.

one of the algorithms that were abandoned Roth also makes a case for the claim that it failed *because* it was unstable, that is, because it provided incentives to circumvent the system. The analysis of the American case leads him to the same conclusion. Before the introduction of the stable system, a different centralized algorithm was proposed but soon abandoned when students pointed out that it created an incentive for misrepresentation.[48] In the next chapter I return to some implications of this analysis.

Preferences are private; they have to be reported by the agent; whence the possibility of misrepresentation. Another private state is *pain*, which is a determinant of many allocative decisions. Similarly, a person's *skill* is to some extent unobservable, enabling people to claim exemption from a task because of lack of skill. Both problems are illustrated in the allocation of household work. "I can't do it because I have a headache," or "I can't do it because I'm no good at it" are excuses that, whether true or false, are difficult to verify. Tolstoy's happy marriages may be those in which work is allocated on the basis of such unobservable criteria, without anyone taking advantage of them for purposes of misrepresentation. Other marriages survive because the family members realize that robust, nonmanipulable criteria are better for everybody in the long run.

LOCAL JUSTICE—GLOBAL INJUSTICE?

The question mark in the title of this subsection is meant to tell the reader that I am not about to engage in wholesale paradox-mongering. My purpose is to draw attention to a lacuna in the theory of distributive justice, not to suggest a systematic discrepancy between the practice of local allocators and theories of global justice. I do believe that sometimes the total effect of local decisions is to create a pattern of burdens and benefits that seems unfair, inefficient, or both. The importance of such effects may be more than marginal, but certainly less than pervasive.

It is widely argued that the task of distributive justice is to compensate for inequalities that arise in decentralized markets. The basis for the market is a certain distribution of skills, a certain distribution of preferences for how people want to use their skills,

---

[48] The specific incentive problem is that described in note 77 to Chapter 2.

and a certain distribution of demand for what people can produce using their skills. Of these distributions, the first and the third are widely accepted as "morally arbitrary." (In Chapter 6 I discuss whether the second distribution is any less arbitrary from the moral point of view.) There is a widely shared intuition that nobody should suffer because they happen to be born without marketable skills. To redress the inequalities that would otherwise arise, there is a need for centrally organized redistribution.

Decisions of local justice are also, however, made in a decentralized and uncoordinated manner. To see the implications of this point, a change of perspective is needed. In the body of this book, allocative problems are considered from the institution's point of view. The institution receives a *stream of applicants* all of whom have a claim on the scarce good but not all of whom can get it. From the individual's point of view, the matter looks different. From childhood to old age, he encounters a *succession of institutions,* each of which has the power to give or deny him some scarce good. In some cases the cumulative impact of these decisions may be grossly unfair. We can easily imagine an individual who through sheer bad luck is chosen for all the necessary burdens and denied all the scarce goods, because in each case he is just below the cutoff point for selection. To my knowledge, this source of injustice has not been recognized so far. To the extent that philosophers have tried to solve problems of local justice, they have not been concerned with the possibility that the solutions might create global injustice. Those who are entrusted with the task of allocating a scarce good rarely if ever evaluate recipients in the light of their past successes or failures in receiving other goods. Local justice is largely noncompensatory. There is no mechanism of redress across allocative spheres.

As I explained in Chapter 2, candidates for kidney transplantation are awarded points for "medical bad luck." Similarly, I mentioned in Chapter 3 that elite colleges sometimes give preference to applicants from disadvantaged backgrounds, on the grounds that they have been deprived of good educational opportunities in the past. These examples show that in one sense, local justice *is* compensatory—but only for local bad luck, as it were. Cross-compensation occurs rarely. It seems fit to award custody to a mother because she has taken care of her child—but not because she has sacrificed her career to take care of her mother who could not find a place in a nursing home. Being laid off through no fault of one's own does not entitle one to move up in the queue for surgery, immigration, or kindergarten. Veterans receive more help for service-related medical problems than for others. In general, allocators tend to see their role as specialized providers of specific services rather than as promoters of overall welfare. If they are aware that there is a bigger picture, they leave it to others. Often, however, nobody feels responsible for the big picture.

As a practical matter, this may be a gap that cannot be filled. To a large extent, life itself is a series of uncorrelated stochastic events, including not only the allocation of goods and burdens, but also windfalls and accidents of all sorts.[49] For most people, events will turn out so that they can say to themselves, "You win some, you lose some." But by the nature of chance events, some individuals will miss every train: they are turned down for medical school, chosen by the draft lottery, laid off by the firm in a recession, and refused scarce medical resources; in addition, their spouse develops cancer, their stocks become worthless, and their neighborhood is chosen for a toxic waste dump. It is neither desirable nor possible to create a mechanism of redress to compensate for all forms of cumulative bad luck. For one thing, the problems of moral hazard would be immense. For another, the machinery of administering redress for bad luck would be hopelessly complex and costly. At a more fundamental level, pleasant surprises and good luck would cease to exhilarate and stimulate us; much of the zest of life would go with them.

These objections do not, however, exclude all forms of interinstitutional compensation. Some forms already exist. Although I just mentioned veterans as an instance of the lack of cross-compensation, veterans do receive preferential treatment in many areas that are unrelated to their service. Other forms might be envisaged. Young workers who have been laid off might get preferential access to higher education (unlike present systems that give points for work). There is probably not much we can achieve along these lines, but thinking about the issues might have some value.

---

[49] In addition, there are many correlated stochastic events, such as discrimination on grounds of race and gender, for which redress is easier.

5 / Explaining Local Justice

In this chapter I shall develop a framework for explaining principles of local justice, that is, for explaining why, at a particular time and place, a particular institution adopts a particular principle for allocating a particular good. On the one hand, we need to understand why allocators, authorities, recipients, and public opinion develop certain preferences with respect to the allocative principles. On the other hand, we must try to understand how these preferences are aggregated to yield the final allocative scheme. As mentioned in the Introduction, I shall not try to offer a *theory* that could serve across the board, somewhat in the manner of the postulates of profit maximization and utility maximization in economics. Instead I shall discuss a number of *mechanisms* that govern preference formation and preference aggregation.

METHODOLOGICAL PRELIMINARIES

Elsewhere, I have distinguished between three main kinds of explanation: causal, intentional, and functional.[1] The explanations

---

[1] See my work, *Explaining Technical Change,* Part I.

of allocative principles are, by and large, of the intentional variety. The principles result as the outcome of deliberations of, and conflicts among, conscious actors. In some cases, the motivations of these actors will be subjected to further, causal analysis, but for the most part they will simply be taken for given.

Functional explanations assert that the allocative principle or mechanism can be explained by its consequences.[2] This is the approach adopted by Calabresi and Bobbit in *Tragic Choices*. As I mentioned in the Introduction, they tend to explain allocative principles in terms of their effect on obscuring the necessity for making hard or "tragic" choices. Lotteries, for instance, are unstable because they make it all too clear that some are chosen and others are rejected. Other mechanisms are alleged to be more stable. (1) The allocation is more acceptable when it is based on absolute worthiness (as distinct from relative worthiness), if the public is persuaded "that individuals who are denied the scarce good could, through their own behavior, put themselves in the favored category."[3] Although this argument might work in nontragic situations such as access to education, the authors do not explain how dialysis, military service, or procreation rights could be allocated by manipulable criteria. (2) I have already cited their claim that "Imposing a complicated procedure functions as a system for allocation, limiting the resource to only a fraction of those whom the society has said are entitled to it."[4] (3) A mixed scheme, involving both time and money, "is often used precisely because it renders imperceptible the bases of both the market and collective elements of the allocation."[5]

Let me grant, for the sake of argument, that these procedures do in fact have the effect of hiding or obscuring the need for hard choices. How could that feature help to explain why they are adopted? An intentional account would be absurdly conspiratorial. A functionalist explanation might, however, seem feasible, based on two ideas.[6] (1) A procedure that does *not* have this fea-

[2] I limit myself to consequences for "society." When the impact of allocative principles on specific groups is used to explain why they are adopted, the explanation is usually couched in straightforwardly intentional terms.

[3] *Tragic Choices*, p. 73.

[4] Ibid., p. 96.

[5] Ibid., p. 98.

[6] For a fuller account of this mechanism, see *Explaining Technical Change*, p. 61 ff.

ture will not survive for long. (2) When the nonviable procedure is replaced by another, the new one emerges "as if" by a random choice. Given sufficient variability in the range of possible procedures, these premises ensure that sooner or later a viable or stable procedure will emerge. The emergence of the matching program for medical interns described in Chapter 4 illustrates the general idea behind this proposal, but not, of course, the specific survival criterion stipulated by Calabresi and Bobbit.

This mechanism has some plausibility, but not much. I do not think the public or the group of potential recipients will be fooled indefinitely or even for long by a semblance of nonselection. I have more faith in another idea mentioned by Calabresi and Bobbit, that of an indefinite cycling of procedures. "Society," they say, does not simply adopt to the tragic choice by using a mixture of pure principles. Instead, "it" uses the "strategy of successive moves" or an "alternation of mixtures."[7] Shorn of its unfortunate language, this description is in many cases appropriate. Because any scheme will create objections in some quarters, and because the faults of the system in place tend to be more vivid than the flaws of the alternatives, we often observe unstable oscillations and perpetual modifications. To the extent that this description is correct, one might say that *there is nothing to explain*. There is no explanandum, in the sense of a stable dependent variable to be understood in terms of context-specific independent variables. Instead, to exaggerate, any solution will be tried to any problem, and no solution will prove lasting.

In many ways, this idea is close to the perspective adopted here. In particular, the idea of a mechanism naturally suggests the idea of perpetual policy changes, as one mechanism is replaced by another. The explanandum, then, will have to be redefined as policies that are in force for a certain time, rather than as stable solutions to a given structural problem.[8] Even then, however,

---

[7] *Tragic Choices*, p. 195.

[8] Of course, if the parameters of the problem change, we would expect changes in the solution as well. For instance, the National Resident Matching Program described in Chapter 4 has become increasingly unstable as a growing number of married couples seek two positions in the same vicinity. Developments in military technology may force the move to a professional army. However, I am concerned here with changes that are adopted even though the problem remains essentially the same. The 1989 change in the point system for kidney allocation is a good example.

successive solutions will almost always have a large common core. The importance of grades in selecting students for higher education or of physical fitness in selecting young men for military service are permanent features of these arenas. There is a need to understand, therefore, both the stable and the changing elements in allocative policies.

A final remark about the explanandum may be in order. At the most general level, I want to understand why a given principle—pure or mixed—is used in a given country in a given period to allocate a given good. This way of stating the explanandum can, however, be misleading or question-begging. As mentioned in the Introduction, there can be considerable variation within a given arena, time, and country. By and large, the factors discussed below suffice to explain such local variations. But they may not fully explain why there is not more variation than there actually is. What are the forces that constrain relatively autonomous institutions to behave in a relatively similar way?

There seem to be four main explanations of this relative degree of homogeneity. Three of them are discussed below: professional norms, national culture, and political regulation. College admission practices may be more similar than university presidents want them to be, simply because admissions officers form a professional group who develop common norms through meetings, journals, and individual mobility. Similarly, specifically national values may explain the emergence of spontaneous similarity without coordination or constraint. The achievement of uniformity by political regulation is too obvious to require further comment. In addition, *competition* can force institutions to adopt the same principles. Firms, private universities, and for-profit dialysis centers compete with each other for customers, students, and patients. If they adopt criteria that emphasize equity at the expense of efficiency, they might go out of business. In the typical case, several of these forces interact to create considerable homogeneity within each arena—and correspondingly sharp differences across arenas.

Earlier, I mentioned that the explanations offered below will be mainly intentional, that is, based on the conscious acts and deliberations of the main actors. A brief survey of these actors will provide a useful introduction to the following discussion of factors and mechanisms. My point of departure is the distinction, advanced by Calabresi and Bobbit, between first-order and second-order decisions, the first determining the total amount of the good to be allocated and the second specifying how to allocate it. I want first to modify this distinction, and then to expand it into a trichotomy by adding the concept of third-order decisions.

In my revised terminology, first-order decisions include *all* choices made or induced for the purpose of affecting the total amount of the good.[9] Whereas Calabresi and Bobbit focus on political first-order decisions and artificial scarcity, I also include decentralized individual choices and quasi-natural scarcity. The most obvious example is voluntary donation of bodily parts, such as blood, sperm, bone marrow, kidneys, hearts, and livers. The supply of children for adoption also belongs to this category, as do private donations to create medical treatment facilities or endow institutions of higher education. By extension, we may count the voluntary assumption of a burden and the voluntary abstention from a good as first-order decisions.[10] Although these decisions do not increase the absolute amount of the good to be allocated, they do affect the prospects of non-volunteers in much the same way.

Individual first-order choices can be of two kinds: whether to give, and to whom. Donation of bodily parts is of the first kind, since the donors are not allowed to stipulate that recipients be restricted to, say, a particular ethnic group. The choice to offer one's child for adoption involves both aspects, as mothers are to some extent allowed to choose the family into which their child is to be adopted. Benevolent donors are, of course, free to choose between funding an endowed chair or an endowed dialysis center. If one is concerned with increasing the total supply of scarce

[9] I do not, however, extend it to all those decisions that simply have the *effect* of increasing the supply. In that case, a decision to increase the speed limit on the roads would count as a first-order determination of the supply of organs for transplantation, since most such organs are taken from victims of car accidents.

[10] For volunteerism in the army, see Chambers, *To Raise an Army*, passim. For voluntary abstention from dialysis, see Swazey and Fox, *The Courage to Fail*, pp. 274–275. Only in the latter case, however, are we dealing with a voluntary act for the sake of helping others.

good, allowing donors to have a say in the selection of recipients may be efficient. The distributive effects may, however, be undesirable. If donors are allowed to express a preference, many will do so who would have donated in any case. The effect may be a net loss for some recipient groups.

Political first-order decisions concern the allocation of fungible (monetary) resources among various activities. The primary consequence of such decisions is to favor certain goods or services at the expense of others. A secondary consequence may be to favor certain individuals at the expense of others, that is to say, those who can benefit most from the favored good. Although the effect on individuals also depends on the second-order allocative principle, some goods are such that many groups cannot benefit from them at all. Thus devoting a large share of public funds to public housing is tantamount to preferential treatment of the poor, almost regardless of what allocative scheme is chosen. Giving priority to education necessarily occurs at the expense of the elderly, since they will not be young again. By contrast, heavy funding of life-saving medical equipment mainly utilized by the elderly will eventually also benefit the young.

When I speak of "first-order actors" I shall usually refer to political authorities, unless otherwise indicated. Although I define the first-order actors by their impact on the supply of the scarce good, political actors also play other roles in systems of local justice. In particular, unlike individual first-order actors, they can influence the principle by which the good is allocated no less than the amount to be allocated. This is not to say that the behavior of individual first-order actors is irrelevant to the choice of principle. Anticipating their behavior, the institution may adopt a principle that sets up an incentive for them to give more than they would otherwise have done. This kind of impact is not properly speaking an influence, however. For an actor to exercise an influence on another he must act in a purposive way—by coercing, constraining, inducing, bargaining, seducing, or persuading[11]—to

---

[11] For the distinction between coercion, seduction, and persuasion, see my *Ulysses and the Sirens*, p. 81 ff. Seduction (e.g., introductory offers) differs from inducement in that a reward is offered for the purpose of changing behavior via a change of preferences, whereas inducement takes preferences for given and acts directly on behavior. Constraining differs from coercion

make the other behave differently from what he would otherwise have done. But if a potential organ donor refuses to sign a donor card when told that organs will be allocated by medical need rather than, say, race, he is not trying to influence transplantation policy. Only if individual first-order actors are organized, or if a single actor affects a large portion of the supply, can the command over the supply be used as leverage on the choice of principle. These conditions being rarely if ever fulfilled, we can look at individual first-order actors as purely parametric, incapable of adapting a strategic attitude toward the institution.

By "third-order" decisions I shall mean decisions by potential recipients of a scarce good that affect either their need for it or their likelihood of receiving it (under a specific allocative scheme). Consider first need-enhancing decisions.[12] Smoking makes it more likely that one will develop heart disease and hence one day need a heart for transplantation; similar relations obtain between alcohol and drug abuse on the one hand, and liver and kidney disease on the other. The decision to have a child creates a need for a place in nursery school, and reinforces the need for better housing and the need to keep one's job.

Third-order decisions can also, for a given allocative scheme, affect one's chances of receiving the scarce good. Workers who are married or work in industries that are vital for the war effort are likely to be exempt from military service, as are young men suffering from obesity. The obese are also less likely to be transplanted or to be chosen as adoptive parents. Soldiers who show valor in battle can be demobilized before others. Students who have worked hard in high school are more likely to get into selective colleges. Those who go into certain professions may be more likely to receive an immigration visa. Workers who have invested in acquiring skills are less likely to be laid off in a recession, as are those who have deliberately stayed in the same firm in the

---

in that it works by removing some elements from the other's feasible set, whereas coercion (like inducement) changes the rewards associated with some elements.

[12] For the present purposes, "need" refers to the extent to which a person can benefit from the scarce good, assuming that post-allocation trade is impossible.

face of outside opportunities. Behavior during marriage, ranging from adultery to time spent caring for the child, can affect the chances of getting custody. Couples who can demonstrate stable behavior in the past are more likely to be allowed to adopt children. Good behavior is also supposed to help one get to heaven.

Sometimes, decisions that increase the need for a scarce good will also (under the given scheme) make it less likely that one will in fact get it. One might imagine schemes (although none exist today) to deter abusers of nicotine, alcohol, or drugs by giving them low priority for transplantation.[13] More realistically, patients who resume their substance abuse after a first transplantation might get low priority for retransplantation. This is already the case in some countries, including Norway. In India, as mentioned before, public housing is preferentially given to families with fewer than three children. In such cases, *deterrence* and *need* point in opposite directions. As further explained in Chapter 6, act-utilitarian considerations will underwrite the criterion of need, whereas rule-utilitarianism tends to support deterrence.

When behavior by third-order decision makers affects their chances of getting the good, incentive effects arise automatically. Anticipating these effects, the institution may choose the allocative principle so as to encourage or prevent them. These forms of strategic behavior are discussed below. Here I want to point out another way in which the behavior of third-order decision makers can affect the choice of an allocative principle. By joining forces in a collective effort, potential recipients of the good can engage in bargaining with the allocating institution over the principle that will select the actual recipients. The outstanding example, and almost the only real example, is union-management bargaining over layoff principles. This issue, too, is further considered below.

The remarks just made about the relation between second- and third-order actors have a parallel in the relation between second- and first-order actors. On the one hand, incentive effects can arise in this case as well. The choice of an allocative principle may shape the supply of the scarce good to be allocated. On the other hand,

---

[13] I may add, although it probably goes without saying, that the reason the obese are not transplanted is purely medical, and does not form part of a deterrence scheme.

first-order authorities and second-order institutions may engage in bargaining over the principle to be used in allocating the scarce good. Here, unilateral imposition of a principle by the first-order actors may be seen as a degenerate case of bargaining, with all bargaining power on one side.

In explaining principles of local justice, this framework of *three levels of decision making,* related by *two modes of interaction* (incentive effects and bargaining), will play a central role. In addition, *public opinion* can be seen as a quasi-actor that is capable of constraining and limiting the range of acceptable principles. These various actors have different portfolios of motives. Political first-order actors tend to care mainly about overall efficiency; second-order actors about equity and local efficiency; public opinion is mainly concerned with equity and third-order actors with self-interest. These statements are valid at best as first and rough approximations. Exceptions and nuances are provided below and in Chapter 6.

PREFERENCE FORMATION

The process leading to the adoption of an allocative principle has as its main input the allocative preferences of the various actors that are involved. In this subsection I survey some of the factors that enter into the explanation of these preferences. Corresponding to the focus of the book as a whole, my main concern is with the preferences of second-order, institutional allocators. The factors I shall be considering are:

- structural variables
- professional norms
- national culture
- institutional politics
- organized interest groups
- public opinion
- incentive problems
- information problems

Structural variables. By this uninformative phrase I have in mind three quantitative aspects of allocative situations. First, what is the absolute number of people who could benefit from the scarce good? Second, what is the ratio of that number to the number of units that are available for allocation? Third, how urgent or important is getting the good (or escaping the burden) for the individual? Clearly, these variables in themselves cannot explain anything. To make a difference, they have to be filtered through the minds of the various actors enumerated above.

Let me begin with the second variable. According to Calabresi and Bobbit, "at very high and very low first-order levels, relatively easy second-order choices are possible, while this is not so at intermediate levels."[14] It is not clear exactly what is here said to be first an increasing and then a decreasing function of the proportion of unsatisfied demands: Is it frustration among the nonrecipients or discontent in the general public? On the first reading, the hypothesis receives some support from general Tocquevillian reasoning.[15] It seems less plausible on the second reading, which is, however, the more natural one, given the constant references in *Tragic Choices* to "society."

I now consider the first and the third variables together. Some issues affect many, others a small minority. Some issues are of momentous importance to the individuals who are concerned, whereas others are more trivial or at least not vitally important. The issue of organ transplantation is a small number/high importance problem. The opposite combination is offered by a high number/low importance problem such as college admission. Almost all applicants to college eventually end up somewhere. Although many do not get into their first choice, this is much less of a blow than not getting a liver transplant. To convey an idea of the difference in numerical importance, the University of Texas at Austin each year has about three times as many applicants for admission to college as there are people on waiting lists for transplantations. High number/high importance problems include selection of soldiers for military service in wartime and rationing of consumer goods in disaster situations. Closer to the opposite

---

[14] *Tragic Choices*, p. 21.
[15] For the general idea, see Boudon, "The Logic of Relative Frustration." For an application to immigration, see Mackie, "Frustration, Preference Changes, and Immigration Demand."

end of the spectrum, layoffs represent a medium-sized problem for a medium-sized number of persons.

The small number/high importance cases might be expected to have some distinguishing features. In particular, one might expect selection to be highly information-intensive and discretionary. Since the decisions are so important, one should try to pay great attention to details of the individual case. Since there are relatively few decisions to be made, such attention is actually affordable. By contrast, high number/high importance cases cannot afford discretion and fine-tuning, whereas low importance cases do not need them. This is not, however, the pattern that one finds. The college admissions procedure at Harvard College is more information-intensive and much more discretionary than the selection of patients for transplantation. The allocation of kidneys follows, as we have seen, a highly mechanical and nondiscretionary procedure. The allocation of hearts, which ranks even higher on the urgency scale, also follows a mechanical pattern.

I have tried to speculate about some possible explanations for this paradox, if it is one, but without much success. One account might go as follows: There is always fear that a discretionary procedure might lend itself to corruption and bribery. In small-number/high-importance cases this fear is likely to be especially strong. Since the number of available places is small, even a single instance of corruption is seen as a threat to oneself; and the high stakes make the idea even more intolerable. Or there might be a feeling that since discretionary procedures consider the whole person and not simply a few selected traits, rejection means that one is found to be inferior as a person. Since mechanical principles always are arbitrary to some extent, they might be better for the self-respect of the losers. Once again, the feeling might be more intolerable when the stakes are high.

Professional norms. These define the first-best conceptions of the allocators.[16] "Naturally, professional soldiers prefer a format based only upon military criteria, as physicians might prefer to think only in strictly medical terms."[17] Walzer's idea of "spheres

---

[16]Later, I discuss whether allocators might have different first-best conceptions.

[17]Chambers, *To Raise an Army*, p. 3, adding that "reality is usually more complex."

of justice" corresponds closely to this idea, expressed in the following passages from his book.[18] "The distributive logic of the practice of medicine seems to be this: that care should be proportionate to illness and not to wealth."[19] "To serve educational needs, without regard to the vulgar irrelevancies of class and income . . . is a part of the teacher's honor."[20] "Special education is necessarily a monopoly of the talented."[21]

Walzer would be the first to recognize that these tacit understandings can be violated. Discussing the inadequacy of the American welfare state, for instance, he observes that "the established pattern of provision doesn't measure up to the internal requirements of the sphere of security and welfare, and the common understandings of the citizens point toward a more elaborate pattern."[22] Hence the "internal logic" of a sphere is not sufficient to explain the principles actually adopted there. Moreover, I think Walzer may be mistaken in identifying this inner logic with the common understandings of the *citizens*. The principle that medical care should be proportionate to ill health and not to wealth is certainly held by many health professionals. To treat the sick is the natural telos of their profession, just as to teach the talented is the natural goal of the teacher. It is not at all clear to me, however, that the citizens in general share this view. It seems at least as plausible that the citizens are mainly opposed to great inequalities of income, and not to the idea that those who earn more can use their money to buy more and better treatment or education, provided they bear the full costs of the extra resources. Be this as it may—I do not want to engage in a contest of armchair sociology—it seems to me that what Walzer captures in many of his examples is the attitude of the professional dispenser of goods ("the teacher's honor"), and not necessarily that of the citizens.

In many cases, professional norms are self-explanatory. There is no need to ask why colleges want good students, why firms want to retain the most qualified workers, or why generals want their soldiers to be fit for combat. The norms of medical ethics,

[18] Walzer, *Spheres of Justice*, p. 9.
[19] Ibid., p. 86.
[20] Ibid., p. 202 (quoting R. H. Tawney).
[21] Ibid., p. 211.
[22] Ibid., p. 85.

however, are somewhat more puzzling. I shall offer some conjectures concerning the origins of two central medical norms with important allocative consequences. Neither norm is outcome-oriented, in the sense of aiming at the most efficient use of scarce medical resources. Instead, one might say that the norms are *patient-oriented,* in a sense that will become clear in a moment.

The first is what I have called "the norm of compassion," that is, the principle of channeling medical resources toward the critically ill patients, even when they would do more good in others. In addition to spontaneous empathy, I believe some cognitive factors could be involved in the origin of this norm. For the critically ill patients, there is a "clear and present danger" which has a special salience, compared to the more uncertain and conjectural risks of patients farther down the continuum. Cognitive psychologists talk about a "certainty effect" that can distort judgment.[23] Also there may be some "framing effects."[24] Instead of comparing the fates of different individuals if treated, doctors compare their fates if left untreated. A similar framing effect can occur in public policy, if the allocation of funds to social issues is a function of how important the problems are, not of how effective the funds would be in solving them. Some educational programs for disadvantaged groups fall in this category.

Next, there is what I shall call "the norm of thoroughness." Rational-choice theory tells us that when allocating scarce resources, whether as inputs for production or as goods for consumption, one should equalize the marginal productivity or the marginal utility of all units. The point may be illustrated by a simple case of consumption. Even if we disregard nutritional constraints, it would be strange to spend all one's income on milk and bread, and nothing on meat and vegetables. Because consumer goods have decreasing marginal utility, the utility derived from the last unit purchased of bread and milk will certainly be smaller than the utility derived from the first unit of bread and vegetables. A rational consumer would, therefore, spread his income more thinly over a large number of goods, rather than concentrate it on just a few.

[23] Kahneman and Tversky, "Prospect Theory."
[24] Tversky and Kahneman, "The Framing of Decisions and the Psychology of Choice."

We can apply similar reasoning to the behavior of doctors. With respect to any given patient, the doctor's time has decreasing marginal productivity, at least beyond a certain point. The functional relationship is probably S-shaped. This implies that if the doctor makes a very thorough examination of the patient, his behavior is not instrumentally rational with respect to the objective of saving lives or improving overall health. Other patients might benefit much more from the time he spends on the last and most esoteric tests. Nevertheless, doctors seem to follow a norm of thoroughness, which tells them that once a patient has been admitted, he or she should get "the full treatment." It is as if a consumer, once he had decided to make milk a part of his daily consumption, decided to drink milk up to the point where the marginal utility of milk becomes zero.

In Norway, a recent parliamentary commission found that eye specialists tend to admit too few patients and treat each of them excessively thoroughly. When I confronted my own eye doctor with this claim, she refuted it by telling me about a case in which she had been able to diagnose a rare eye disease only after exhaustive examination, thereby saving her patient's sight. I did not remind her of the cases that go undetected because the patient never gets to see a doctor at all.

In transplantation, the norm of thoroughness seems to affect behavior in two cases. First, there are cases of multiple transplants. Recently, one patient in Pittsburgh received as many as five different organs, which in theory could have been used to save the lives of five other people. Secondly and more importantly, there is the issue of retransplantation. Success rates tend to be lower for retransplantations than for primary transplantations. This differential is due not just to a sample effect, in the sense that the patients who need a second transplant had smaller chances in the first place. There also seems to be a genuine aftereffect, in the sense that the failure of transplantation in itself lowers their chances. Instead of being given to a patient who has already been transplanted once, scarce organs could be given to others who stand a better chance of success.[25]

Again we may speculate about the origins of the norm of thor-

---

[25] Matthieu, "Introduction to Part 2," pp. 44–45.

oughness. In the American context, fear of litigation may be at work. But I believe that the norm is too old and too widespread for this to be the whole explanation. To some extent, the sunk-cost fallacy may be responsible. Here as elsewhere, it is hard to cut one's losses, even when it is the rational thing to do. The most important factor may be that doctors are exposed to a biased sample. They observe patients who benefit from their thoroughness, whereas they know nothing about the nonadmitted patients who could have benefited from a brief examination.[26]

National culture. This is an important and elusive factor in the shaping of local justice. I am fully aware that the idea of differences in national character has a bad name. Many would say that it belongs at best to after-dinner conversation and certainly not to scholarly work. Perusal of the pages of the now defunct *Journal de Psychologie des Peuples* would to a large extent justify this judgment. Methodologically, such differences, if they exist, are hard to study. The value of direct observation is reduced by possible observer prejudice and biased samples; the value of surveys, by the difficulty of knowing whether people really say what they think and do what they think they do; and the value of direct studies of behavior, by the difficulty of keeping everything else constant. Theoretically, the argument has been made that people's values are essentially the same everywhere, so that any observed differences in their behavior must be due to differences in the opportunities they face.

Nevertheless, I believe, and I believe that most readers believe, that national value differences are substantial and important. A simple example from Chapter 3 will suffice to prove their reality: Whereas China has offered exemption from military service to young men without siblings (who have to take care of their parents), the United States has exempted fathers (who have to take care of their children). I shall offer a few specimens of the kind of hypotheses one might pursue, leaving the actual pursuit to another occasion (or to others). The first two examples illustrate the narrower kind of hypothesis, that in the allocation of good A, value 1 is more important in country X and value 2 more important

---

[26] Recall, from Chapter 3, that a similar bias may explain why patients on dialysis hesitate to get on the waiting list for transplantation.

in country Y. The last two illustrate the more general hypothesis that in one country one value may be especially important across all allocations.

I suggested earlier that British medicine has a more utilitarian orientation than its American counterpart. If this observation proves correct, several explanations suggest themselves to account for the difference. Most obviously, the greater scarcity, not to say penury, of resources in Britain reduces the scope for the norms of compassion and thoroughness. Under such conditions doctors are forced to think in terms of incremental benefits and to spread themselves thinly over more patients. An alternative or complementary explanation could be that Britain has a National Health Service, organized so as to have hard budget constraints.[27] The American system of third-party reimbursement provides no such constraints. "Because care is essentially free when demanded, incentives encourage the provision of all care that produces positive benefits whatever the cost."[28] At a more speculative level, one might seek the explanation of British utilitarianism in the traditional culture of the Civil Service, or even in the pervasive influence of Bentham and Mill on British officials.

We observe interesting differences between American and European layoff practices. On both continents seniority—a desert-based principle—is widespread. On both, exceptions are made, but on different grounds. In Europe, need is often a factor in layoff decisions, whereas this criterion is never used in the United States. By contrast, American employers have more freedom to retain the most skilled workers. The American system reflects the spirit of free enterprise, whereas European layoff policies are an extension of the welfare state. The state does impose constraints on layoffs in the United States, to prevent discrimination against women, minorities, the elderly and (in the near future) the handicapped—but not to protect married workers or workers with many dependents. In the American labor market, desert is rewarded, status is banished, and need is irrelevant. The state may interfere, but only to ensure equal opportunity for all—not to change the outcome of fair competition.

[27] For a brief description, see Aaron and Schwartz, *The Painful Prescription,* p. 18 ff. For some implications, see ibid., p. 100 ff.
[28] Ibid., p. 113.

Equality is highly valued in social democratic countries, sometimes to the point of refusing to all what not all can get. Two examples from Norway will indicate what I have in mind. The government's report on nursery schools seriously discussed whether one should allow private firms to build such schools for the children of their employees.[29] "The question is whether it is acceptable that some obtain the good before others, or whether one should wait 15–20 years to achieve a consistent 'justice.'" Reluctantly, the report concluded that the need for nursery schools was so acute that some injustice had to be accepted. Norwegian immigration policy is to admit very few foreign workers. One reason often adduced is that Norway should not admit foreign workers unless they can achieve the same standard of living (jobs, housing, welfare services) as that of the average Norwegian. Norway should not be split into an A-team of Norwegian-born citizens and a B-team of foreign-born ones. The argument overlooks the fact that most potential immigrants would rather be on the Norwegian B-team than on the A-team in their own country.

Status has been the major allocative principle in many societies, including, for instance, classical Athens.[30] Male citizens, metics, women, and slaves were treated differently in most allocative respects. The category of need and the idea of needs-based allocation were largely absent: people were left to look after themselves. "To make it possible for each and every citizen to participate in political life, the citizens as a body were prepared to lay out a large sum. Obviously, this appropriation benefited the poorest citizens most, but of poverty itself the city took no direct notice."[31] By contrast, in modern societies status matters mainly because it is not fully eradicated as a criterion. Some status categories have simply disappeared, and most of the others have been classified as morally arbitrary and irrelevant for purposes of distributive justice.

---

[29] The reason that this is an issue at all is that private nursery schools, like the municipal ones, receive state subsidies. The subsidy system is not, however, organized so that more state support for private schools means less for the municipal ones.

[30] See Walzer, *Spheres of Justice*, pp. 53 ff., 69 ff. for useful discussions.

[31] Ibid., p. 71. See also Veyne, *Le pain et le cirque*, for a magisterial argument to the same effect.

Institutional politics. Up to this point I have spoken as if second-order institutions are monolithic, unitary actors with a single preference. Real institutions, of course, consist of departments and divisions that often disagree over the choice of an allocative principle. In such cases, bargaining within the institution will decide who gets what—allocating goods to applicants as a side effect of the allocation of applicants to departments.

Hospitals are always anxious to discharge older patients who absorb many of their resources although they can no longer be usefully treated. If the patient cannot take care of himself, a place in an institution for the elderly must be found. In Norway, where places in such institutions are scarce, a selection among dischargeable patients is inevitable. In one large hospital in Oslo they are selected by rotation among the wards, on the principle that each ward should have a fair chance of being relieved of its most difficult patients.

The American system for sharing kidneys was set up to ensure the equitable and efficient allocation of kidneys. Except when there is a perfectly matched patient (with six antigen matches), the criteria applied to the local allocation of organs exclusively. The national sharing, however, was not equal. The more productive organ procurement organizations complained that, because of the disparate impact of the six-antigen matching rule, the hospitals with which they were affiliated sent out many more kidneys than they got in return. The pressure for inter-center equity, and the need to induce compliance with the six-antigen-matching rule, eventually forced a change in the system, through the "Kidney Payback Policy" introduced in January 1990.[32]

Point systems lend themselves naturally to compromises among different groups of second-order actors. The point system for allocating kidneys has been depicted as a trade-off between the values of equity and efficiency. Perhaps it may be more accurately seen as a compromise between groups advocating the one

[32] Dennis, "Reflections on the Unintended Consequences of Planning Local Justice" notes that a side effect of the drive for a more equitable distribution across centers may be that more kidneys are procured. The efficiency gains on the supply side might offset the tendency (created by the same reform) for each kidney to be less efficiently used (as measured by graft survival rates).

or the other value, that is, between doctors and hospital administrators or between different groups of doctors. As reported above, doctors in inner-city hospitals in one large city successfully fought for giving more points for time on the waiting list, to ensure better chances for black patients. Whereas the serologists who carry out the practical tasks of antigen matching stress the need for a good match between donor kidney and recipient, transplantation surgeons emphasize that, with the advent of cyclosporine, goodness of match is less important. In this perspective, the point system can be seen as a compromise between two *factual* views rather than between two values.[33] Other mixed systems might also have their origin as compromises among groups of actors within the institution.

Organized interest groups. Usually, interest groups organize to promote goals that are common to all members. We would not expect, therefore, a group to organize for the sole purpose of deciding which of its members should be excluded from a scarce good. If, however, the group is organized around another purpose that *is* common to all members, it might take on the bargaining over allocative principles as an additional task. It might organize for the purpose of increasing the supply of the scarce good, and then also engage in bargaining over allocation. Since the task is inherently divisive, the organization might nevertheless hesitate to take it on. The British Kidney Patient Association, for instance, strives to improve the patient's quality of life and to alter policy so that everyone requiring treatment will receive it,[34] but not (as far as I know) to change allocative principles. The main exception is the inclusion of layoff provisions in collective agreements between unions and firms. Although these tend to favor the more senior workers, the divisive impact is blunted by junior workers knowing they will gain seniority with time. Also, unions perform other valuable functions for these workers.

Outside the labor market there are few if any genuine instances of third-order groups organizing themselves to advocate a particular allocative principle, for three main reasons. First, as I said, the allocative issues tend to be inherently divisive. Second, these

[33] I am indebted to Michael Dennis for this observation.
[34] Halper, *The Misfortune of Others*, p. 76.

groups have no bargaining power that would enable them to make credible threats. If patients take themselves off the waiting list or high-school students withdraw their applications to college, they harm nobody but themselves.[35] Third, many recipient groups—students, draftees, patients on the waiting list for operations, parents with small children, the elderly—form a transient population, with little capacity to organize in the first place.[36] In all these respects, workers and trade unions are more advantageously placed.

In addition to organizations that include all and only the potential recipients, there are two other cases to be considered. First, an organized subgroup of the potential recipients may try to change the allocative system in their favor, directly through bargaining or indirectly by lobbying or an appeal to public opinion. Blacks and other minorities have often claimed the right to do military service.[37] Recently, feminist groups have made the same demand. Other groups have neglected to press their claims. For instance, "though diabetics have suffered heavily from the United Kingdom's ESRD policy, the British Diabetic Association until recently has given little time to this issue."[38] Second, pressure groups may form *on behalf* of subgroups among the potential recipients. Although blacks have never organized to get a larger share of kidneys, doctors, acting on their behalf, have done so. Earlier, I referred to the local variant of the UNOS point system adopted by one regional organ bank. The leading actors behind this policy were doctors in inner-city hospitals who saw that their black patients rarely managed to leave the waiting list. Although children who need special education cannot organize themselves, their parents can and do.[39] The exemptions for American farmers and

[35] This statement, though broadly valid, has one important exception. Apparently pointless "strikes" by patients or students might drum up public opinion in their favor, and the threat of taking such action could therefore confer bargaining power. Although such self-hurting strategies are well known from other domains, I do not know of cases in which they have been used to promote a specific allocative principle.

[36] Cp. my *Logic and Society*, p. 134 ff.

[37] Petersen, "Rationality, Ethnicity and Military Enlistment"; Chambers, *To Raise an Army*, p. 156.

[38] Halper, *The Misfortune of Others*, p. 79.

[39] Handler, *The Conditions of Discretion*, especially Chapter 3.

agricultural workers in World War I were not obtained by young men from the countryside acting on their own behalf, but through pressure from the agricultural interests. The two cases point to a further subdivision: group A's motive in acting on behalf of group B may be found in the interest of B (as in kidneys for blacks) or in the interest of A (as in exemptions for agricultural workers).

Public opinion. For Calabresi and Bobbit, public opinion is a major explanatory category. At least, this is how I interpret their constant references to what "society" can accept or cannot accept, and to the need for "society" to deceive itself about the necessity of making hard choices. Although I have objections to the functionalist framework of their analysis, I do not deny the importance of public opinion. First, however, I have to distinguish this category from that of national culture. Roughly speaking, national culture constrains the allocative proposals that are made, whereas public opinion constrains those that are accepted. To the extent that the reaction of public opinion is anticipated by second-order decision makers, it may also stop proposals from coming to the floor, but this is a secondary effect that should be distinguished from the primary effect of culture in stopping a proposal from coming to anybody's mind. The distinction may seem tenuous. In many cases it is certainly not clear whether one is dealing with culture or opinions; but there exist paradigm cases of each kind that cannot be confused with the other.[40]

The debates in the spring of 1917 over modes of enlistment in the United States Army offer a good example. Initially, there were two proposals before Congress: the President's proposal for exclusive reliance on the draft and a proposal that relied largely on volunteers. Later, a compromise or two-track system was also proposed. Massive publicity campaigns were organized for the draft and against volunteerism, notably by the Hearst press. The problem with volunteerism, according to one Hearst editor, was that

---

[40] Public opinion also needs to be distinguished from the attitudes of the potential recipients. While including those attitudes, it goes beyond them to encompass sizable segments of the population at large. Attitudes of recipients are discussed separately below.

Those who are most patriotic and most intelligently loyal are necessarily sacrificed in the defense of the least patriotic and least loyal—so that in the very process of defending the land we automatically lower its future standard of citizenry and leave its destinies in the hands not of the brave and freedom-loving but in the hands of cowards and those fit to be slaves.[41]

The argument has a curious and familiar ring, recalling Catch 22 and Solomon's judgment.[42] The editorialist comes close to saying that those who volunteer for service by that very act show themselves to be such good citizens that they ought to be exempt from service. The appeal, in any case, was very successful. "Like a summer thunderstorm, a deluge of letters and telegrams battered Capitol Hill. Half a million came from the 300,000 Navy League alone. Except for the declaration of war, the draft led to more constituent mail than any other issue in 1917."[43] These were not self-interested reactions by potential draftees (they would, if anything, have supported volunteerism), but disinterested protests coming from many parts of the population. In the end, the President's draft bill was adopted with 394 votes against 24, largely because of this popular pressure.

Another selection procedure was actually implemented before it had to be abolished because of public reactions. This was the screening of candidates for dialysis done by the Seattle Artificial Kidney Center's Admission and Policy Committee, sometimes referred to as "the Seattle God committee" because the members had wide discretion not only to apply but also to formulate guidelines. Hence the only principles involved were those that went into the selection of committee members, who were "envisaged as representing a broad socioeconomic spectrum of the Seattle community, in hope that this would mitigate any bias in favor of candidates with certain social backgrounds or occupations." Instead of choosing patients by lot (a proposal often made but never implemented), the Seattle Center came close to choosing the choosers by lot. The committee, in fact, worked very much like a jury, members of which are regularly selected by lot, partly

[41] Cited from Chambers, *To Raise an Army*, p. 162.
[42] See my *Solomonic Judgements*, pp. 127–129.
[43] Chambers, *To Raise an Army*, p. 163.

for the cited reason of "representing a broad spectrum of the community."[44]

The committee started working in 1961. In 1962 an article appeared in *Life* magazine, which reported that the committee weighted factors such as "sex of patient; marital status and number of dependents; income; net worth; emotional stability, with particular regard to the patient's capacity to accept the treatment; educational background; nature of occupation, past performance and future potential; and names of people who could serve as references."[45] In addition, of course, medical criteria were used. Although the article created "an avalanche of criticisms,"[46] the committee was not immediately disbanded. It was eventually modified, however, to include more doctors and no permanent lay members. Revelation of the committee's practices and those of similar laymen's committees was a factor behind the Social Security Amendment of 1972 that extended Medicare to cover the costs of dialysis, thus making it accessible to all patients.

In the 1920s, Harvard's admission policy for Jews also had to be changed because of public outcry:

> President A. Lawrence Lowell of Harvard . . . was urging the adoption of a quota system to resolve what he saw as Harvard's Jewish problem. Between 1900 and 1922 the proportion of Jewish students at Harvard College had tripled, rising from 7 percent to 21.5 percent. Through the carelessness of the Harvard publicity manager, word of the impending Jewish quota was allowed to leak out. Falsification of character and psychological tests, the manager implied, might also be options for limiting the proportion of Jews. Once the news became public President Lowell, a firm believer in the justice of a ceiling on Jewish admissions, steadfastly defended his proposals, and a public relations nightmare ensued.[47]

In the end, Lowell had to back down. Other universities, among them Yale, learned from his mistake. When Yale came to limit the number of Jews, they proceeded with "utmost secrecy

---

[44] On this and other reasons for selecting juries by lot, see my *Solomonic Judgements*, p. 95 ff.

[45] Cited after Swazey and Fox, *The Courage to Fail*, p. 245.

[46] Calabresi and Bobbit, *Tragic Choices*, p. 188.

[47] Oren, *Joining the Club*, p. 46.

and caution,"[48] achieving informal quotas by the use of facially neutral criteria, as explained in Chapter 4.

Incentive problems. Incentive effects can arise at all levels in an allocative scheme. To help the reader orient himself in the rather complex discussion that follows, a brief preview may be useful. First, I discuss first- and second-order responses to third-order incentive effects: how authorities and institutions react to strategic behavior by the recipients. Second, I discuss the responses of second-order and first-order political actors to incentive effects among first-order individual actors: how authorities and institutions may try to increase supply by adopting allocative principles that motivate individual donors. Third, I consider second-order responses to second-order incentive effects: how institutions respond to the fact that their own officers may have an incentive to deviate from the official policy. Fourth, I discuss whether first-order political actors might not also have their own personal incentives to shape principles.

(1) In considering higher-order responses to strategic behavior among the recipients, I shall first discuss moral hazard in the allocation of medical resources. In Chapter 4 I argued that this problem is a relatively unimportant one. Organizers of health care do not seem to believe in them either. It is an important fact about modern systems for providing health care that incentive-based reasoning has very little force. The only possible example I have encountered is the practice in Norway and some other European countries of refusing reimbursement for dental work. Perhaps people take better care of their teeth when they know they have to pay for the trip to the dentist, but I cannot help thinking that vanity is a stronger motivation. The assertion that medical need justifies treatment only if it is not knowingly self-inflicted is seldom heard outside libertarian circles, where it is based on arguments from desert rather than on incentive-effect reasoning.

In Chapter 4 I mentioned that there might be a partial positive analogue to moral hazard. The idea is this. Think of the welfare state like a circus with a safety net. As more acrobats fall in arenas that have nets than in those that don't, there is a moral hazard effect. For some acrobats, though, the fear of falling when there

---

[48] Ibid., p. 48.

is no net might be psychologically destabilizing and thus make them fall more easily. The strong desire not to fall causes their hands to shake and makes them more likely to fall. This is not an incentive effect, but the result of a nonintentional causal mechanism.[49] Unconditional access to free medical treatment could have a similar effect. While possibly leading people to behave more recklessly than if they knew they had to pay for self-induced illness, it also reduces worry and stress with their concomitant medical problems. To the extent that health officials think along such lines, they may help explain why incentive-based schemes are so common. However, the other reasons adduced in Chapter 4 against believing in incentive effects are certainly more important. And even if credible incentive schemes could be counted on to deter almost everybody, I do not believe that health care providers would refuse treatment to the occasional patient with a serious but self-induced problem. Simple humanity and compassion, as well as fear of media scandals, would keep them from carrying out the threat of denying treatment. But this means that the scheme would not be credible.

Consider next problems of wasteful investment in entitlements. Sometimes the response is to make such behavior illegal. In many countries, including Spain and Norway, there have been severe laws against those who tried to escape military service through self-mutilation. The punishment may or may not include denial of the scarce good in question. In child custody cases, for instance, it has been debated whether abduction of a child for the purpose of increasing the chances of getting custody should be punished by denial of custody, even when this action would go against the interest of the child.

Alternatively, the response may be to adopt another principle which is expected to yield a better outcome *in terms of the first-best criterion* than that criterion would yield if applied directly. All things considered, to award custody by a mechanical rule (a maternal presumption or even a lottery) may be better for the child than to let custody follow the best interest of the child. If self-

---

[49] For such "nonstandard causal chains" in the analysis of action, see D. Davidson, *Essays on Actions and Events*, p. 79. Tocqueville offers a dictum in a similar spirit: "Rien ne sert plus au succès que de ne point le désirer avec trop d'ardeur" (*Souvenirs*, p. 108).

mutilation is a widespread response to selection for physical fitness, selection by lot might yield fitter soldiers. If the use of present dwelling conditions to allocate public housing induces people to move into slums, income might be used instead to select the genuinely needy recipients. More generally, a principle can be abandoned if it has incentive effects that, while not necessarily counterproductive in its own terms, result in an unfair allocation. If foreigners marry citizens just to be allowed to immigrate, the clause favoring relatives might be limited to marriages in which there are children.

What is wasteful from the social point of view may be desirable or neutral from the institutional perspective. An institution tends to focus on the effect of incentives on those who actually receive the good, and neglect the effect on those who are turned down. First-order authorities are in a position to take a larger view. They might intervene, for instance, to prevent people from investing in job-specific skills that are useless if they do not get the job, insisting instead that training be done on the job. Conversely, they might insist on principles that, while not necessarily optimal from the institution's point of view, encourage successful and unsuccessful applicants alike to acquire generally useful skills. Moreover, first-order actors might be more sensitive to the wastes generated by queuing and waiting lists. I do not know how important such considerations are in practice, but I suspect they are somewhat marginal.

Finally, consider the problem of misrepresentation. In practice, the most important problems do not arise because the relevant information is essentially private, as is the case with information about preferences, pain, or skills. Rather, they arise when the relevant information is public, but independent verification is costly. In such cases, the institution can either trust the applicant or carry out its own investigation—or decide to ignore such information altogether. Applicants to kindergarten in Norway sometimes ask a friendly doctor or psychiatrist for a letter saying that admission of their child to kindergarten is vital for their mental health. Should the admissions committee ask for a second opinion? Or should they eliminate this category of need from the list of admissions criteria? A similar problem arises for immigration authorities when citizens from the Third World apply for permission to join relatives in Norway. Although the information they provide about relatives can in principle be independently verified, this is a difficult and time-consuming task. As a result, immigration restrictions have been greatly tightened. Similar semi-sordid examples could be multiplied indefinitely. Toward the end of this subsection I return to the intricate interaction between incentive problems and information problems.

(2) Principles can also be chosen because of their incentive effect on individual first-order decision makers (i.e., donors). One clear illustration is the French practice of giving priority in the allocation of sperm to women who can also provide a sperm donor. Under Singapore law, "those who object to serving as posthumous kidney providers are given second-priority access to the cadaver kidney pool in the event of need; that is, only if an available kidney is not able to be used by a needy non-objector (i.e., a presumed consenter), will it be offered to a needy objector."[50] In countries that do not have the principle of presumed consent, the converse scheme could be used: to prefer as recipients for organ transplantations those who have indicated their willingness to donate organs.[51]

In a related yet different line of argument, fear has been expressed that if one allows transplantation of foreign nationals, the willingness of citizens to donate might fall,[52] or that if patients have to pay for transplantations, the poor might be less willing to give their organs. "How can we request organ donations from underinsured families? We certainly cannot attempt to obtain organs for transplantation from families whose members cannot participate in a transplantation program as potential recipients."[53] These supply-related arguments for allocative schemes are not based on incentive effects, as that phrase is commonly under-

---

[50] Peters, "A Unified Approach to Organ Donor Recruitment, Organ Procurement, and Distribution," pp. 177–178.

[51] This proposal is made in Kamm, "The Report of the U.S. Task Force on Organ Transplantation."

[52] Childress, "Some Moral Connections Between Organ Procurement and Organ Distribution." This fear is probably not well founded. (See Evans and Manninen, "U.S. Public Opinion Concerning the Procurement and Distribution of Donor Organs.")

[53] Strom, "Letter to the Editor."

stood, but on what we might call "group-based fairness effects"[54] or "group interest effect." The refusal to donate in such cases would not be based on self-interest, as the impact of any single refusal on the probability that the program would be extended to cover that group is negligible. Nor would the refusal simply be grounded in a concern for fairness, since such concerns would presumably extend to any form of unfair distributions. For more on these group-based arguments the reader is referred to the discussion of ethical individualism in Chapter 6.

(3) Principles may also be rejected if they have negative incentive effects on the officers in the second-order institution itself. In particular, the risk of corruption, whim, and favoritism in discretionary systems may force the adoption of new and safer procedures. There may be a minor paradox at work here. I conjecture that the less a society has reason to fear arbitrary behavior among second-order allocators, the stronger the pressure to move toward principles that make such behavior impossible. As the general level of professional competence and trustworthiness rises, the indignation caused by the few transgressions that inevitably occur rises even faster. (Readers of Tocqueville's *Ancien régime* may recognize the logic.) Be this as it may, to reduce the incentives for corrupt behavior, institutions have adopted the following devices: reducing the scope for discretionary decisions, making selectors accountable for their decisions, and giving applicants and recipients more insight in the process.

First, one can move from discretionary to nondiscretionary criteria. As Robert Klitgaard writes, "Mechanical systems—such as centrally graded, standardized tests—are a guard against . . . abuses. They hamstring the selectors, reducing their freedom of movement and providing fewer incentives and opportunities for corruption and coercion."[55] Instead of leaving evaluation of "leadership qualities" to the discretion of the admissions officer, one can give explicit points for a finite set of activities such as being president of the high school debating society and the like. Or one

---

[54] Matthieu, "Introduction to Part 3," p. 144, explicitly claims that "it would not be fair to ask the poor to denote organs that will then only be used to aid the affluent portion of the population." She does not, however, go on to express a fear that the poor might, for this reason, refuse to cooperate.

[55] Klitgaard, *Elitism and Meritocracy in Developing Countries*, pp. 100–101.

can move away from leadership qualities altogether and use grades and test scores only. The fear of discretionary behavior (or of being accused of such behavior) was a major factor behind the introduction of the point system for allocating kidneys. The fear of discretionary foreman behavior was no less important in the move toward seniority in layoff decisions. As mentioned earlier, literacy tests and head taxes, as screening devices for immigrants, were preferred to discretionary evaluation by the immigration officers. In fact, examples of this tendency away from discretionary behavior can be found in virtually all issues of local justice. It is supported by the need, noted below, to economize on costs of decision making.

Sometimes, however, discretion must be harnessed rather than eliminated. Let me quote Klitgaard[56] again:

> The Chinese recognized that the complicated and highly valued examination system was only a partial answer to choosing its administrative leadership. Examinations could measure intellectual power and cultural formation, but they did not purport to measure how well a person would meet the practical challenges that faced a high official of government. To augment the exams, an elaborate system of recommendations was instituted, but recommendations with safeguards against corruption and whim. The recommender was held responsible for the person he recommended. If you recommended someone for a job and he did well, you could receive "requitement and commendation" yourself, but if he did badly, you could be liable. Table 1 shows how the penalties to the recommender were related to the penalties incurred by the person recommended. This system was administered scrupulously, and the evidence is that in early Sung China at least this method of incorporating subjective judgments about personal character into the selection process was relatively free from corruption and abuse. [see Table 1, page 164]

The mechanism used here is that of accountability. If the selectors can be held responsible for their decisions, the danger of discretionary decision is much reduced. Transplantation centers might be evaluated by graft survival rates.[57] Similarly, centers for

---

[56] Ibid. I am grateful to Patricia Conley for directing me to this passage.

[57] This proposal is a hotly debated issue within the transplantation community. A memorandum from the United Network for Organ Sharing states that "Requiring minimum institutional survival rates was rejected as a basis

TABLE 1. / **Recommended Liability in China** (c.a. A.D. 1020)
[Klitgaard]

If the Person Recommended Was Later Punished With:	The Recommender Could Be Punished With:
Death	Deportation
Deportation	Forced labor
Forced labor	Beating with a heavy or light rod
Beating with a heavy rod	None
Beating with a light rod	None

artificial insemination might be evaluated according to the proportion of women who become pregnant.[58] Admission officers might be evaluated by the final grades of the students they admit. Judges whose decisions are often overturned on appeal might lose their jobs. For such schemes to work, success itself must be measurable in a nondiscretionary manner, since otherwise little would be gained. Despite the admirable example set by the Sung dynasty, this technique for containing discretion is little used today. Most institutions have complex, multidimensional objectives that do not allow for easy monitoring. Fear of litigation tends to make institutions move away from discretion rather than to try to use it more wisely.

Finally, discretion can be tamed by offering applicants insight into the selection process, together with some power to influence, contest, or appeal. In custody disputes parents take part in the decision process, by testifying and producing expert witnesses and character witnesses. Unions not only negotiate the clauses in

---

for developing membership standards but not without making a provision for the importance of outcomes in program evaluation. Several reasons . . . were put forth: first, no historical data exists to sufficiently and comprehensively produce a national baseline correlating transplant outcome and quality. . . . Second, it is unfair and unwise to impose minimum outcome criteria on all programs in the national network; such criteria would unfairly discourage the transplantation of highly sensitized or high-risk patients and may not be uniformly applicable to the diverse types of transplant programs" (UNOS, Sept. 1989, "Statement of Policy, UNOS Policies for Institutional Membership: Clinical Transplant Programs," p. 12).

[58] For reasons similar to those given in the preceding note, this proposal might discriminate unfairly against the centers who take on the more difficult cases, notably older women.

the collective bargaining agreement that specify how layoffs are to be made, but are also heavily involved in implementing and interpreting those clauses. In the admissions process at Harvard College, all applications, after passing through a subcommittee, go before the full committee with about sixty members, making any bias or hidden collusion very improbable. In many cases, though, admitting claimants or their representatives to the decision procedure would render it extremely unwieldy and time-consuming. References to student power and patient power are frequent, but in practice the power rarely extends to allocative issues.

(4) I have discussed cases in which incentives arise at two levels: given their goals, higher-order actors have an incentive to adopt principles that will create incentives for recipients, donors, or administrators to behave in ways that the former find desirable. And I have tacitly assumed that these higher-order actors were motivated by concerns of efficiency or fairness. But could they not also be motivated by personal self-interest, by the desire to favor themselves, their children, or their cronies? Since politicians (to whom I shall limit myself in the following) form a subset of the potential recipients of scarce goods, they no less than others have an incentive to act so as to increase their chances of getting them. On the one hand, they may use their power to increase the total supply of the good (or diminish the size of the burden); on the other, they may try to impose a principle that favors individuals with a profile similar to their own. The first strategy treats the principle as a parameter but the amount of the good as a variable; the second modifies the principle but leaves the scarcity unaffected. If the scarcity is natural or quasi-natural (Chapter 2), the second strategy may be the more feasible.

A hypothetical example of the first strategy is the following: "If random selection or the market were the main basis of scarce resources allocation, there is all the more likelihood that scarcity would be significantly alleviated as holders of political and economic power attempted to reduce the chance that they would themselves be excluded."[59] Closer to the real world, it has been argued that the introduction of the draft lottery and the end of

---

[59] Kilner, "A Moral Allocation of Scarce Lifesaving Medical Resources."

deferment for most students contributed to political pressure to end the Vietnam War, as influential parents faced the prospect of seeing their children sent to die. Other, more clear-cut cases may exist, but I have not come across any. Nor can I cite any examples of the second strategy. Since politicians in most countries have the power to skip the queue, why should they use the much more cumbersome method of replacing the principle of queuing with one that happens to pick them out before others? Both strategies, in fact, are forms of overkill, implausibly roundabout ways of making sure that one is chosen to receive a scarce good. The incentives to use them may be present, but in the presence of a better way of achieving the same end they are not acted on.

In fact, the whole discussion of categories (1) through (4) suggests that incentive effects do not figure prominently in the explanation of allocative principles. Although no doubt pervasive, such effects are also very elusive. Given people's ingenuity in finding loopholes or turning rules to their advantage, as well as their occasional propensity to neglect their self-interest, they are hard to anticipate in advance. When a principle has been adopted, one cannot always demonstrate an incentive effect by comparing actions before and after its introduction, because behavior may have changed for other reasons; by the same token, incentive effects may be present even if behavior does not change. To identify them one must rely on complicated counterfactual arguments, comparing the actual with the hypothetical rather than the present with the past.

In Chapter 4, I claimed that second-order actors act naively if they assume that principles have no incentive effects. Perhaps I did them an injustice? The problems of anticipating and identifying such effects suggest that it is equally naive to believe that allocative schemes can be fine-tuned so as to take full account of them. If, as I believe, incentive-based schemes are relatively rare, the reason may be that second-order actors are sufficiently sophisticated to be aware of these difficulties. If they appear to act naively, it may be because they are aware of their limits. I leave it to the reader to reflect on this problem.

Information problems. These are often relevant and sometimes decisive for the choice of principles and procedures. Although information-intensive procedures usually lead to better selections among the applicants (but see below), these benefits must be weighed against two drawbacks. In the first place, the costs incurred in gathering and processing information are not always justified by the additional discriminatory power. In the second place, when the information is to be provided by the applicants themselves, some may be deterred by the complexity of the procedure from seeking to obtain what is rightfully theirs.

The first-best principle of second-order actors is almost invariably an individualized criterion interpreted in a discretionary manner: to have applicants judged and ranked by professionals on the basis of medical need, productive skills, fighting ability, scholastic merit, past contributions, or whatever criterion is seen as appropriate. Such procedures can be very information-intensive and hence expensive. In addition to written documentation, decision makers may need extensive tests, interviews, and direct observation before they feel they know enough about the applicants to make a confident choice among them. To gather the information is costly; and processing it may be even more so. At Harvard College, it has been estimated that in 1982–1983 the budget for the admissions office might have been cut from $450,000 to half that amount "if folders were given only one reading and committee discussions were eliminated, as at some schools."[60] At Harvard Medical School, each of the 926 students who applied in 1980 had two interviews. At Harvard Law School, each faculty member on the admissions committee read about 1,000 applications. At Harvard Business School, each applicant must submit seven essays. These are highly discretionary, information-intensive, and costly procedures.

Harvard and other universities using similar procedures presumably believe the costs to be justified. In other cases, similarly extensive investigation and careful discussion of each applicant would be absurdly expensive, compared to the expected gains. The institution may then follow one of three paths. First, it may stick to a discretionary procedure, but reduce the information input and the amount of redundancy in the processing. Instead of using several readers for each application, there might be only

---

[60] Klitgaard, *Choosing Elites*, p. 311. The following facts about Harvard admissions procedures are all taken from Chapter 2 of this book.

one; instead of several interviews, there might be one or none; the requirement of essays might be dropped; and so on. Next, the institution might stick to the basic principles, but implement them in a nondiscretionary manner. High school grades and standardized test scores can be used as sole indicators of academic merit, as in the computerized system used by the University of Texas at Austin to select among its fifty thousand applicants to college. Finally, the institution may use a different principle altogether, such as lottery (as in Holland), queuing (as in French faculties of letters), or open admission combined with draconian selection after one year (as in French medical schools). If the first and the second alternatives to information-intensive discretionary selection are thought insufficiently reliable in selecting the most able applicants, and that principle itself is judged to be too costly, the institution may decide to take a wholly different route.

A fact that may reinforce this tendency is that discretionary decisions also have nonmonetary costs associated with them. For one thing, they invite suspicions of arbitrary and corrupt selection practices, sometimes even litigation. Ultimately these moral costs may also entail financial costs, as litigation costs rise, applications drop, and private benefactors show less interest. For another, information-intensive procedures also tend to be time-consuming. If the selection has to be made urgently, as in cases of medical triage, it may be self-defeating to wait until one has all the information needed to make the correct diagnosis. Earlier, I noted that a partially similar problem arises in child custody cases: the attempt to determine what is in the best interest of the child may not be in the child's interest. In business matters and war, similar remarks apply. Note, however, that this dilemma need not take us all the way to nondiscretionary decision making; it might be better still to have a swift discretionary decision based on less information.

I have written so far as if more information about individual recipients always enables discretionary allocators to form better judgments, and as if mechanical formulae are inferior substitutes with nothing to be said for them except their lower costs. Some types of information seem to be largely useless, however. The use of interviews in admitting students or hiring applicants for a job is not only costly, but arguably irrelevant as well.[61] Sometimes, less can even be more. For many purposes—predicting future performance of students or diagnosing an illness—a mechanical formula based on a limited number of characteristics does better than the trained judgment of a professional with access to a larger range of information.[62] Even more surprisingly, it has been shown that this difference remains when the formula is based on decisions made by that professional himself. In Chapter 3, I distinguished the normative weights used in a mechanical point system from the descriptive weights that capture the implicit trade-offs in discretionary decisions. The "bootstrapping" results to which I just referred affirm that a professional can improve his performance by using the weights that describe his past decisions to improve his choices in the future.[63]

We see, therefore, a number of converging pressures to move away from heavily discretionary principles toward mechanical formulae or impersonal mechanisms. The latter are less costly; they may save time and, when time is of the essence, life and suffering; they are less vulnerable to corruption and bribery, and therefore to suspicions that such practices occur; they are less controversial and less prone to litigation; and they may be no less effective and sometimes more effective than discretionary methods. Yet there is also much to be said for discretion. A professional exercising his judgment can take account of unusual features of an applicant that would never make their way into a mechanical formula. To show the need for discretionary selection, the Federal Labor Court in Germany (see Chapter 3) cited the case of a worker whose child

---

[61] Klitgaard, *Choosing Elites*, p. 137 ff.

[62] The classical study is Meehl, *Clinical versus Statistical Prediction*.

[63] "For example, a decision-maker may be weighing aptitude, past performance, and motivation correctly in predicting performance in graduate school and beyond, yet he may be influenced by such things as fatigue, headaches, boredom, and so on; in addition, he will be influenced by whether the most recent applications he has seen are particularly strong or weak. A [linear model] of this behavior would not be affected by these extraneous variables, and as long as these variables are not systematically related to the relevant variables of aptitude, past performance, and motivation, the model will attach the appropriate weights to these relevant variables" (Dawes, "A Case Study of Graduate Admission," p. 182).

had a speech defect that required attendance at a special school, and it is indeed hard to imagine that a mechanical formula for layoffs would assign points for children with such defects. Also, I cannot help thinking (and, more relevantly, I believe that many second-order actors cannot help thinking) that *good* professionals are better than any formula, including formulae based on their own past decisions. In thinking about the optimal procedure for selecting good professionals to whom these judgments are to be entrusted, the dilemma of discretionary versus mechanical procedures arises again. I cannot here pursue this matter.

Information about applicants can be gathered by observing them, testing them, interviewing them, asking them questions, or having them fill out an application form. In the last case—which arises regularly in the administration of the welfare state—a well-known dilemma arises. Assume that the good is to be allocated on the basis of need, that is, by using the welfare level criterion. To determine need, questions have to be asked about income, dependents, housing, education, health, and the like, each of them subdivided into further questions to sort out the truly needy. The first "folk theorem" of the welfare state asserts that the most needy are those who are so disadvantaged that they cannot complete the application form. Here, too, there is a Catch 22 effect: if a person is able to understand and fill out the application form, the facts about himself that he writes down will show that he does not need the good.[64] More generally, obtaining scarce goods may require actions that nobody who needs them could possibly perform.[65] The second folk theorem asserts that if welfare officials respond to this dilemma by simplifying the procedures,

[64] "The Social Security Administration has erected mind-boggling obstacles to poor, homeless and disabled people who need its help. . . . About 4.6 million people receive the benefits, but various studies have concluded that as many as 50 percent of those eligible for [Supplemental Security Income] are not participating" ("Red Tape Deters Aid Applicants," *Chicago Tribune,* April 6, 1990).

[65] "A one-legged man seeking a state mobility allowance had to struggle up four flights of stairs to the room where a tribunal was to decide the claim. When he got there the tribunal ruled that he could not have the allowance because he managed to make it up the stairs" (*Observer,* February 17, 1980). See also the moving report by Malcolm MacEwan, "Stranded Without a Leg to Stand on" (*The Independent,* March 14, 1989), relating the difficulties in obtaining artificial limbs in Britain.

access to the good will be enhanced not only for those who did not understand the more complicated rules that entitled them to it, but also for those who did not qualify under those rules. The third folk theorem, therefore, is that no scheme singles out all and only those who need the good.

More generally, simplified procedures based on incomplete information create *loopholes*—an allocation of the scarce good to some individuals who on first-best principles should not have it. Examples include blanket exemptions for military service based on occupational or marital status; award of child custody on the principle of maternal presumption, used as a proxy for the interest of the child; a general preference for veterans, some of whom may have done nothing to deserve the good to which their service entitles them; allocation of rationing cards for gasoline to individuals who sell their quota to others because they never use their car; and arbitrary age limits for adoption, artificial insemination, place in nursery school, or transplantation. In all these cases there may well be good reasons for not seeking the first-best allocation, but there is nevertheless a gap between the ideal and the reality.

Incentive problems can also create loopholes, albeit of a different sort. In many cases, scarce goods ought ideally to be reserved for individuals who would qualify for them even if the principle of allocation were a secret.[66] Thus a man who gets exemption from military service because he has cut off a finger should not really have it: he has exploited a loophole. Similarly, a person who could afford to save money for an apartment but fails to do so because he knows he can count on public housing, does not really deserve it. These problems, too, can be seen as due to incomplete information. If information about applicants is extended to their past behavior, some who are now accepted might be rejected, either by a direct argument from desert or *pour décourager les autres*.

On arenas of local justice we observe an endless chase between third-order actors in search of loopholes and first- and second-order actors trying to close them. The latter are in a difficult position, as the remedies for loopholes of one kind tend to open up

---

[66] Not in all cases: there is nothing wrong in admitting students to college on the grounds that they have obtained high grades by working hard in high school in order to get into college.

others. The incentive-induced loopholes can be plugged by switching to nonmanipulable status criteria and impersonal mechanisms. These principles, however, almost as a rule give rise to information-induced loopholes. The basic dilemma is that the criteria which are most relevant from the first-best point of view also tend to be highly manipulable. If they are included because of their relevance, some people will exploit the system. If they are excluded because of their manipulability, others will get an undeserved windfall gain. Other things being equal, the latter ill is the smaller. More disturbing than either, however, is the possibility that some individuals who really deserve the good might be denied it, either because relevant information is excluded (as in the German point system for layoffs) or because the procedure is so complicated that the most needy applicants are unable to tell the authorities what they need to know. Actual allocative schemes are to a considerable extent the outcome of second- and first-order authorities trying to cope simultaneously with all these problems.

PREFERENCE AGGREGATION

I have tried to sketch some of the motives of actors involved in the choice of allocation systems, and some of the practical constraints they are facing. I now conclude by considering the larger explanatory issue: How do the motives and constraints facing the different actors come together to produce a final outcome? As I said, I shall limit myself to a discussion of some frequently occurring patterns or mechanisms, thus falling far short of anything like a general theory. I shall discuss three main such patterns: coalition-building, bargaining, and accretion.

Coalition-building. In Chapter 3, I observed that allocative principles and procedures tend to be overdetermined, in the sense that they can often be justified from several, sometimes very different, perspectives. When a scheme corresponds to the values or interests of several groups, the task of building a coalition around it is much facilitated. Coalitions can also form by logrolling and similar procedures, one group supporting a principle advocated by another in return for support of some of its own, more important, goals. Although clearly important in practice, this mechanism operates so generally, across the whole spectrum of political issues, that it would take me too far to discuss it here. I shall concentrate, therefore, on coalition-building by overdetermination.

As further explained in Chapter 6, there is a general tendency for desert-based arguments and rule-utilitarian arguments to yield similar conclusions. As a result, consequentialist and antecedentialist arguments are often less opposed in practice than one might expect. The solid employer-employee coalition around seniority as a principle for layoffs offers a clear illustration. Workers believe that senior employees deserve preferential treatment, and management finds it efficient to accord it to them. In addition, as I mentioned in Chapter 3, under many circumstances seniority would be adopted by majority voting among workers based on simple self-interest, further cementing the alliance. There is little that outside forces can do to overturn or substantially modify the seniority principle. One might argue, for instance, that it would be socially desirable to retain the *least* senior workers in layoffs, to stabilize what is often a fragile insertion into the work culture and the work ethic.[67] In face of a strong worker-management alliance, however, this proposal would not stand much of a chance.

The alliance for seniority is based on equity, efficiency, and self-interest. In other cases, different conceptions of equity may be involved. Consider again the importance of time on the waiting list in the point system for kidney allocation. Some may emphasize waiting because they believe in the inherent fairness of queuing. Others may advocate more points for waiting to compensate people for the bad medical luck of having unusual antigen patterns. Still others may support the policy because some of the persons with bad medical luck also happen to be disadvantaged on other grounds. None of these are self-interested arguments. None of them are based on efficiency considerations. They represent different conceptions of distributive equity, which in this particular case happens to point in the same direction.

The alliance for preferential admission of students from economically and culturally disadvantaged backgrounds may be similarly heterogeneous. Some may believe that this policy can be justified on efficiency grounds, arguing that high school grades

---

[67] For an argument to this effect, see my "Is There (or Should There Be) a Right to Work?"

may underpredict the college performance of such students. Others may believe in pure compensatory justice; and still others may support the policy as a remedy for the low representation of ethnic minorities. Some may even support it out of a diffuse fear of public opinion and concern that the college might be viewed as insufficiently progressive.

Under certain conditions (specified in Chapter 3), the level and increment welfare criteria point in the same direction. This allows for a coalition between those who want to allocate scarce resources on humanitarian grounds and those who are more guided by efficiency considerations: the worst-off individuals are also those who can benefit most from the scarce good. In terms of Figure 3.2, for instance, both criteria would tell us to prefer patients at B over patients at C. In the choice between patients at B and patients at A, where the two criteria point in opposite directions, a compromise solution might be expected instead (see below).

Immigration policy is largely shaped by coalition-building. The literacy test, for instance, had broad appeal "in selecting on the basis of individual merit (the liberal tradition), discouraging Central, South, and East European immigration (ethnocentrism), and, it was believed, in sharply lowering numbers (labor welfare)."[68] An increased head tax was seen "as both a source of revenue and a means to a better class of immigrants."[69] However, one also observed the formation of opposing coalitions, with "right-wing ethnocentrists and racists and left-wing laborites advocating restriction, and right-wing business interests and left-wing liberals and humanitarians advocating expansion."[70] In such cases alliance formation cannot be the whole story.

Bargaining and compromise. When no winning coalition can form, a compromise must be reached. In practice, this implies the agreement on some mixed principle that incorporates several considerations. In one ideal-typical case, we may imagine the outcome being a point system, with each dimension corresponding to a specific group demand and the weights reflecting the bargaining

---

[68] Mackie, "U.S. Immigration Policy and Local Justice."
[69] Hutchinson, *A Legislative History of American Immigration Policy*, p. 145.
[70] Ibid.

strength of the different groups. In another, the outcome might be reached through rational discussion, through which the parties come to realize that fairness and efficiency demand a more complicated scheme than each of them had initially envisaged.[71] In the following I limit myself to the polar case of pure bargaining, knowing well that in practice it is always intermingled with more argumentative elements, and that sometimes the element of bargaining is largely absent.

Bargaining power rests on the ability to make credible threats. Roughly speaking, credibility rests on the ability to harm the other party without conferring excessive harm on oneself. This is not the occasion to go more deeply into this issue.[72] Instead, I shall suggest some sources of bargaining power for the main actors that are involved: first-order actors ("the government"), second-order actors ("the institution"), and third-order actors ("the recipients").

The government has considerable leverage that it can use to impose certain allocative principles on the institution. Most obviously, it can impose or forbid the use of certain principles and use its monopoly on legitimate violence to force compliance. In Germany, the law requires all firms over a certain size to employ a certain proportion of handicapped workers. Fines are imposed on violators. In the United States, Title VII of the Civil Rights Act of 1964 prohibits discrimination against women and minorities in layoffs. Workers can seek redress, compensation, and punitive damages. In many arenas, market transactions are explicitly forbidden. In addition, the government often has control of the scarce good to be allocated or of other resources vitally needed by the institution. Private colleges in the United States often receive state or federal funding that is contingent on special admissions

---

[71] For this discussion, see my "Arguing and Bargaining."

[72] All modern thinking about credible threats starts from Schelling, *The Strategy of Conflict*. For some recent discussions see Nalebuff and Dixit, "Making Strategies Credible" and my work, *The Cement of Society*, pp. 272–287. A special consideration that applies in the present case is that the government is uniquely able to make credible threats, since the separation of powers enables it to precommit itself to apply laws even when, in a given case, it would be in its interest to make an exception. Also, the source of credibility that derives from the need to maintain one's reputation becomes especially important in this case.

programs for disadvantaged groups. To receive state subsidies, municipal nursery schools in Norway have to comply with admission priorities laid down by the government. If a transplant center violates UNOS bylaws, UNOS has the legal authority to deny Medicare reimbursement. When the United States government does business with private contractors, it can and does insist on certain racial proportions in the work force. Finally, the government can use its control over the jobs of second-order administrators as leverage in its bargaining. Suppose that the government decides that those who are active in the work force shall have priority in public hospitals; or that a municipality decides that children of municipal employees shall have priority in the nursery schools it runs. If these instructions are not fulfilled, the responsible administrators will be reprimanded and, after repeated violation, will lose their jobs.

Bargaining between the government and institutions often turns on the degree of precision and specificity in the instructions issued by the center. Institutions usually want guidelines to be vague, to leave maximal scope for local adjustments. The government wants them to be precise, to ensure that its intentions are faithfully carried out.[73] There are, however, important exceptions to both statements. Sometimes, the government prefers vague principles because of a need to accommodate conflicting political forces. Conversely, institutions may prefer very precise instructions so as to be able to blame the government for any perceived unfairness. This strategy is especially tempting if the degree of scarcity is such that any scheme for allocating it will appear as unfair. Knowledge of this problem may in turn induce a preference for vagueness among first-order actors ("I don't want to know the details").

Suppose that the center wants to impose precise principles, such as point systems, blanket exemptions, or quotas, and to have them strictly and uniformly applied. The local institution, knowing that these principles will sometimes yield absurd or unfair allocations, can then threaten to make such cases known to the

---

[73] A good example of this conflict is provided by the relations between the federal government and the local rationing boards in World War II (Maxwell and Balcom, "Gasoline Rationing in the United States, Part II," p. 581 ff.).

public or, if need be, actually make them known. By virtue of its information, the institution can play on public opinion to get its way vis-à-vis the center. The best-known form of this strategy is the crisis maximization policy of refusing to make hard choices, so as to force the center to increase the budget. But the strategy can also be used to make the center refrain from attempts to adopt a very precise and specific set of principles. Groups of recipients (or groups organized on their behalf) can also use public opinion and the media as resonance boards for their claims. A public scandal may force the institution to bend or break its rule in the particular case that is perceived to be scandalous—or to change the rules to prevent this particular kind of scandal from occurring again. If the change occurs at the expense of other groups, the next scandal may not be late in coming.

Public opinion matters because politicians want to get reelected. Because of its numerous forms of leverage, enumerated above, the government might appear to be overwhelmingly the strongest actor in this game. It is vulnerable, however, because of the need for public support. The legitimacy provided by public opinion may also be necessary for compliance, especially in wartime. Draft evaders and black marketeers will proliferate if exemptions, deferments, and rations are granted on grounds that are perceived to be inequitable.

Accretion. By now, I hope I have conveyed that allocative schemes can be incredibly complicated. The exceptions and adjustments that, over time, grow up around such schemes create a local culture of allocation that can look bizarre and baroque to the outside observer. Even without any pressure from politicians and interest groups, allocative officers constantly find themselves discovering that the total supply or demand has unexpectedly changed; that some proxies are less reliable than they thought; that claims for the scarce good are made on good grounds which they had not anticipated; and that the practical difficulties of administering the scheme are larger than expected. In the numerous cases in which all these problems arise simultaneously, stability becomes a will-o'-the-wisp. In addition, many schemes have to accommodate a large number of outside demands, pressures, and interests. Constraints related to race, gender, and, increasingly, age are omnipresent. Often, funding depends on compliance. Occasionally, the usually diffuse force of public opinion is focused and crystallized in a way that forces the institution to mend its ways.

A frequent response to these internal and external pressures is change by accretion. New categories are added to the list, without any of the old ones being dropped. Immigration law is perhaps the best example. The following is a list of excludable classes of aliens, numbered as in section 212a of the 1952 Act, with an indication of the year in which the class or its equivalent first became excludable:

1. Mentally retarded (1882)
2. Insane (1891)
3. With one or more attacks of insanity (1903)
4. With psychotic personality or a mental defect (1917)
5. Narcotic drug addicts (1952), chronic alcoholics (1917)
6. With any dangerous contagious disease (1891)
7. With physical defects, disease, or disability that may affect ability to earn a living (1907)
8. Paupers, professional beggars, or vagrants (1891)
9. Convicted of crime involving moral turpitude (1875)
10. Convicted of two or more offenses, with aggregate sentence of five years or more (1952)
11. Polygamists and related classes (1891)
12. Prostitutes and related classes (1875)
13. Coming to engage in any immoral sexual act (1952)
14. Skilled or unskilled laborers, if sufficient workers already available or if it would adversely affect wages and working conditions (1952)
15. Likely to become a public charge (1952)
16. Previously excluded and deported within one year (1917)
17. Previously deported for any of various reasons (1952)
18. Stowaways (1917)
19. Entry by means of false statements (1952)
20. Without proper documents (1924)
21. Without proper preference classification (1937)
22. Ineligible for citizenship (1924)
23. Narcotics laws violators (1952)

24. Arrival by nonsignatory line (1924)
25. Illiterates over sixteen years of age (1917)
26. Certain nonimmigrants without proper documents (1924)
27. Admission prejudicial to public interest or safety (1948)
28. Subversive classes (1903)
29. Suspected of subversive intent (1950)
30. Accompanying excluded alien (1903)
31. Aid to illegal immigration (1952)[74]

The exclusion clauses are not fully cumulative: some get dropped over time. The exclusion of Chinese was repealed in 1943. Epilepsy as a ground for exclusion was dropped in 1965. Restrictions on persons with tuberculosis have been eased over time. By and large, however, the picture is one of change by accretion.

I believe that the admission policies of private colleges often evolve in the same fashion. Here, evidence is harder to come by, as these institutions are not obligated to make their policies public. Also, there is immense variety across institutions, making it hard to generalize. But one would probably not be much wrong in saying that, in the typical elite college, traditions develop of giving preferential treatment on the following grounds:

- grades and test scores
- high school
- athletic skills
- artistic skills
- community service
- leadership abilities
- relative of alumni
- relative of staff and faculty
- age
- race/ethnicity
- socioeconomic status
- character as assessed by interviews

[74] Hutchinson, *A Legislative History of American Immigration Policy*, p. 441 ff.

Usually, these criteria will have been adopted at different times in the past, the newer being added to the old ones rather than substituting for them. Although some criteria, such as the use of ceilings on Jewish enrollment, are dropped over time, the overall picture is one of cumulativity.

Accretion of grounds for exclusion, as in immigration, might seem the more plausible mechanism, as it does not create a pressure on the total capacity of the institution. By contrast, accretion of grounds for inclusion, as in college admission, might be expected to be controversial. For each new category of preferred applicants to college, some applicants from the old categories must be evaluated more severely. Although colleges do feel this strain, it is eased by the fact that changes occur gradually.

Let me try to pull some strands together, by regrouping from another perspective the explanations offered. As I said in the first pages of this chapter, I rely heavily on intentional or motivational explanation in my accounts of the emergence of allocative principles. At a very general level, we may distinguish between three types of motives based, respectively, on the desire to promote self-interest, equity, and efficiency. In trying to identify the subjects who *have* these intentions and motives, we may distinguish between four major categories: actors at the first, second, and third orders of decision making, as well as public opinion.[75] Crossing these two classifications, we obtain twelve categories altogether. Although some are marginal, most have been repeatedly illustrated in this book.

Political first-order actors tend, on the whole, to be motivated by efficiency concerns. Being under relentless pressure from innumerable interest groups as well as administrative agencies, they will be reluctant to allocate funds for a particular scarce good unless they can be confident that the funds will be efficiently used. At the highest level, efficiency is measured against the use of the same funds in other sectors. In practice, cross-sector com-

---

[75] In the following I ignore individual first-order actors. Although they have an important place in the conceptual framework, their factual importance is not very large.

parisons are often difficult, since for operational purposes there is no common coin for health, education, and jobs. Cross-sector trade-offs are then determined by political struggles, not by comparative efficiency. Within the sector, efficiency is measured by the impact of the good on the individuals who receive it. First-order actors do not want to subsidize public housing for the most destitute if the predictable outcome is vandalism; nor do they want to channel massive funds to the education of disadvantaged groups if such efforts seem to have little impact.

At the first-order level, self-interest plays a very minor role. If politicians want to get access to a scarce good, they can do so through their connections or wealth; to get access by forcing a change in the principle of allocation would be pointlessly complicated. Equity does, however, matter, but mainly because politicians are constrained by public opinion, in which equity concerns are paramount. Politicians fear allocative scandals; and more scandals arise from the sight of seeing a good withheld from a needy or deserving person than from seeing it allocated to a person who does not use it efficiently. This difference in scandal-arousing capacity of inefficiency and inequity is probably due to the fact that costs and damages are dispersed in the former case, and concentrated in the latter.[76]

Second-order actors are motivated by equity as well as by efficiency. Their concept of efficiency tends, however, to diverge from that of first-order decision makers, being local rather than global. Thus in the allocation of medical resources, efficiency means allocation according to increment of welfare in the recipient, not according to the increment in social welfare. In the allocation of penicillin in World War II these two conceptions of efficiency and the conception of (welfare-level) equity pick out three different groups of soldiers. The local conception of efficiency tells us to give penicillin to those whose survival chances would be most increased; the global conception to the soldiers with VD who

---

[76] I am grateful to Claus Offe for this observation. He adds that the generalization is not very robust, a point also made by John Roemer (personal communication), citing Senator Proxmire's "golden fleece" awards for irrelevant science and reports of welfare recipients driving Cadillacs. I continue to believe, however, that the intensity of indignation is stronger when equity is violated.

could be made ready for combat; whereas equity (another local idea) would prefer those who are most unlikely to survive in the absence of penicillin. As for the role of self-interest, I have not come across a single case in which second-order actors have changed a principle to get the good for themselves or their friends and relatives. The self-interest of second-order actors does, however, come into play whenever the good is allocated by discretionary procedures that allow for bribes and corruption.

Third-order actors are typically moved by self-interest.[77] They lobby, bargain, or vote for principles that favor the subgroup of potential recipients to which they belong. In doing so, they may appeal to considerations of equity and efficiency, but the correspondence with their self-interest is rarely accidental. As always, there are exceptions. When women and minority groups lobby for equal access to institutions of higher education, arguments from equity provide an independent reinforcer of self-interest. Also, recall from Chapter 2 that in the survey among enlisted men used to construct the point system for demobilization in the Army, 24 percent of single men thought that preference should be given to married men with children.

Public opinion tends to be aroused by *scandals*, allocative episodes perceived as grossly unfair or wasteful. By and large, as I said, inequity has a higher scandal-arousing potential than inefficiency. Typical examples of inequity-generated scandals are those created by the Seattle God committee, draft deferment for students, and Harvard's quota for Jews. Scandals generated by revelations of waste tend to involve individuals who are exploiting the system, as in the innumerable stories of individuals on welfare who, in the absence of this safety net, could and would have had a job. Rarely if ever are scandals created by bona fide recipients who use the good less efficiently than others could have done. Nobody, for instance, was outraged when Dr. Starzl's team in

---

[77] This statement should not be taken quite literally, since potential recipients swayed *wholly* by self-interest would usually choose to be free riders. To the extent that they overcome that temptation, they are motivated by group interest rather than self-interest. Yet in this context the relevant fact is that they are concerned with increasing the share of their subgroup rather than with bringing about a more equitable or efficient allocation for the whole group of potential recipients.

Pittsburgh made a quintuple transplantation of heart, lung, liver, kidney, and pancreas to one person, in spite of the fact that these organs might have saved the lives of several other people.

One ideal type scenario, therefore, could be the following: First-order actors prefer principle P because of its global efficiency properties. Second-order actors would prefer principle Q on grounds of equity or local efficiency. Self-interest induces various third-order actors to advocate principles R, S, and T. It so happens that Q and S select pretty much the same recipients, thus allowing a coalition to form. Another coalition is formed around principles P and T, which also happen to coincide roughly in their consequences. The final selection of a principle is achieved by bargaining between these two coalitions, constrained by the fact that principle R has great appeal to public opinion. Over time, the bargaining compromise is modified or eroded by addition of ad-hoc clauses to take account of new claims or of changing circumstances. Other combinations and permutations can be envisaged, ad infinitum.

6 / Local and Global Justice

In the preceding chapters I have been concerned with the nature, causes, and consequences of local justice. In this chapter I return to an issue briefly mentioned in the Introduction, concerning the relation between patterns of local justice and philosophical theories of global, society-wide justice.

The main purpose of the chapter is to improve our understanding of the justice-related arguments of the main participants in allocative systems. Actors at all three levels of decision making, as well as the general public, often argue for allocative schemes in terms of efficiency and fairness. Even when ultimately moved by self-interest or partiality, actors are forced by the nature of public debate to argue their case in these more general terms. An illustrative example, cited in Chapter 4, is the search for impartial arguments to support use of the literacy test to exclude immigrants from Southeastern Europe. Only in bargaining behind closed doors can self-interest and bias come fully out into the open.[1] Because the normative arguments for and against allocative policies are rarely based on comprehensive theories, they often

---

[1] On this point see my "Arguing and Bargaining."

contain ambiguities and downright contradictions. Philosophical theories, which strive for clarity and consistency, can help us locate and identify problems that arise in the layman's conception of justice and, in consequence, help us understand policy patterns that might otherwise puzzle us.

For readers unacquainted with philosophical writings on justice, a caveat may be in order. After having read the following survey, they will know very little about what is at the core of these theories: chains or networks of *arguments*. They will have a rough understanding of some of the conclusions reached by those arguments. They will know some respects in which the theories differ, and others in which they are similar. They will know something about a range of difficulties—uncertainty, incentive problems, the nature of welfare, the question of determinism—that the theories have to confront. This knowledge may, as I said, prove useful for the study of local justice, but it should not be confused with an understanding of the theories themselves. A Gothic cathedral can be a wonderful work of architecture. Nobody could appreciate it, however, if he were shown only an air photograph of the edifice and some individual pieces of stone that went into it.

I have singled out three theories for separate discussion, although others will also be mentioned in various places. First, utilitarian theories of justice in various forms; second, John Rawls's theory of justice; third, Robert Nozick's libertarian theory of justice. In addition—the only claim to originality in this medley—I discuss what I believe to be the *commonsense theory of justice* among professional decision makers in Western societies. Strictly speaking, this is not a theory, but a number of widely and strongly held views about justice that may not be mutually compatible, and a fortiori need not be deducible from a single general principle. Before considering these theories, however, I shall make some classificatory and meta-ethical observations.

THE SCOPE AND DEPTH OF JUSTICE

What is the scope of theories of justice? What aspects of society are they intended to regulate? A rough first answer might be: the system of liberties and obligations and the distribution of income.

I begin with the latter. For some purposes, income is indeed the relevant *distribuendum*, or thing to be distributed. To implement a theory of justice, we need to know what taxes, transfers, and subsidies it implies; and sometimes we do not need to know much more. For other, more theoretical purposes, the focus on income can be misleading. Some theories care more about the distribution of what generates income, namely, productive resources. Others care more about what income generates, namely, goods for consumption or self-realization. Still others care more about what those goods generate, namely, subjective welfare.[2] From the point of view of local justice, this is an important point. I have defined local justice in part by the fact that it concerns *in-kind allocation*—of primary resources like education or final goods like public housing—rather than distribution of money. The concerns of those who allocate these goods may be expected to be closer to the theories that emphasize resources or goods as the distribuendum than to those which emphasize money or welfare.

In pursuing this issue, we may first note that the term "distribution" is ambiguous, in that it can denote a *process* of distributing or redistributing goods among individuals as well as a *state* which is described by specifying the quantities of goods possessed by individuals. Using "allocation" for the first sense and "distributon" for the second, we may distinguish between three kinds of goods. First, there are goods which can be allocated, like money, material goods, and services. Second, there are goods that cannot be allocated, but whose distribution can be affected by the allocation of other goods. The distribution of self-respect, welfare, knowledge, or health depends largely on the allocation of money, goods, and services. Third, there are mental and physical capacities whose distribution cannot be affected by allocation, because they are determined genetically or are subject to irreversible accidents (such as the loss of a limb).[3] Theories of justice differ in the importance they assign to these kinds of good. For utilitarianism, welfare—a good of the second type—is paramount. Rawls emphasizes income and self-respect—goods of the first and second

[2] For a full discussion see Cohen, "On the Currency of Egalitarian Justice."

[3] In practice, many goods belong simultaneously to the second and third types. Knowledge can be modified; intelligence cannot; but the capacity for problem-solving which matters in practice is a function of both.

types, respectively. (I simplify.) Amartya Sen has argued that the morally relevant goods are "basic capabilities"—goods belonging partly to the second and partly to the third type.[4]

Egalitarian conceptions of distributive justice differ in their policy implications for these three types of good.[5] For the first type, the implication is simple: the good should be allocated equally or, if indivisible, by a lottery. For the third type, the implication also seems to be clear. Since the disadvantaged cannot be helped by direct or indirect equalization of the good, they must be compensated through allocation of other goods. A difficulty arises, however, when we ask how much they should receive in compensation. The obvious answer—that they should be compensated up to the point where their welfare equals that of others—may not be available for theories that focus on capacities rather than welfare. Sen's argument for basic capabilities, for instance, takes off from what he sees as basic flaws in welfarist conceptions of the good; hence he cannot use that conception to solve problems arising within his own theory.

For goods of the second type, an egalitarian policy might be to seek an equal distribution through the appropriate allocation of other goods. As a general solution this proposal is defective. Even when allocation of one good can affect the distribution of another, there may be no allocation that will bring about an equal distribution. And even if there are such allocations, equality may be purchased at an excessively high price. To judge what is "excessive" and to propose an alternative policy, we again have to appeal to welfare. We might retain the unequal allocation of the good and instead compensate the disadvantaged by giving them more of other goods, up to the point where they are as well off as others, if that makes them at least as well off at lower costs compared to a policy of equalization. Once again, however, the problem is that welfare may not be a good currency in which to measure these losses and gains.

The preceding discussion suggests a general distinction between three strategies for equality—direct equalization, indirect equalization, and compensation. It may be instructive to see how

---

[4]Sen, *Commodities and Capabilities.*
[5]Similar distinctions could be made for non-egalitarian conceptions. The reasons that equality is privileged are discussed later.

they work out in some cases of local justice. Consider the place of blacks in higher education. A direct way of achieving equal (or more equal) representation would be to use quotas or give points for race.[6] Indirect equalization could be achieved by giving black students extra training to help them meet academic criteria of admission. Compensation would imply abandoning the goal of equal representation of blacks in university and offering them other goods instead. In this case, nobody has advocated the third strategy, but the other two are frequently used. In the labor market, the three strategies correspond to employment quotas, retraining schemes, and unemployment benefits. Because of their local bias, institutions tend to prefer the first strategy over the second and the second over the third. Dialysis and transplantation centers do not see it as an important part of their work to put obese patients on a diet so as to make them eligible for transplantation, and the idea of offering nonmedical compensation is probably never envisaged.

In some theories of justice, individual liberties and duties are subordinated to distributive issues. Utilitarianism, for instance, does not value liberties or prescribe duties over and above what is necessary to maximize total welfare. Other theories hold a noninstrumental view of liberties and duties. These values may be given priority over distributive issues. In Rawls's theory, for instance, political freedoms and freedom of religion are prior to distributive issues in the very strong sense that no trade-offs are allowed. This is related to the fact that Rawls is prescribing for societies that have reached a level of development at which rational individuals would not choose to trade off their freedom for a bit more of material wealth. In Nozick's theory, distributive issues have *no* independent weight. If liberties and duties are respected, whatever distribution emerges spontaneously will *ipso facto* be just.

[6]Some colleges assign explicit points for race. Implicit points can be reconstructed from admissions practices. At Williams College, membership in a minority group increases by 53 percent the probability of being admitted, controlling for high school rank and test scores (Klitgaard, *Choosing Elites,* p. 46). At one Midwest university, blacks are 20 percent and Hispanics 31 percent more likely to be accepted than whites, controlling for academic achievement, personality ratings, and type of high school attended (Conley, "Local Justice and the Allocation of College Admission").

Political liberties and obligations have themselves a distributive aspect. Citizenship rights, voting rights, and the duty to do military service can be allocated in various ways over the population that lives on the territory of the nation-state. These are in-kind goods and burdens that, in practice, are allocated by local justice. Global, comprehensive theories of justice are rarely concerned with these issues. An exception is Rawls's discussion of the proposal that justice might be best served by allowing some individuals to cast several votes. He ends up dismissing it—not because he thinks it intrinsically wrong, but because he does not believe this form of unequal liberty would increase the total liberty of those with the least total liberty.[7] Another exception (discussed below) is his rejection of student deferments for military service.

Related to the question of scope is the question of depth, by which I mean the level of detail at which a theory of justice can pretend to issue prescriptions. Some theories would, under perfect information, be able to prescribe everything. Theories that argue for maximal equal welfare, maximal total welfare, or maximal minimum welfare would, under ideal conditions, which include the possibility of comparing the welfare of different individuals, be able to dictate solutions to all questions, subject at most to occasional ties. Similarly, Nozick affirms (mistakenly, as I shall argue) that his theory would, if we knew everything about the past, be able to set everything right in the present. Rawls, by contrast, explicitly says that the subject matter of his theory is nothing less and nothing more than the basic structure of society. The main reason Rawls's theory is relatively coarse-grained is not that, unlike other theories, it takes proper account of the lack of information. Rather, I conjecture that the reason is that he recognizes that the empirical constraints on a theory of justice are too soft or fuzzy to allow for a high degree of precision.

THE EMPIRICAL FOUNDATIONS OF JUSTICE

What are these empirical constraints? Why should there be any constraints at all? Let us distinguish between hard and soft theories of justice. Hard theories start from first principles and then,

[7]Rawls, *A Theory of Justice*, p. 231 ff.

when applying the principles to actual cases, let the chips fall where they may. *Fiat justitia et pereat mundus*—let justice be done, even should the world perish. If the theory tells us that under some circumstances it is permitted or even required to torture infants, then so be it. Our intuitive aversion to such practices is an irrational prejudice that should not be allowed to constrain the theory. Soft theories are more reluctant to go against intuitive judgments of what would be just under particular circumstances. Having limited faith in the power of reason to legislate in the abstract, and more respect for views relating to concrete situations, they assume that such views form empirical constraints on the theory. An acceptable theory of justice must conform with our strong intuitions about what is fair and just in particular cases. Only when intuition is weak or vacillating, can the theory be allowed to arbitrate.

Some qualifications must be added, however. Proponents of hard theories are rarely willing to endorse strongly counterintuitive prescriptions. Instead, they try to show that the theory, when properly understood, does not have the alleged appalling implications. In an article on "the survival lottery," John Harris proposed a scheme that would maximize total welfare by killing some people drawn at random from the population and using their organs to save the lives of other people with organ failures.[8] Since the organs from one could save more than one, the utilitarian calculus seems to require this practice. For a soft theorist, this might look like a reductio ad absurdum of utilitarianism. Utilitarians might reply, however, by denying that this practice is required by their theory. The knowledge that they might be selected by the lottery would create so much anxiety among the citizens as to dwarf the benefits. Also, the availability of organs in case of organ failure would create a problem of moral hazard. By reducing the incentive to take proper care of one's body, the lottery would ultimately necessitate higher numbers to be selected.[9]

Conversely, proponents of soft theories do not advocate that all strong intuitions be unconditionally respected. They acknowledge that some strong intuitions might come to be modified in the

[8] Harris, "The Survival Lottery."
[9] Singer, "Utility and the Survival Lottery."

light of theoretical explorations. Theory can help us see hidden similarities and to ignore superficial ones. As a result, we may come to understand that a strongly held view was based on a misguided analogy and should be discarded. John Rawls argues that we must go back and forth between theory and intuitions, until we reach a "reflective equilibrium." The method is partly similar, he says, to that of constructing a grammar for a language.[10] Although that process is heavily constrained by the intuitions of native speakers about the acceptability of particular sentences, the constraint is not absolute. Sometimes, the linguist is forced by his deeper understanding of the language to revise some of his pre-analytical intuitions.

Now, in neither case are these revisions unique. In moving toward a reflective equilibrium we can either discard intuition A and reach theory T, or discard intuition B and reach theory S. The most reliable conclusions, in such cases, are those that are endorsed both by S and by T. (Such coincidences can then form the basis of a coalition, as explained in the previous chapter.) When S and T diverge, cases arise in which reasonable individuals may differ. This is one reason why a theory of justice is necessarily somewhat fuzzy or coarse-grained. Another reason (not mentioned by Rawls) is that intuitions themselves are blurred at the edges. Cognitive psychology shows that our intuitive responses to choices and dilemmas can vary with trivial and irrelevant changes in the problem formulation and, more importantly, that it is often impossible to correct for these biases so as to arrive at the "real" intuition.[11] For these reasons, search for precision

---

[10] It is only partly similar, because there is nothing in grammar that corresponds to the requirement that a theory of justice, in addition to conforming to the empirical intuitions, should also be independently plausible. Justice is, as it were, constrained to be plausible both from above (by embodying a set of first principles for which good arguments can be given) and from below (by conforming to intuitions about particular cases). As far as I know, linguistics is constrained only from below.

[11] See notably the seminal article by Tversky and Kahneman, "The Framing of Decisions and the Psychology of Choice." An example is provided by the fact that people are less willing to use credit cards when they have to pay a surcharge on the posted price than when cash buyers are given a discount, even though the two practices are equivalent (see Thaler, "Towards a Positive Theory of Consumer Behavior"). For similar phenomena in intu-

would, even assuming perfect information about factual matters, betray a misunderstanding of the nature of the enterprise. This is not to argue against the use of mathematics in arguing about justice, only to claim that in the appraisal and application of mathematical models judgmental elements inevitably enter.[12]

I agree that theories of justice need empirical foundations. I would like to ask, however, whether the intuitions of the philosopher provide the most sturdy basis. Perhaps one could improve on introspection by harnessing the techniques of the social sciences to this task? I believe there are two main ways one could go. On the one hand, one could take the path of experimental studies of perceived justice. I believe it is fair to say that until recently, the large experimental literature on beliefs about justice and equity was somewhat unsatisfactory—long on techniques, short on ideas. To be sure, there were exceptions, but as a generalization I believe the statement is reasonably accurate. On this background, the recent work done jointly by economists and psychologists[13] came as a liberation. While using only rudimentary techniques, these articles are bursting with ideas. Their approach could be taken further. Instead of choosing subjects in a population of students or recruits, one might want to tap the intuitions of justice among people who are in the business of making allocative decisions. I return to this idea below.

On the other hand, one could take the path of local justice. The study of how institutions allocate scarce resources at their disposal might, in addition to being of interest in its own right, pro-

---

itions about justice, see Kahneman, Knetsch, and Thaler, "Fairness as a Constraint on Profit-seeking."

[12] A partly similar problem arises in the attempt to construct a theory of rational choice. In his foreword to Harsanyi and Selten, *A General Theory of Equilibrium Selection*, Robert Aumann writes that "The authors will probably be the first to acknowledge that their selection theory is not the only possible or reasonable one. Although the theory selects a unique equilibrium, as a theory it need not be unique. Every facet of the theory was carefully thought out; but, as in any complex construction project, many decisions were made which, though far from arbitrary, could well have been made in some other way."

[13] See notably Yaari and Bar-Hillel, "On Dividing Justly"; Bar-Hillel and Yaari, "Judgments of Justice"; Kahneman, Knetsch, and Thaler, "Fairness as a Constraint on Profit-seeking."

vide empirical foundations for theoretical conceptions of justice. Clearly, the findings would have to be laundered before one could use them as inputs in a normative theory. As we saw in Chapter 5, allocative principles often reflect the perceptions of justice held by the potential recipients. These views, in turn, often have a clear self-serving bias. Against this drawback we must weigh the fact that principles used in practice are in an obvious sense more robust than intuitions and introspections about hypothetical cases.

It may not be clear, though, why such empirical findings would constrain the construction of a philosophical theory of justice. Rawls says that "for the purposes of this book, the views of the reader and the author are the only ones that count. The opinions of others are used only to clear our own heads."[14] I would argue, however, that knowing what others think (and what institutions do) can help the moral philosopher in what may be a somewhat stronger sense.[15] At the very least, the knowledge that others hold or practice very different conceptions should make him scrutinize his own opinions with extra care. In these matters, more than in most others, intellectual humility is required. Secondly, and perhaps more controversially, he should not use his own views as inputs to theory construction unless he can *understand* why others think differently. When reasonable men hold views that differ from his own, he need not embrace their opinions, but nor should he ignore them unless he can reconstruct the causal or intellectual processes that have led them to these views. In the process of trying to do so, his own opinions might well come to change. I am not, therefore, arguing that other people's intuitions

---

[14] *A Theory of Justice*, p. 50. A similar point is made forcefully by G. A. Cohen in a comment on an earlier draft of this paper: "It's not right, in my view, to counterpose the intuitions of philosophers (and their readers) to other supposed sources of raw material for theory construction where theory of justice is what's involved. For the theorist is proposing his theory as *normatively* true, and that means that it *must* accord with his (equilibrated) intuitions. Of course, he can allow his intuitions, and he should, to be tutored and jogged by those of others both as uttered to investigators and as implicit in practices. But those data have to go through his intuitive set to affect his theory. He can't circumvent his own intuitions in favour of those data without ceasing to be a moral philosopher and becoming a sociologist."

[15] See also Gibbard, *Wise Choices, Apt Feelings*, p. 174 ff.

or institutional practices should enter directly as constraints on a theory of justice. I do claim, though, that empirical facts of this kind have a major role to play in the elaboration and refinement of the philosopher's own moral intuitions.

One additional problem is too important not to be mentioned. When canvassing intuitions or practices, should we limit ourselves to Occidental societies?[16] When Rawls says that he views the construction of reflective equilibrium as a process involving only him and his reader, he is implicitly restricting himself to modern, Western, democratic societies.[17] This procedure points in the direction of relativism, suggesting that for each cultural group there is some theory of justice that captures its ethical intuitions and, moreover, that this is all there is to such theories. Even philosophical theories of justice might be constrained to be "local." This is not a proposal that holds out much hope for peace among nations or for international cooperation on environmental issues. The alternative—to base the theory on "moral universals," intuitions, or practices found in all human societies—is not necessarily more attractive. There might be no such universals; and if there are, they might simply be inborn tendencies produced by evolution rather than the outcome of human reasoning powers. I am not denying that these powers are produced by evolution. But there is a difference between saying that moral behavior is the direct outcome of evolution and saying that it it is an indirect outcome, mediated by reason.[18] It is hard to see why we should respect intuitions about particular cases if they are largely the knee-jerk residue of responses to situations with which the early hominids were often confronted. I leave the question here, being both in deeper waters and on thinner ice than I am equipped to deal with.[19]

[16] For a rare attempt to relate non-Western values to allocative issues, see Kilner, *Who Lives? Who Dies?* pp. 20 ff., 88–89, 263–264. See also Kuran, "Behavioral Norms in the Islamic Doctrine of Economics" and "On the Notion of Economic Justice in Contemporary Islamic Thought."

[17] This restriction is made explicit in his recent article, "Justice as Fairness: Political not Metaphysical."

[18] For this distinction between one-step and two-step evolutionary explanations, see also my *Ulysses and the Sirens*, pp. 15–17.

[19] Gibbard, *Wise Choices, Apt Feelings* has an extensive discussion of these issues.

ETHICAL INDIVIDUALISM AND PRESENTISM

In this subsection I shall discuss the views that for purposes of distributive justice, *groups don't matter* and *the past doesn't matter*. Justice is concerned with living individuals. The view that groups don't matter I shall call ethical individualism (EI); the view that the past doesn't matter I call ethical presentism (EP). As stated, the doctrines are hopelessly vague. I shall not here try to state them more precisely, but instead try to convey their content by means of some examples.[20] I believe that the doctrines are valid constraints on any substantive ethical theory, and that, with some exceptions, most prominent substantive views do in fact respect them. On the other hand, there are allocative practices or (especially) proposals that violate the one or the other doctrine.

Assume that there are two groups, of equal size, each of which is made up of two subgroups of equal size. The groups could be men and women; rich and poor nations; present and future generations; or anything else you like. Using the example of men and women, I shall discuss the idea that the primary goal of social policy should be to equalize the average utility across groups. Consider then the following distributions:

TABLE 6.1 /

	Men		Women	
	I	II	I	II
(A)	10	8	6	4
(B)	9	5	10	4
(C)	8	6	8	6

Assume that the initial state is (A) and that after transfers state (B) is achieved. Men and women now have the same average utility, but this equality has been achieved at the expense of greater inequality among individuals, both overall and within

---

[20] As comments by G. A. Cohen and Cass Sunstein have made me realize, my earlier attempts to state and justify EI and EP in a clear and explicit fashion were vulnerable to compelling counterexamples. In the present exposition, therefore, I have retreated into impregnable vagueness. I continue to believe firmly in the basic intuitions, however. On some later occasion I hope to be able to state them more precisely and persuasively.

each of the two groups. This amounts to a prima facie violation of EI. By contrast, the move from (A) to (C), which also equalizes average utility of men and women, could be justified on the grounds that it reduces inequality across all *individuals.*

For practical purposes we may sometimes have to act in ways that appear to violate EI. To move toward equality of the average incomes of two groups is a feasible, clearly understood goal. To increase equality across individuals in both groups is a much more elusive target.[21] Sometimes, we can say unambiguously that one distribution is more equal than another. In other contexts, it is more difficult to tell, since there are many different ways of measuring the equality of distributions.[22] In some cases, like the numerical illustration used above, they all induce the same ranking of distributions. In other cases, they diverge, for instance because some measures take more account of extreme outliers than others. We usually know what equality means, but the relation "more equal than" cannot be unambiguously and uncontroversially defined.[23]

Insurance systems might seem to violate EI. Thus when young male drivers pay higher rates than drivers in other categories, the majority of young men are made financially responsible for the behavior of a small number in this group. But if no discrimination at all was made among drivers, EI would still be violated. It would still be the case that the careful drivers would be held financially responsible for the behavior of the reckless ones. In a system of no discrimination, the maximal difference between actual risk and imputed risk would probably be smaller, but the sum total of all such differences would surely be larger. In any case, this is a problem that arises because of the costs of gathering information. Under ideal conditions (which is the case that concerns me here), each individual would be rated according to his individual risk.

EI does not exclude theories that affirm that women should be privileged, since being a woman is an individual-level property.

---

[21] Hence, the goal of moving toward equality of average incomes of *many* groups is equally elusive.

[22] See, for instance, Sen, *On Economic Inequality.*

[23] This problem arises in two cases. One, discussed here, is when a homogeneous good is to be distributed over more than two individuals. The other, discussed later, is when bundles of goods are to be distributed over two or more individuals.

We shall see later that EP excludes certain arguments for preferring women (or blacks or citizens of poor countries), but EI is not in itself inconsistent with such views. But it is hard to see what arguments could be made for giving preferential treatment to all women and only to women. The argument that women ought to be compensated for childbearing does not apply to childless women. The argument that women ought to receive support to overcome the negative effects of early socialization does not apply only to women.

Violations of EI regularly arise in debates over race and transplantation. As explained in Chapter 4, blacks are highly overrepresented in the population of patients with end-stage renal disease. They are also heavily underrepresented among organ donors, largely because of reluctance of relatives to give their permission to recover an organ that could be used for transplantation. The reluctance has several causes, one of them being the fact that the organs mainly go to white patients. This argument, however, violates EI. The idea that a white recipient does not deserve a kidney because of the harm that whites inflict on blacks is flawed because it makes each white person responsible for the behavior of the whole group to which he belongs. The converse fallacy is sometimes encountered in discussions of changes in the point system made for the purpose of increasing the prospects of black patients. Since blacks are not willing to donate kidneys, they cannot expect special treatment as recipients. This argument, too, unfairly treats each black patient as if he or she were responsible for the behavior of the whole group. In other words, the fallacy takes the form of making each black person responsible for the fact that some members of the black community commit the same fallacy.

Although one should not make the allocation of organs to members of a group conditional on the average willingness of that group to donate organs, there is no similar objection to a link of this kind at the level of the individual. In Singapore's system for organ allocation, consent is presumed unless the potential donor has explicitly objected to use of the organs. Those who have gone on record as objectors are subsequently given low priority to transplantation in the event that they might need one. Because this rule makes the allocation to an individual contingent on the behavior of that same individual, it does not violate EI.

There might be other reasons why relatives of donors or the donors themselves could give preference to recipients of a particular race, which might or might not be their own. First, a member of group A might give preferential treatment to members of group B, on the grounds that they are more disadvantaged. This form of affirmative action is perfectly compatible with EI, as race, like gender, is an individual-level property. However, there might be equally disadvantaged members of group A, and fairness would dictate that in the long run they, too, should get some organs. Also, some members of B might not be disadvantaged at all, and for that reason have no claim to special treatment. Thus it would be hard to argue for the view that organs should go only to members of group B, and that any member of group B should have the same chance of getting one. Second, members of group B might preferentially donate to members of their own group, on grounds of community and shared fate.[24] This practice already exists with living donors, who are allowed to restrict their donations to relatives. The idea that one's family members and friends stand in a special relationship to oneself that justifies special sacrifices does not violate EI; in fact, the idea is inherently plausible. Nor is EI violated by the idea that any member of one's own race, be it a total stranger, deserves special treatment. The latter idea does not seem very plausible, though. In particular, I do not think the concept of community offers much of a justification.

Consider now EP, and assume the following distributions of income between whites and blacks (assumed to be equally numerous):

TABLE 6.2 /

	Whites	Blacks
Actual Distribution	10	8
Past Distribution	9	4
Counterfactual Past Distribution	7	7
Counterfactual Present Distribution	10	10
Proposal A	9	9
Proposal B	8	10
Proposal C	5	13
Proposal D	6	12

[24] In this case, too, disadvantage might be a consideration.

I make the following assumptions. (1) No currently living whites are discriminating against blacks or otherwise treating them unfairly. (2) All whites in the past engaged in discrimination, exploitation, oppression, or unfair treatment of blacks; and all blacks were subject to such practices. (3) Those unfair practices made the economy less productive than it would otherwise have been, by preventing full utilization of the skills and talents of blacks. (4) They also affected the earning capacity of blacks in the present, by reducing their monetary and cultural endowments below what they would otherwise have been. (5) Redistribution from whites to blacks in the present is costless (the transfer bucket does not leak).

There are two issues to be discussed. Should blacks get more because their ancestors were the subject of discrimination in the past? Should whites get less because their ancestors practiced discrimination in the past? Because of assumption (2), the questions can be treated in a way that is consistent with EI. Each individual white person has come into the world with unjustly earned endowments; and each individual black has been deprived of endowments that he or she would otherwise have had. Hence the question of unfairly taxing a white person whose ancestors did nothing wrong does not arise.

Egalitarianism—an end-state theory of justice—would endorse proposal A. Historical principles might endorse proposals B or C, to compensate for past injustices. A theory like Nozick's, for instance, would endorse B, to ensure that blacks get in the present what they would have had in the present had they not been exploited in the past. This proposal is consistent with EP as I understand it. Proposals C and D, however, are not consistent with that doctrine. They argue that blacks in the present should be compensated for harm done to their ancestors in the past; and that currently living whites should be punished for the harm done by their ancestors. If Proposal C is implemented, not only do the currently living blacks get what they would have had in the absence of discrimination in the past, they also appropriate the surplus exploited from their ancestors. If Proposal D is implemented, not only do currently living whites lose the gains caused by the discriminating practices of their ancestors, but they also lose an amount equal to the exploitative gains of their ancestors. The sins of the fathers are returned on the sons.

EP says, in other words, that past practices are irrelevant to distribution in the present, except to the extent that they have left morally relevant and causally efficacious traces in the present. Lower present endowment as a result of past exploitation is one such trace. To compensate for past injustice that has not left such traces is to treat successive generations as if they were part of a single life. If I am sent to jail for a crime of which I am later proved innocent, the harm can be offset, at least partially, by an indemnity. But if I am proved innocent posthumously, my children cannot claim a compensation, unless they can prove that the stigma of my guilt has affected their earning capacities or other things that they value.

EP is violated in a vulgar feminist argument for giving women priority for jobs over more qualified male applicants: "In the past, men were given priority over more qualified female applicants; now it is our turn." A violation with massive practical implications occurred in the discrimination against children of bourgeois parents that has been widely practiced in China since 1949, denying them access to higher education and other scarce goods. To be sure, bourgeois descent was probably to some extent used as a proxy for current features of these children, but I imagine that some murky ideas of intergenerational justice were at work as well. A more curious example is the Chinese practice of allowing two only children to have two children if they marry. If applied to couples whose parents are all dead, the practice amounts to a posthumous reward for good behavior.

Many claims that violate EP also violate EI. The vulgar feminist argument just referred to is an example. Some claims based on compensation for past injustice violate EI rather than EP. To finance transfers to blacks by taxing whites whose ancestors neither practiced discrimination nor benefited from it is to treat those ancestors as responsible for the behavior of the whole generation to which they belonged, in violation of EI.

EQUALITY AS THE BASELINE FOR JUSTICE

With the exception of rights-based theories like Nozick's, the task of the major theories of justice can be stated as *justifying deviations from equality*. The proposal to distribute liberties, duties, and goods equally seems to need no justification; the burden of proof is on the advocate of an unequal distribution.[25] I shall discuss seven reasons for deviating from the equal distribution.

(1) If the good in question is both scarce and indivisible, equal distribution in the literal sense would mean that nobody got it, as in Solomon's (first) judgment and various other examples mentioned in Chapter 3. Usually, the all-or-none principle for allocating scarce goods is seen as morally unacceptable. The combination of scarcity and indivisibility provides a sufficient justification for deviating from equality taken in the literal sense. If the scarce, indivisible good is allocated by an equal-chance lottery, however, one might argue that equality is respected.

(2) Indivisibility is not the only reason why equality may be an inefficient way of allocating a given amount of a scarce good or a necessary burden. When the good to be divided is a multidimensional bundle, equal division along each dimension can make everybody worse off than they would have been under some other division. Thus in the allocation of household tasks, equal division of each task is inefficient because it does not allow one to take account of the fact that some members of the family are better than others at some task or less averse to doing it. In theory, efficiency could be achieved by first dividing equally and then allowing family members to trade to equilibrium.

(3) Sometimes, inequality of X is accepted because what one really cares about is equality of Y, to which X is a means whose efficacy varies across people. Suppose that what we care about is equality of welfare, and that some people are inherently less efficient in converting money (i.e., the goods money can buy) into welfare than are others. The handicapped fit this description, as do other individuals for more idiosyncratic reasons.[26] There is

---

[25]See, however, the powerful argument in Kolm, *The General Theory of Justice*, to the effect that the principle of insufficient reason can justify inequality as well as equality. See also Westen, *Speaking of Equality*, Chapter 10.

[26]In a comment on an earlier draft of this chapter, Cass Sunstein pointed out that the handicaps of the handicapped depend heavily on man-made features of the physical environment. "We tend to think of the handicapped as facing lots of inherent obstacles, or obstacles resulting from their handicaps, when in fact the obstacles are produced by human decisions." In addition, the obstacles facing the handicapped depend on their own decisions as to what careers to pursue.

then a prima facie case for giving more money to the inefficient converters. Here, a natural inequality is offset by an artificial one, so as to yield equal outcomes. In other cases, the original inequality is socially caused, as when children from an impoverished background start out with poorer qualifications when applying to college or for jobs. Again, equality of outcome may require preferential—that is, unequal—treatment of these individuals, so as to offset the original inequality.

(4) In all such cases, however, it is an open, empirical question whether *any* amount of compensation can achieve equality of outcomes. It is likely—although nobody can really know—that severely retarded individuals can *never* attain what we think of as a normal level of welfare, however many resources we put at their disposal. This provides a further reason for deviating from equality that can be summarized in the philosopher's slogan, "Ought implies can." There can be no duty to do the impossible. It is nonsense to demand equality of mental and physical skills, because this goal cannot be attained, except by the extreme measure of deskilling the skilled. Similarly, it may be nonsense to demand *full* compensation for unequal skills.

(5) A further general argument for inequality relies on the link between production and distribution. Some allocative situations are zero-sum, at least in the short run; there is a given quantity of the scarce good which is available for distribution. In other cases (and in the long run almost always), the way the good is allocated has an impact on how much of it there will be to allocate.[27] Widely used metaphors for this fact are "the problem of the shrinking pie"[28] and "the problem of the leaky bucket."[29] In principle, it might be possible to transfer income from some individuals to others without affecting the earning incentives of the former. If they are taxed a lump sum according to their earning capacity, rather than some percentage of their actual earnings,

[27] This can happen in two different ways: either because the allocative process itself uses up some of the (given) resources, with less being available for distribution; or because the incentive effects of the allocation scheme imply that fewer resources will be produced.
[28] Bargaining, for instance, "has an inherent tendency to eliminate the potential gain which is the object of the bargaining" (Johansen, "The Bargaining Society and the Inefficiency of Bargaining," p. 520).
[29] See, for instance, Okun, *Equality and Efficiency: The Big Trade-Off.*

they can keep for themselves 100 cents in the dollar of what they earn beyond that sum. The scheme is flawed, however, by its tendency to induce misrepresentation of skills and by its violation of the principle of self-ownership (see below). Instead, one must adopt a percentage scheme. Beyond a certain level of taxation, such schemes reduce the incentive to work and hence the total that is to be redistributed. When incomes are equalized, total savings also go down, because the wealthy usually save a higher percentage of their income than do the less well off. Lower savings in turn cause lower investment, lower rates of economic growth, and smaller totals to be redistributed in the future.

Let me briefly recapitulate some links between production and distribution in local justice contexts. The supply of scarce goods through voluntary donations can depend on how they are to be distributed. If young men are exempted from military service on grounds of social standing rather than on physical fitness, the war may go on for longer and more people may need to be called up. If workers are laid off by inverse seniority rather than by productivity, the earnings of the firm may fall and more workers might have to be laid off. If hospitals give priority to those who are active in the work force and nursery schools to children of nursery school teachers, more places can be made available to other applicants. If willingness to donate organs is used as a criterion for organ allocation, more organs may be donated.

(6) Another argument for inequality is that unequal outcomes must be accepted when caused by factors fully within the control of the individual. Some people prefer leisure over income; others prefer enjoyment in the present over enjoyment in the distant future; still others are unwilling to take risks; and some just don't like to work hard. As a result of these dispositions, such persons may end up earning less than those with different propensities. It is a central part of Ronald Dworkin's version of egalitarianism that when inequality of income is caused by such factors, there are no grounds for redistribution.[30] Even labor exchanges that technically qualify as exploitation in the Marxist sense may be perfectly acceptable if they have this pedigree.[31] To those who

[30] Dworkin, "What Is Equality? Part 2: Equality of Resources."
[31] See Roemer, "Should Marxists Be Interested in Exploitation?"

complain about the outcome, one can say, 'You have made your bed, so you can lie in it." In earlier chapters this issue has mainly been discussed in the context of incentive schemes. By telling individuals ahead of time that they will be denied a scarce good if their need for it is the predictable outcome of their own behavior, one might reduce the total demand for the good and hence the total amount of suffering among nonrecipients.

(7) A final, and very different, argument for accepting inequality is that any attempt to eliminate it is likely to create new forms of inequality. Opponents of communist or radically egalitarian regimes often claim that the attempt to create social and economic equality necessarily gives rise to political hierarchy and inequality.[32] It is not possible to create economic equality once and for all, and then expect it to maintain itself without further interventions. Inequalities of skill or of willingness to take risks and work hard always tend to re-create income inequalities. To nip them in the bud, permanent supervision and control are necessary. Such control in itself constitutes an objectionable form of inequality. Human nature being what it is, or so the argument goes, the supervisors and controllers will not only enjoy special power but also soon use that power to get economic privileges as well.

VEILS OF IGNORANCE

When implementing a theory of justice, we want as much information as possible. But when choosing a theory of justice, we may decide to ignore some of the information we have about the individuals to be regulated by the theory. This methodological device of assuming a veil of ignorance is best known from Rawls's *A Theory of Justice*, but was used several years earlier to justify utilitarianism. As we shall see, the device can be used to justify quite different theories, depending on the properties that we decide to neglect. We may distinguish between veils of different thickness or number of layers, and observe the effect on the outcome as we successively shroud more and more aspects of individuals in ignorance.

One purpose of the device is to show how to obtain consensus

[32] See, for instance, Walzer, *Spheres of Justice*, pp. 15, 160.

for a theory of justice among rational individuals not motivated by anything beyond self-interest. Now, actual individuals may be assumed to know everything about themselves. Let us also entertain the thought experiment that they know everything that will happen to them in the future. Under these assumptions, no consensus on justice or redistributive schemes could ever emerge, since those who are and expect to remain well off would simply use their veto. Let us now forget about the thought experiment, and allow for the very real veil of ignorance that derives from uncertainty about the future. Prudent individuals will then engage in risk-pooling, and set up insurance schemes to secure themselves against illness, unemployment, fires, and the like. Because of information and incentive problems,[33] the scheme will be less than perfect, but much better than having no scheme at all. They might also be able to agree on political schemes that, in the long run, will benefit everybody. Even those who are currently in the minority may agree to a scheme of majority voting, knowing or hoping that their turn will come later.[34] This is the thinnest of the four veils of ignorance we shall be considering. It is also very different from the others, in that here the ignorance is a real feature of the choice situation rather than, as in the others, a methodological fiction.

The reasoning behind the other veils of ignorance may be expressed by an analogy. Suppose Peter and Paul are playing tennis

---

[33] It may be difficult to get individuals to reveal the information about themselves that would allow the insurers to place them in different risk categories and to adjust premiums accordingly. As a result, low-risk individuals end up subsidizing high-risk ones. Also, the knowledge that one has insurance lessens the incentive to take care of oneself and one's property. As a result, more accidents happen than would otherwise have occurred.

[34] Reasoning of this kind was deployed in the debates of the Federal Convention in Philadelphia in 1787. According to Madison's notes, George Mason made the following argument: "We ought to attend to the rights of every class of people. He had often wondered at the indifference of the superior classes of society to this dictate of humanity & policy, considering that however affluent their circumstances, or elevated their situations, might be, the course of a few years, not only might but certainly would distribute their posteriority through the lowest classes of Society. Every selfish motive therefore, every family attachment, ought to recommend such a system of policy as would provide no less carefully for the rights and happiness of the lowest than of the highest orders of Citizens" (Farrand [ed.], *The Records of the Federal Convention,* vol. I, p. 49).

in five sets for a prize, and that rain interrupts the game at the beginning of the fourth set, when Paul has a lead of two sets to one. For some reason, it is not possible to continue the game on a later occasion. How should the prize be divided? Paul might say that he should get it, since he is ahead. Others may propose to give two thirds of the prize to Paul and one third to Peter. As for Peter, he might argue for equal division, backing his claim by asserting that he had been deliberately saving his forces for the last two sets. Clearly, the matter ought to have been settled beforehand, when nobody could know the exact circumstances under which the match would be interrupted. Since it was not settled beforehand, the players have to try to forget what they know about the game, and think about the matter under a self-imposed veil of ignorance. To reach agreement they will have to abstract from their individual features. If Paul is the better player, or if he tends to play badly in the endgame, or if he just likes the thrill of risk-taking, he will insist on the whole prize going to the player who is ahead when the game is interrupted. If Peter differs, he might insist differently. Also, if he is very poor he might insist on dividing the prize equally rather than giving the whole prize to whoever is ahead. To reach an agreement, they will have to put themselves in the place of players who ignored their own wealth, capacities, and preferences. This corresponds to the thickest veil of ignorance, that of Rawls.

Let me begin, however, with the thinnest of three fictional veils, the meritocratic conception of justice. Although this view is probably widely held in the population at large, it has not been much defended by philosophers. On this view, family background and wealth ought not be relevant for justice. To ensure equality of opportunity and allow the best to rise to the top, one should compensate for economic and social handicaps that are external to the individual. On this meritocratic conception of justice we assume that behind the veil of ignorance people know their skills and preferences, but not their social background. In this hypothetical choice situation they would agree on the need for some insurance against bad social luck. This agreement, in turn, justifies transfers from the rich to the poor in the actual choice situation.

The next step is to pull down another veil, so as to ignore

inborn skills and capacities. In Dworkin's phrase, outcomes should be "ambition-sensitive" but not "endowment-sensitive," whether the endowments be social or genetic.[35] Unequal endowments are grounds not for equalization—this would be impossible—but for compensation. Dworkin phrases his arguments in terms of the insurance scheme for handicaps that would be chosen behind the veil of ignorance. His view corresponds to the argument for inequality made earlier, that unequal outcomes must be accepted if caused by factors within the control of the individual. It is also a prominent component in what I describe below as the commonsense theory of justice. To justify the line drawn between these two features of individuals, skills and preferences, we may note that the latter cannot coherently be used in the first person singular to excuse bad performance and to ground claims for compensation. I return to this idea.

Finally, we may follow Rawls and abstract from preferences and ambitions no less than from wealth and skills. On a determinist view of the world, this would seem to be an inescapable conclusion. Preferences are no more uncaused than skills. Even though their proximate cause may be a decision to cultivate certain desires, their ultimate causes are to be found in factors outside the control of the individual. Hence one cannot hold individuals responsible for being lazy, unable to defer gratification, extremely risk-averse, extremely risk-loving, or for having whatever other character traits that keep them at low levels of welfare. At the very least, they have what one might call a third-person claim to compensation. Other people, understanding that these individuals are not to blame for their misfortune, might well want to subsidize them, assuming that one can distinguish genuine cases of need from those who just fake the relevant character traits. I have already hinted, however, that third-person arguments may not be good enough.

Utilitarians, too, argue that distributions ought to be chosen behind this thick veil. They differ from Rawls in their conception of what rational individuals would prefer if they knew nothing

---

[35] As shown by Cohen, "On the Currency of Egalitarian Justice," Dworkin tends to confuse the distinction between ambitions and endowments with the morally more relevant distinction between what is and what is not within people's control.

about their wealth, skills, and preferences. Rawls argues, as we shall see, that they would opt for the distribution that would make them as well off as possible if, when the veil is lifted, they find themselves in the position of the worst-off. Utilitarians argue that they would believe themselves equally likely to occupy each position, and hence would choose the distribution with the highest average level of welfare.[36]

We have seen that in local justice contexts, wealth, abilities, and preferences are often disallowed as grounds for allocation. To promote equality of opportunity, special programs are offered to students from disadvantaged backgrounds. Often, the most productive workers are laid off before workers with higher seniority.[37] The fact that some people choose to drive without safety belts does not exclude them for medical treatment. Although these policies are rarely if ever justified by explicit veils-of-ignorance arguments, they share with such arguments the premise that properties that are arbitrary from the moral point of view are not allowed to count for distributive purposes. A more direct application of veil-of-ignorance reasoning can be made to the question of whether to prefer the old or the young in the allocation of scarce lifesaving medical resources. For illnesses whose onset is equally likely at any age, the choice behind the veil is clearly to have treatment reserved for the young. For illnesses that disproportionately affect the elderly, the opposite priority might seem rational—until we remember that under this policy the competition for the scarce good would also be much greater.

CONSEQUENTIALISM AND WELFARISM

Suppose that we are to assess the justice of some proposed action, like a new tax scheme or a law against defaming the flag. Often, we ask, what are the consequences? Assuming ethical individualism, this means the consequences for individual human be-

---

[36] A compelling criticism of this argument for utilitarianism is made in Weymark, "A Reconsideration of the Harsanyi-Sen Debate on Utilitarianism."

[37] Following Cohen's argument (see note 35, above), this example would not illustrate the point made here if the skills of the more productive workers are acquired rather than inborn.

ings. To assess the consequences for individuals, we often ask, how do they affect their welfare? And we might endorse the proposal if it has better welfare consequences than any other we can think of, including the status quo. It is important to see that this answer need not be a utilitarian one. A theory is welfarist[38] if it asserts that the only consideration that is relevant for the allocation of goods to individuals is the way they affect the welfare or utility—these terms being here used synonymously—of individuals. Utilitarianism is welfarist, but so are theories which assert that goods ought to be allocated so as to achieve the highest level of equal welfare for all, or to maximize the welfare of those at the lowest level of welfare.

In Chapter 3 we came across another type of nonutilitarian welfarist principles, those, namely, that only consider the welfare of a subset of the population. According to present law, litigation over child custody is to be guided by the consequences for the child; the welfare of the parents (and society in general) is not allowed to count. People have been exempt from military service or received scarce medical goods because of the benefits to their dependents, whereas benefits accruing to society at large are disregarded. An unskilled worker who is married and has five children might take preference over a brilliant but childless painter. In local justice contexts this *agent-restricted utilitarianism*[39] is quite important. The reasons for restricting the consequences differ. In child custody cases, the child's innocence and vulnerability make the salient difference. In other cases, I conjecture that many believe that severe welfare losses for a few people count for more than small losses for many, even assuming that the sum of the latter exceeds the sum of the former.[40]

If utilitarianism is a species of welfarism, so is the latter a species of consequentialism. Decisions can have an impact on morally

[38] Sen, "Utilitarianism and Welfarism."

[39] The phrase is not entirely felicitous. In the literature (see, for instance, Scheffler, *The Rejection of Consequentialism*), "agent-restricted ethical theories" are theories that assign special importance to individuals who stand in some privileged relation to the moral agent. They would not, for instance, single out children in general as contrasted with adults, but the agent's children as contrasted with other children (and adults).

[40] For an argument to this effect, see Thompson, *The Realm of Rights*, pp. 166–167.

relevant aspects of people other than their welfare. People's *autonomy* would be negatively affected if we do things to them without their consent, whether or not they also suffer a welfare loss. Given the choice between two evils, one might choose the action that involves the smallest amount of violation of individual *rights*.[41] This would involve treating rights-violation as a consequence to be minimized by action. As mentioned earlier, we might also assess actions by their consequences for the distribution of *material goods and resources*, quite independently of the impact of the latter on welfare. All these would be consequentialist, non-welfarist arguments.

Some conceptions of justice are squarely non-consequentialist. The notion of *fairness* (see comments below on the commonsense theory of justice) does not appeal to consequences, but rather to some idea of equal treatment. Most rights-based theories do not see rights-fulfillment as a consequence to be maximized by action, but as an absolute constraint on action.[42] Some of these theories might be called *antecedentialist*, in that they emphasize how the justice of present distributions is shaped by past actions.[43] Robert Nozick's theory falls into this category, as we shall see. Other rights-based theories justify their claims by different arguments. Some claim respect for natural rights, others for rights that have been established by an unfettered and unbiased democratic process (see comments on John Hart Ely below).

As we have seen over and over again, local justice is very much alive to this distinction between forward-looking and backward-looking arguments. If veterans are given priority in college admission, it is because of their service in the past, not because of their expected educational achievements in the future. They *deserve* it, we often say, quite independently of the future effects on themselves and others.[44] Similarly, workers often understand the seniority system in terms of merit or desert, although management may welcome it on forward-looking grounds. In the allocation of lifesaving medical resources, some argue that the elderly

---

[41] Sen, ''Rights and Agency.''
[42] Nozick, *Anarchy, State and Utopia*, pp. 28–29.
[43] Sher, ''Antecedentialism.''
[44] Sher, *Desert*.

should take priority because of their past contributions to society, whereas outcome-oriented considerations suggest that priority be given to the young. When child custody is allocated on the basis of past contributions to childcare, this criterion is seen both as the best proxy for future fitness and as reflecting merit and desert. The French practice of selecting patients for transplantation on the basis of time of entry on dialysis (rather than as in the United States on the basis of time of entry on the waiting list) can be interpreted on antecedentialist lines: since these patients have already suffered a great deal, their claim to a better quality of life is stronger. As several of these examples show, a principle can have the simultaneous support of antecedentialist and consequentialist arguments. The importance of such multiple backing was noted in Chapter 5.

I now proceed to survey three theories of justice. I devote most space to utilitarianism, because problems of local justice resonate especially well with utilitarian thinking. For decision makers with scarce resources at their disposal, the notion of using them to produce the largest total good comes naturally. Substituting profits for utility, managers would like to run their firms in the way a utilitarian planner would run a society. Doctors and hospital administrators are often concerned with saving as many lives as possible. Admissions officers do not want to waste college places on applicants who lack the qualifications to benefit from them. Draft boards induct some and exempt others on the basis of where they will do the most good for the war effort. There are exceptions to these rough generalizations. The importance of *need* and *desert,* in particular, has been a constant theme in this book. Yet even these criteria gain a great deal in power when efficiency considerations point in the same direction. (Recall the discussion in Chapter 5 of need-efficiency coalitions and desert-efficiency coalitions.)

UTILITARIANISM

There are many doctrines that have been referred to as utilitarian, often with some prefix such as "X-utilitarianism." Common to them all is the view that the sole ground for allocation of goods—in the widest possible sense, which also includes political liberties and exemptions from obligations—is the maximal promotion of the utility of the members of society, so that "each is to count for one and no one for more than one." This formulation is somewhat vague, as it had to cover the several varieties of utilitarianism. More precision will be provided as we go along.

I shall define five different conceptions of utility, all but one of which have an important role to play in some welfarist theory. All but one of the four also have an important role to play in some variety of utilitarianism. The fifth is included because it can impinge on distributive issues.

First, there is *classical utility*, which is the conception invoked in *classical utilitarianism*. On this conception, utility is a property that attaches to experiences. If positive, we call it pleasure; if negative, pain. Between pain and pleasure there is the zero point of neutrality or indifference. Utility can be represented, therefore, by positive and negative real numbers, with the usual properties of such numbers. We can add them to each other and subtract them from each other, not only within each person, but across people. On this view, utility is a kind of "psychic stuff" that, although not transferable across people, is fully comparable across them. We cannot take two "utiles" from A and give them to B, thereby increasing B's level from, say, 5 to 7. We can, however, assert that in a situation in which A has 6 utiles and B has 5 there is the same total utility as one in which A has 4 and B has 7.

With classical utility, the notion of the sum total of utility in society is fully meaningful, as is the prescription of maximizing that total. Classical utilitarianism is not, however, necessarily defined by that goal: it can also be defined by the goal of maximizing average rather than total utility. The two goals coincide when the population size is given, but not when that size itself is to be chosen by the utilitarian calculus. Let us assume, however, that the population is given. In that case, we do not really need the full classical conception of utility. We need a conception that allows for *unit* or *increment comparability*, but we can do without *level comparability*. Lack of level comparability means that we cannot define a zero point of utility, except by an arbitrary stipulation. Suppose that there are two individuals, A and B, at utility levels u_A and u_B, compared to some arbitrarily chosen baselines, and that we must choose one of them to receive a unit of some good.

If A would reach utility level $(u_A + 3)$ if given the good, and B would reach $(u_B + 5)$, then utilitarianism requires that B should get the good. We are not, in this case, maximizing total (or average) utility, because that total is not just unknown, but undefined. We are, however, allocating the good where it will produce the largest increment in utility. The requirement to do so in all cases we may call *increment utilitarianism*. If the individuals have decreasing marginal utility and the good in question is infinitely divisible, we should allocate it so as to *equalize the marginal utility* of the two parties.[45] To "equalize at the margin" is a basic tenet of utilitarian theory. Only in the special case of equal utility functions does it also imply that individuals should get equal amounts of the good.

Issues of redistribution of income are often discussed in this framework. Let us suppose that there are two individuals A and B, at initial income levels 4 and 25. Let us suppose that if we take 2 units from B, we can transfer only one unit to A, for reasons indicated earlier. (The bucket is quite leaky.) For specificity, assume that utility is the square root of income. In the initial situation, their utilities add up to 7. If we take 2 units from B, the distribution of income will be 5 and 23, with utilities about 2.23 and 4.8, adding up to a little more than 7. If we take as much as 8 units from B, the sum of the utilities falls below 7. Using elementary calculus, we can show that the maximum total utility is achieved when we take 3 units from B. Hence we see that on utilitarian grounds, some transfer of income is allowed. That it lowers total income doesn't matter as long as it increases total utility. Utilitarianism does *not* favor the rich over the poor.[46]

Other theories, however, can favor the poor even more. Consider the theory of *maximin utility* according to which redistribution ought to take place up to the point where further transfer would make the worst-off worse off. Or equivalently: one should choose the level of transfer that would make the worst-off as well off as possible. Note first that this theory requires only *level comparability* of utility, and can dispense with unit comparability. An analogy might be the perception of sounds: although we can of-

---

[45] This may not always be possible, if one individual derives more additional utility from the last unit of the good than the other from the first unit.

[46] By contrast, *bargaining* between rich and poor does indeed follow the principle of justice according to Saint Matthew: Unto everyone that hath shall be given. See Chapter 2 of my *The Cement of Society*.

ten tell if one sound is louder than another, we may be hard put to say how much louder it is. Observe next that the theory is indeed more generous than utilitarianism in its treatment of the poor. Consider the numerical example of the previous paragraph. If we take everything from the rich, the (formerly) poor achieve a utility level of about 4, well above their initial level of 2. Yet the (formerly) rich are now the worst-off group, well below the level of 2. To raise the worst-off to the highest possible level, we should take 14 from the rich, bringing both groups up to a level of about 3.3.

In this case, maximin utility implies equal incomes and equal utilities. This implication does not hold true if the poor benefit to some extent from the wealth of the rich, for instance because the savings of the rich form a more-than-proportional part of total investment. Now transfers have two opposed effects on the poor: they get a short-term gain from the transfer itself, but they incur a long-term loss. In that case, the maximin distribution would yield higher levels of income and utility to the rich than to the poor. If the poor insisted on transfers until equality was achieved, they would be cutting off their nose to spite their face, taking a loss in order to impose an even greater loss on the rich. I shall return briefly to the issue of envy.

As we saw in Chapter 3, level and increment comparisons also arise in many problems of local justice. Giving allocative priority to the person who is worst off along the relevant dimension (health, education) bears some resemblance to maximin utility; favoring the person who can benefit most from the scarce good bears a similar resemblance to utilitarianism. The relation is one of resemblance, not of identity. In local justice context only one aspect of the person is singled out. One would never give scarce medical resources to the person who is worst off, all things considered, including education and income: only the medically critical cases may be favored. Also, current procedures for allocating medical goods according to increment of welfare do not take account of the impact on the welfare of others than the recipient.

I now turn to two conceptions of utility that do not allow for any kind of interpersonal comparison. I begin with the most impoverished notion. This is the *ordinal* conception of utility, which is little more than a shorthand for preference rankings that satisfy three formal conditions.

We assume first that an individual can rank his options in a consistent and complete manner. Completeness means that given any pair of options, he will either prefer one of them or be indifferent between them. He will never say, for instance, that he knows too little about the options to be able to compare and rank them. This condition often fails to obtain when one has to make a big decision, rather than a marginal adjustment. The task of expressing a preference for one parent over another for custody provides an example.[47]

Next, we assume that the preferences are consistent, that is, that the individual never prefers A to B, B to C, and C to A. Recall from Chapter 2 that the authors of *The American Soldier* thought they discerned individually inconsistent preferences in the patterns of response to survey questions about order of dismissal. Although an explanation in terms of aggregation problems is perhaps more plausible, the hypothesis of individual inconsistency cannot be eliminated.

Finally, we may impose a technical condition called continuity, which essentially says that the individual must be able to make trade-offs among all the goods that are objects of his preferences. It must always be possible, that it, to compensate for the loss of one good by providing more of another, leaving the individual indifferent between the two combinations of goods. Lexicographic allocative schemes, discussed in Chapter 3, do not satisfy this condition. For instance, the "preferences" embodied in collective bargaining agreements which stipulate that seniority is to count in layoff cases only when ability is equal, cannot be represented by an ordinal utility function.

When these three conditions are satisfied, preferences can be represented by an ordinal utility function that assigns numbers to options in such a way that higher numbers are assigned to more preferred options. Since there are innumerable functions that will serve this purpose, no significance should be attached to the actual numbers, beyond their ordinal properties. They do not mea-

---

[47] See my *Solomonic Judgements*, p. 134 ff.

sure quantities of "psychic stuff," nor levels or increments of such stuff. Classical utility is prior to preferences: people are thought to prefer one option to another because it offers more utility. With ordinal utility, it is the other way around: we can assign higher utility numbers to an option because it is the more preferred one. Hence ordinal utility functions do not allow us to make intrapersonal comparisons such as "Individual A prefers x to y more strongly than he prefers y to z," nor interpersonal comparisons such as "Individual A prefers x to y more strongly than does individual B." Their main role in economic theory is to enable us to construct *indifference curves,* a very useful tool for many purposes. Suppose that a consumer has to allocate his budget over two perfectly divisible commodities, bread and milk. Assume, moreover, that he is indifferent between a bundle that consists of three pints of milk and two pounds of bread and another that consists of two pints of milk and four pounds of bread. In that case these two bundles, as well as many others, will be on the same indifference curve.

"Ordinal utilitarianism,"[48] more frequently referred to as *social choice theory,* attempts to evaluate social options in terms of how they are ranked by individual preferences.[49] To be more precise, the task of social choice theory is to find a function that to any set of individual preferences over given options assigns a unique ranking that can be reasonably interpreted as society's preferences over these options. Individual preferences are required to be complete and consistent, but not necessarily continuous. (Hence ordinal utility functions, which require continuity, have no role to play in the construction of a social preference order.) For obvious reasons, the social ranking is required to have the same properties. In addition, the following conditions, first laid down by Kenneth Arrow forty years ago, are standardly imposed.[50]

The condition of unrestricted domain says that the function must assign a social ranking to any set of individual preferences. One is not allowed, in other words, to assume that self-interest will

[48] The phrase is from Kenneth Arrow's review of Rawls's *A Theory of Justice.*
[49] The best exposition of social choice theory remains Sen, *Collective Choice and Social Welfare.* A survey of some controversial issues is in Elster and Hylland (eds.), *Foundations of Social Choice Theory.*
[50] Arrow, *Social Choice and Individual Values.*

exclude "perverse" preference orderings from occurring, or that culture will exclude excessive diversity of preferences.

The condition of Pareto-optimality says that if all members of society prefer one alternative to another, society has the same preference.

The condition of non-dictatorship says that there should be no individual who is such that the social ranking always coincides with his preferences, whatever the preferences of other individuals.

The condition of independence of irrelevance alternatives says that the social ranking of two alternatives should depend only on how individuals rank those alternatives against each other: how each is ranked against further alternatives is irrelevant. Thus, for instance, the social ranking of x and y should not change just because some individuals who formerly preferred y to z now prefer z to y.[51]

Arrow showed that it is not possible to satisfy all these conditions simultaneously. In more rudimentary form, this problem had been known for a long time. At the end of the eighteenth century, the Marquis de Condorcet identified the problem of cyclical majorities, which is illustrated by the following example. Consider a municipal assembly that has to choose between building an indoor swimming pool, subsidizing the local symphony orchestra, or setting up a golf course. Suppose there are three blocs in the assembly, of approximately equal size, representing the business community, industrial workers, and the health and social service professionals. Let us also suppose that, conforming to the stereotype of these groups, they rank the options as follows:

TABLE 6.3 /

	Businessmen	Workers	Professionals
Golf Course	1	2	3
Orchestra	2	3	1
Swimming Pool	3	1	2

[51] Young, "Equitable Selection of Kidney Recipients," shows that the earlier point system for allocating kidneys violates a condition similar to this one: the relative ranking of two persons on the waiting list can be reversed if a third person drops out.

One majority, made up of businessmen and workers, thinks it better to have a golf course than to subsidize the orchestra. Another majority, made up of businessmen and professionals, thinks it better to subsidize the orchestra than to build a pool. A further majority, made up of workers and professionals, thinks it better to have the swimming pool than the golf course. Majority choice is circular, or inconsistent. Again, I refer to the American demobilization scheme for a local-justice example that exhibits the same pattern.

What Arrow showed is that similar problems can be expected to arise in any attempt to aggregate individual preferences into an overall social ranking, as long as we insist on a purely ordinal framework and impose the quite reasonable conditions listed above. Arrow also argued that the ordinal framework is the appropriate one. Modern economists have little faith in theories that require comparison of the utilities of different people, either because they think such comparisons are meaningless or because they cannot see how they could be implemented.[52] In my opinion, few people really believe that such comparisons are meaningless. The more telling argument is that we are often unable to carry out the comparisons in practice. We may think of this as an informational problem, compounded by an incentive problem. The attempt to elicit individual preferences for the purposes of constructing a social ranking runs into the problem that, knowing the purpose of this elicitation, people might misrepresent their preferences. Essentially all aggregation schemes are vulnerable to such strategic misrepresentation.[53] If—contrary to fact—there existed techniques that allowed us to compare the utilities of different individuals, assuming they would answer truthfully to certain questions, we would find that telling the truth was not in their interest.

In practice, we never attempt to carry out interpersonal comparisons of utility on a case-by-case basis, partly because of information problems (we do not know which measurements to take of individuals nor what questions to ask them about their nonmea-

---

[52] For the pros and cons of this debate, see the essays in Elster and Roemer (eds.), *Interpersonal Comparisons of Well-Being*.

[53] Gibbard, "Manipulation of Voting Schemes."

surable properties), partly because of incentive problems (we do not know whether they would answer truthfully), and partly for reasons that flow from the purpose of making these comparisons in the first place. Suppose we want to use them as grounds for compensating people at low utility levels. The first step would be to establish certain observable features of individuals, such as physical handicaps, that are known to be highly correlated with low welfare. As I said, one would have to be something of a nihilist to deny the possibility of establishing such correlations.

That step might well also be the last step. We might stop short, that is, of more individualized measures, even assuming that there were no information and incentive problems to prevent us from carrying them out. Some handicapped people might, because of a naturally sunny disposition, be at high levels of welfare. Or, because of their greater flexibility, they might have adapted successfully to their handicap. Some of the non-handicapped might, because of a naturally morose disposition, be at a lower utility level than most handicapped people. Or, as in an example of Ronald Dworkin's, they might be unhappy because their religion makes them afraid they might be damned to eternal pain. In all these cases, we might feel disinclined to use this individualized information, even assuming it could be costlessly obtained. Most of us have strong intuitions that, for purposes of compensation, such things as natural tempers, the ability to adapt to difficult circumstances, and religious beliefs neither offset handicaps nor constitute the analogue of handicaps. Hard welfarists might say that these intuitions are just wrong. Alternatively, they might try to reconcile these intuitions with welfarism, by invoking incentive arguments of a kind further discussed below. Others, denying that they can be so reconciled and believing that theories of justice are constrained by intuition, would use them to refute welfarism.

In problems of local justice, one never goes beyond the first step, even in the occasional cases where it might be feasible to do so. One would never turn away a patient from kidney transplantation on the grounds that his sunny disposition enables him to overcome the discomforts of being on dialysis. Nor would one exempt an individual with a depressive temper from military service on the grounds that he had already suffered enough. There comes a point, of course, where a depressive temper turns into a clinical illness. In that case, depression might constitute grounds for treatment, but not for compensation. If it also constitutes grounds for exemption, it would not be out of regard for the individual, as part of a compensation or treatment scheme, but out of regard for military efficiency. The point is not simply that institutions shy away from discretionary decisions such as those involved in gauging the welfare of individuals. It is true that for the reasons discussed in the previous chapter, institutions often prefer mechanical and automatic procedures over those that require clinical judgment and trained discretion. In addition, however, they tend to see their role as specialized providers of specific services rather than as promoters of overall welfare.

I come, finally, to the fifth and last conception of utility, often called *von Neumann-Morgenstern utility* after the two writers who contributed most to the diffusion and popularity of this concept.[54] Like the purely ordinal variety, this conception of utility does not allow us to make interpersonal comparisons of utility. Unlike ordinal utility, it does allow us to make intrapersonal comparisons of the strength of different preferences. To explain this conception, let us consider the notion of *quality-adjusted life years.* "Assign a year at full function a utility of 1, and a year without life the utility of 0. An individual has a choice between living the rest of his life with a specific impairment or having an operation. The operation has a probability x of restoring full function (this will not extend his life span, however), and probability 1-x of being immediately fatal. The value of x that would leave the patient indifferent between having and not having the operation is the [quality-adjusted life year] level for his particular level of impairment."[55]

Ordinal utility information would tell us only that the patient prefers life without the impairment to life with the impairment, which is in turn preferred to no life at all. The von Neumann-Morgenstern construction allows us to quantify the value of the intermediate option. If a person with a hip displacement is indif-

---

[54] von Neumann and Morgenstern, *The Theory of Games and Economic Behavior.* For an outstandingly lucid exposition, see also Chapter 2 of Luce and Raiffa, *Games and Decisions.*

[55] Zeckhauser and Shepard, "Where Now for Saving Lives?" pp. 11–12.

ferent between going on as he is and undergoing an operation that has a 25 percent chance of being fatal, we can infer that, for him, a year of living with the displaced hip is equivalent to nine months of full functioning. Suppose that another person, with the same life expectancy, also with a hip displacement, would not be indifferent unless there was a 90 percent chance of success. For that person, a year of impaired living is worth about eleven months of unimpaired life. Suppose finally that in reality hip surgery is riskless, but that the authorities have decided it is too costly to be made available to all. They might then decide to operate on the first person, on the grounds that this would maximize the sum of quality-adjusted life years. Observe that in doing so, they would not be comparing the overall utilities which the two individuals experience under perfect or imperfect functioning. In line with what was said earlier about the specialized role of providers of medical care, they would adjust only for the part of the utility difference that is due to their handicaps.

This is an attractive scheme, but it suffers from three fatal flaws. First, it creates an incentive for the patient to underreport the value of x that would leave him indifferent between having the operation and not having it. Secondly, even assuming that he tried to report truthfully, he might not be able to do so in a reliable way. In many cases the point of indifference reached when we begin with a low value of x and move upwards is lower than the point reached when we begin with a high value of x and move downwards. It is not clear how one would go about eliminating such anchoring effects.[56] There simply may not *be* anything there to be measured. Thirdly, even assuming that there is something there and that we can measure it reliably, the measure might not be valid. Although it is supposed to measure the intrinsic desirability of options and the intrinsic strength of preference with regard to them, the method by which it is constructed makes it inevitable that it will also take account of the individual's attitude toward risk. The person who required a probability of a 90 percent chance of success, might just be more risk-averse than the person

[56] Tversky and Kahneman, "Judgment under Uncertainty." Although this article refers mainly to the anchoring effect evidenced in the elicitation of probabilities, it is reasonable to expect it also to operate in the elicitation of von Neumann-Morgenstern utilities.

who was content with a 25 percent success. The actual quality of their lives might well be identical.

To conclude this section, I shall explain an important distinction between *act-utilitarianism* and *rule-utilitarianism*.[57] The former enjoins us, on every single occasion, to perform the act that will maximize total utility on that occasion. The latter tells us to act according to the rule that, when followed invariably, will maximize total utility over time. In many circumstances, the rule of acting according to act-utilitarianism will not maximize total utility over time. Instead, utility will be maximized by following some other rule, even if in each individual case that rule yields results that are less than optimal. Consider the "survival lottery" mentioned earlier. An isolated act of selecting and killing one individual for the purpose of using his organs to save the life of several others might appear to be justified on utilitarian grounds. But consider what would happen if this practice were made into a general rule. First, there would be an undesirable *uncertainty effect*. Some people could have their lives ruined by the constant fear of being selected. Secondly, there would be undesirable *incentive effects*. Some people would neglect to take care of their organs if they knew that they could always get new ones. Finally, there are sometimes strong *precedence-setting effects*. These do not arise in the survival lottery, but are important in many other cases. Many of the alleged counterintuitive implications of utilitarianism disappear when we note that virtually all utilitarians defend the rule-oriented rather than the act-oriented version.

In local justice, act-utilitarianism (or agent-restricted act-utilitarianism) is rampant. The program of end-stage renal dialysis may, in isolation, have seemed to be worthwhile. Today we know[58] what was already suspected[59] earlier; namely, that the program has set an undesirable precedent for uncontrolled growth of expensive medical care. Legal decisions in custody cases are

---

[57] For an excellent exposition, see Harsanyi, "Rule Utilitarianism and Decision Theory."

[58] Evans and Blagg, "Lessons Learned from the End-stage Renal Disease Experience."

[59] "Renal dialysis may serve as the opening wedge for other, even more expensive, technologies for saving lives" (Zeckhauser and Shepard, "Where Now for Saving Lives," p. 7, note 7).

often constrained to do what is thought best for the particular child in question. As a result, harm may be done to the wider category of children, by creating incentives for parental procrastination and even abduction.[60] When profits are threatened, employers are easily tempted to override seniority and dismiss the least productive workers. They often overlook the fact that the ensuing uncertainty is bad for morale and that the loss of an incentive to remain in the firm leads to higher turnover, effects that may damage the firm more than retaining some inefficient workers. Admitting students on a case-by-case basis on grounds of expected academic excellence may not serve the end of promoting academic excellence, if there are interaction effects among different categories of students.

JOHN RAWLS'S THEORY OF JUSTICE

There is no canonical exposition or representative of utilitarianism. Today, John Harsanyi comes perhaps closer than anyone to embodying the utilitarian philosophy,[61] but others have had approximately equal influence. Utilitarianism is not one theory, but a general approach to justice which can be spelled out in many different ways, as we have seen. By contrast, the views set out in John Rawls's *A Theory of Justice*—probably the greatest work in moral and political philosophy of this century—form very much a single coherent theory. The architectonics of the book is complex, so much so in fact that even after several rereadings it is hard to keep in mind the many connections between different parts of the book. Although it is sometimes presented as constructed around a principle of maximin justice, this is only one part of a vast edifice. It is, nevertheless, the part on which I shall focus here, because of the special purposes guiding the exposition.

Let me begin, however, with the main criticism leveled by Rawls at utilitarianism, its lack of respect for individuals. In classi-

---

[60] As this example shows, it is sometimes more appropriate to refer to act-consequentialism or act-welfarism, since a similar distinction between act and rule can be made for these more general cases.

[61] See notably his classic article, "Cardinal Welfare, Individualistic Ethics and Interpersonal Comparisons of Utility."

cal utilitarianism,[62] a person is not seen as valuable and worth protecting in his own right. Rather, he is just a drop in the ocean of overall social utility. Sometimes one might have to accept very low utility levels for some people if that forms part of the scheme that maximizes total utility. This is more than a hypothetical possibility. As mentioned earlier, it is sometimes argued that rich countries should reduce their aid to poor countries, so as to create the right incentives for economic growth. Even assuming that this policy would maximize total long-term utility, the transitional period would lead to a great deal of suffering. The rich countries would have to take a hard stand to make it clear that they are not going to bail out the poor countries each time they get into difficulties. Similar rule-utilitarian arguments are also often made with respect to welfare recipients within the rich countries.

In this respect utilitarianism fails to respect Kant's principle, "Do not use other people only as means and not also as ends in themselves." Rawls observes that this instrumental attitude toward individuals may in itself be a source of disutility. The worst-off may feel even more miserable if they know that their situation, though improvable, is deliberately left unimproved because their gains would impose greater losses on others. (It seems to hold quite generally that people are more willing to accept bad outcomes if they are the unintended result of anonymous social processes than if they are the intended result of deliberate intervention.) They might well say, "What's their welfare to us?" For that reason, utilitarianism is psychologically unstable. It might achieve greater stability, perhaps, if the utilitarian planners could keep their theory secret. Against this proposal Rawls, again following Kant, argues for a *condition of publicity:* it is a constraint on any theory of justice that it must be possible to state it publicly without reducing its psychological appeal and, hence, the possibility of realizing it.

Rawls argues that his own theory respects individuals as ends in themselves, and that it is, therefore, psychologically stable. He argues that individual rights, such as freedom of expression, freedom of association, and freedom of religion, should never be

---

[62] Ordinal utilitarianism differs in this respect. See Arrow, "Extended Sympathy and the Possibility of Social Choice."

traded off against material goods. The argument is not that such trade-offs would, in the long run, be detrimental to material wealth itself.[63] Rather it is that rational men behind the veil of ignorance would not choose to restrict their liberties. The knowledge that when the veil is lifted they may find themselves to have some religion, combined with ignorance about which religion they might have, makes them agree on a constitution that allows for the free worship of all religions. The knowledge that the religion they might turn out to have could be more important to them than anything else prevents them from allowing repression of religion for the sake of economic growth.

I shall not pursue Rawls's arguments about rights, but focus from here onward on his theory of the distribution of primary goods. The theory is explicitly non-welfarist. Rawls is not concerned with the direct promotion of equal, minimal, or total welfare, but with enabling individuals to engage in the pursuit of happiness. To this end they need certain resources, or primary goods. Foremost among these is income, but Rawls also lists among the primary goods power, equality of opportunity, and, crucially, self-respect. Surprisingly, perhaps, Rawls does not list health among the primary goods. Nor does he say, as one might have expected, that working or holding a job is a primary good, not just for the income it provides, but as a main source of self-respect.[64]

The distribuendum, in Rawls's theory, is not a single homogeneous good like income or welfare, but a multidimensional bundle of primary goods. This creates a problem for his theory. On the one hand, as we shall see, he needs to be able to make ordinal comparisons of the bundles of primary goods held by different individuals (or by the same individuals in different situations). On the other hand, many pairs of bundles might be noncomparable. One bundle might be higher on income, another higher on self-respect. Unless Rawls can propose a common coin in which all bundles could be measured, his theory risks being indetermi-

---

[63] This argument was made by Tocqueville, in *L'ancien régime et la révolution*, p. 217.

[64] On this point, see my "Self-realization in Work and Politics" and "Is There (or Should There Be) a Right to Work?"

nate. One common coin could be welfare, but Rawls does not want to use this measure. It might, for instance, allow an unacceptable place for utililty derived from spiteful or envious preferences.[65] In the end, Rawls does not try to resolve the question.

Primary goods ought to be distributed according to "the difference principle," which means that they should be allocated so as to maximize the amount of primary goods held by those with the least primary goods. This principle ensures that nobody would be left to suffer or starve for the sake of a higher good. For reasons explained in the last paragraph, it is not quite clear how much redistribution would be required by the difference principle.[66] The numerical example used earlier suggests, however, that it would require substantially more redistribution than what is demanded by utilitarianism. It is restricted only by the interests of the beneficiaries from redistribution, not by the interests of society as a whole.

[65] Another objection to using the coin of welfare is that people with few primary goods might adapt their preferences so as to feel reasonably content, as in the fable of the fox and the sour grapes. On this point, see Chapter 3 of my *Sour Grapes*. For other arguments against using the coin of welfare see Sen, *Commodities and Capabilities*.

[66] An additional difficulty is pointed out by Krouse and McPherson in "Capitalism, 'Property-owning Democracy,' and the Welfare State." When Rawls says that political liberties should be equalized, he adds a clause saying that sufficient resources must be made available to everyone so that the *value* of these liberties does not become excessively unequal. "There is a maximum gain permitted to the most favored on the assumption that, even if the difference principle would allow it, there would be unjust effects on the political system and the like excluded by the priority of liberty." (*A Theory of Justice*, p. 81.) But this creates a problem. Assume that under the difference principle the worst-off earn a and the best-off b. Assume, moreover, that any earnings in excess of c give the best-off an unacceptable power to influence political decisions through their wealth. Assume, furthermore, that when the earnings of the best-off are limited to c, those of the worst-off are d. Assume, finally, that the minimal level of income required to participate effectively in politics, to form autonomous preferences and the like, is e. If, as Rawls implies, $c < b$, it follows (as G. A Cohen points out to me) that $d < a$. To move toward equality of the value of liberty, the income of the worst-off might have to be reduced below the level at which they are as well off as possible. That implication might be acceptable. If, however, it is also the case that $d < e$, the theory is in deep trouble. One would then face the choice between ensuring effective political liberty for the worst-off and preventing the best-off from illegitimately using their wealth to shape political decisions. If, in addition, we have $a < e$, the ideal of effective political liberty for the worst-off is unattainable.

This last remark suggests a natural justification of the difference principle. In variable-sum situations, we can distinguish between three norms of equality. *Non-envious egalitarianism* tells us to divide equally up to the point where further equalization would make some worse off without making anyone better off. This is equivalent to the difference principle, with an added clause which says that of two states that make the worse-off equally and maximally well off, one should prefer the state that makes the group above the worse-off best off, or, if they are equally well off too, the state that makes the next group best off, and so on.[67] *Weakly envious egalitarianism* tells us to divide equally up to the point where further equalization would make everybody worse off. This norm is consistent with changes that make some worse off without making anyone better off ("If I can't have it, nobody shall"). *Strongly envious egalitarianism* insists on absolute equality even if it makes everyone worse off ("cutting off one's nose to spite one's face"). The difference principle can be justified as a form of non-envious egalitarianism. Nevertheless, as we shall see, it does not fully exclude envy as a determinant of just distribution.

Rawls's own argument for the difference principle is more elaborate, but not very convincing. He argues that in what he calls *the original position*, defined by the thick veil of ignorance discussed earlier as well by some assumptions about risk-averse motivation, rational individuals will incline to a maximin policy and, accordingly, select the difference principle. They would not follow utilitarian reasoning and consider it equally likely that they might turn out to occupy each position in society. Instead, they would act as if it were certain that they would end up in the worst position or, as Rawls said in an earlier article, as if their place in society would be assigned to them by their worst enemy. Rawls's reasoning on this point is notoriously elliptical or worse. The original position is a useful framework for formulating questions of justice. The difference principle is in many ways an attractice idea. But there is no sure path from the one to the other.

I said earlier that Rawls's theory is relatively coarse-grained. The multidimensional character of his proposed distribuendum illustrates this point. Another illustration is provided by what he

---

[67] This is often called the leximin principle for distributive justice.

says about the delimitation of "the worst-off." He does not mean literally the worst-off individual. Rather, he is talking about large groups of individuals, such as (his examples) the group of unskilled workers or the group of those whose income is less than half the median income in society. Within each group there might, of course, be some individuals who have very much less than the group average. Why does not Rawls tell us to assist these individuals, over and above the transfers offered to the group to which they belong? Isn't the broad definition of the worst-off a violation of ethical individualism, as well as inconsistent with the argument from rational choice in the original position?

I have a conjectural answer to this question. Suppose that Rawls had defined the worst-off narrowly, as the worst-off individual in society. In some conceivable situations, he might then have been led to the counterintuitive prescription that we should impose large sacrifices on many other people to ensure a small gain for that one person. Because Rawls is never very clear about the actual mechanics of redistribution, it is hard to identify such situations, but they cannot be ruled out of court. The severely handicapped, for instance, might require the commitment of vast social resources.[68] By using a broader definition of the worst-off, Rawls avoids this counterintuitive consequence, but at some cost. He now has to face the equally counterintuitive implication of offering no special protection for the physically or mentally handicapped, the unemployed and unemployable, and similar groups.[69] Also, many people might still find it counterintuitive to impose large taxes on those who are well off if the bucket is so leaky that it allows only for small gains in the situation of the worst-off. Rawls might respond that the bucket is not, or need not be, that leaky. In the near-ideal society to which his theory is supposed to apply, it might not be; but then again it might.

---

[68] Harsanyi, "Can the Maximin Principle Serve as a Basis for Morality?"

[69] Two separate problems arise in the case of the handicapped. First, what resources are needed to bring their bundle of primary goods up to a higher or indeed maximal level? Perhaps the provision of self-respect to the handicapped would require extensive and very expensive redesigning of the urban environment. This is the problem discussed in the text. Secondly, Rawls has been criticized by Sen ("Equality of What?") for neglecting the fact that the handicapped need more primary goods than others to realize their life plans.

I return to the question of envy. According to Rawls, self-respect is the most important primary good. Clearly, large income differences can induce loss of self-respect in the worst-off, not only because they are badly off, but because others are so much better off. Let us assume, for simplicity, that there are two primary goods, wealth and self-respect, and that the self-respect of an individual is a function of the difference between the wealth of others and his own. Two profiles of distribution of these goods between two individuals might be A = [(6,4), (3,2)] and B = [2,3), (2,3)], with self-respect as the second good. Since self-respect is the most important primary good and since one ought to prefer the distribution which is most favorable to the worst-off, one must infer that B is to be preferred over A. This conclusion amounts to a justification of envy. "When envy is a reaction to the loss of self-respect in circumstances where it would be unreasonable to expect someone to feel differently, I shall say that it is excusable."[70] Rawls goes on to argue that a well-ordered society is unlikely to give rise to feelings of envy, because material inequalities are likely to be relatively small and because the worst-off are more likely to accept them since they know inequalities work to their advantage and, indeed, are allowed to exist only because they work to their advantage. This might be the case; but then again it might not.

As I said earlier, Rawls's theory is not directly relevant for local justice. Its proposals are too broad to have clear implications for small-scale problems. We may ask, nevertheless, whether, as in the case of utilitarianism, the general spirit of the theory could not illuminate issues of micro-allocation. The concern for the worst-off certainly suggests specific policies in many arenas. Employment offices might give priority to those with the longest periods of unemployment; doctors to those with the shortest life expectancy; admissions officers to the educationally disadvantaged; and so on. In most cases, however, it would clearly be a mistake to defend specific allocative policies by claiming that they are supported by Rawlsian reasoning. The main exception is not based on the difference principle, but on the lexicographical priority of liberty over material goods. One cannot, Rawls claims, "justify a selective

[70] *A Theory of Justice*, p. 534.

service act that grants educational deferments or exemptions to some on the grounds that doing this is a socially efficient way both to maintain the armed forces and to provide incentives to those otherwise subject to conscription to acquire valuable skills by continuing their education. Since conscription is a drastic interference with the basic liberties of equal citizenship, it cannot be justified by any needs less compelling than those of these equal liberties themselves."[71]

ROBERT NOZICK'S THEORY

Anarchy, State and Utopia is the best-known statement of libertarian thought. Brilliant and frivolous, it generates excitement, provocation, and irritation in equal measures. Some people find it hard to take seriously. Others take it very seriously indeed, and devote much effort to refuting it or propagating its ideas. While it is sometimes believed to provide philosophical foundations for laissez-faire and unrestricted property rights, it does not take a careful reading to see that it has virtually no implications for policy.

Nozick's theory is summarized in three principles: justice in appropriation, justice in transfer, and justice in rectification. It asserts that a distribution of goods is just if it is the end result of an unbroken chain of just transfers, beginning from a just original appropriation. If these conditions are not satisfied, justice in rectification requires that we establish the distribution that would have occurred if all unjust links in the chain had been replaced by just ones. We shall see that, given Nozick's notion of just appropriations and transfers, his idea of justice in rectification is entirely indeterminate, whence the lack of policy implications.

For my purposes, I need not say much about Nozick's idea of original appropriation. It is essentially a "finders keepers" principle, with an important proviso. The basic idea is that anyone has the right to appropriate, exploit, and enjoy the fruits of any unowned piece of nature. The proviso says that one is not allowed to do this if others are harmed thereby. Harmed compared to what? Compared to their pre-appropriation state, to the hypothet-

---

[71] *Justice as Fairness: A Restatement*, § 13.

ical state in which they do the appropriation, or to some other state again? The issue is indeterminate, and Nozick's resolution in favor of the first answer is essentially arbitrary.[72]

The principle of just transfer is more important. It says that the outcome of any voluntary, uncoerced transaction between two or more individuals is *ipso facto* just, assuming that the property titles entering into the transaction can be traced back to a just original state, either directly or indirectly through a series of just transfers. Justice in transfer, then, is equated with lack of coercion. If two or more individuals get together and agree on a transfer of goods or entitlements because all prefer the agreement to no agreement, the only fact that could invalidate the contract is the use of power by some of the parties for the purpose of making the non-agreement state worse for other parties than it would otherwise have been.

In a famous phrase, Nozick asks who can object to "capitalist acts between consenting adults." It is easy to see how "just exploitation" might come into existence by such acts.[73] Suppose that a society equalizes all external resources and assures, by genetic engineering, equality of skills and talents. Only different preferences are left undisturbed. Some people will work hard, because they care more about income than about leisure or because they care more about the future than about the present. After a while, they will have accumulated more capital than they can use for themselves. Others, who have different attitudes, will remain poor because they spend all they earn. At some point, the rich offer the poor to work for them at an hourly wage in excess of what they could earn for themselves. If the poor accept, we have exploitation in the technical Marxist sense of the term—but what's wrong with it? Should the egalitarian police step in and block a transaction that would benefit both parties? The distribution is "ambition-sensitive," but not "endowment-sensitive," as prescribed by Dworkin and (as I argue later) by commonsense conceptions of justice.

In a perfect world, with no transaction costs, collective action problems, information problems, or weakness of will, Nozick's

---

[72] Cohen, "Are Freedom and Equality Compatible?"
[73] Roemer, "Should Marxists Be Interested in Exploitation?"

argument would be hard to refute. In the real world, these conditions are not satisfied. Suppose first that there are many poor individuals, who all engage to contract with the same rich person. In so doing they might collectively endow him with much more wealth than they would have desired individually.[74] Their reason for not wanting him to be too wealthy might be fear that he would use his wealth for coercive purposes, or, less respectably, envy. In either case they would find themselves in a Prisoner's Dilemma. Each individual would know that *his* contribution to the wealth of the rich man would have a negligible negative impact on his own welfare, less in any case than he would gain working for him. Hence he would, knowingly and willingly, do his share of what he knows will harm him. The obvious reply—that the poor could organize themselves and pledge to abstain from such contracts—runs into two problems. First, a new Prisoner's Dilemma arises: Why should any individual keep his pledge? Secondly, assuming willingness to keep the pledge, the costs to the poor of organizing themselves might be prohibitively high. Under these circumstances, the government might be justified in prohibiting the transactions or, less drastically, in enabling the poor to take collective action.

Suppose next that some individuals are imperfectly informed about the consequences of entering into a given transaction. They might not know that smoking is harmful to their health or that prolonged exposure to high-decibel music will impair their hearing. Although they believe they are engaging in a mutually beneficial transaction, only the other party will in fact benefit. In many such cases there are real asymmetries that work against the principle of *caveat emptor*. No single buyer can be expected to acquire technical information about each of the large number of products offered on the market.[75] Under these circumstances, the government might at the very least be justified in requiring that the information be provided, as it does in countries where cigarette advertisements are required by law to include warnings on the

[74] Cohen, "Robert Nozick and Wilt Chamberlain."

[75] For an insightful discussion of such transactions between natural persons and corporate actors, see Coleman, *Foundations of Social Theory*, p. 548 ff.

dangers of smoking. It might also be justified in prohibiting the transactions, if the cost of providing the information would be very high. (It might also prohibit them if it believes that the information would not be heeded. But that belongs to the argument of the next paragraph.)

Finally, and more controversially, some apparently voluntary transactions might be subject to a Prisoner's Dilemma within the individual.[76] An ordinary Prisoner's Dilemma is characterized by the following features. By engaging in, say, polluting activities, the individual imposes a small harm (or a small probability of harm) on each of a large number of persons. He also extracts a gain for himself, which exceeds the harm (or the harm discounted by its probability). In consequence, it is in his self-interest to pollute. If motivated exclusively by self-interest, he will pollute. If others are similarly placed and motivated, they will pollute too. As a result, each person becomes the target of many small harms (or a large probability of harm), which outweigh the private benefits of polluting. Similar phenomena can occur within the individual, if we distinguish between what a person does at any given moment and the consequences of the action he suffers at later moments. By accepting a cigarette now, I get a momentary pleasure now. I also impose a small harm on each of my future incarnations. If I care more about the present than about the future, that harm will not keep me from smoking. As we move on in time, each incarnation will, for the same reason, decide to smoke. It will also be the target of many small harms imposed on it by earlier incarnations. As a result, I am always worse off if I smoke than if I never smoked. This is an instance of the problem of weakness of will.

Libertarian philosophers tend to dismiss this phenomenon as a ground for governmental intervention or compensation. If people act imprudently, they should be prepared to take the consequences. As a general principle, this proposition is not unreasonable (see below). Sometimes, however, imprudence is caused by poverty or other circumstances outside the control of the individual. As I said (Chapter 4), impulse control is a complicated matter.

---

[76] See my "Weakness of Will and the Free-rider Problem."

It would be unfair to blame the victims of poverty for their inability to take account of the long-term consequences of their actions.[77] In any case, even assuming that those who act imprudently are not in a position to complain, those who count on and benefit from their imprudence may be in a position to be blamed.

I shall not say much about Nozick's account of justice in rectification. Suppose we have decided that the present state of affairs is unjust, because it is the end result of some chain of actions one or more of which were unjust. We then have to identify the point in time at which the earliest violation occurred, be it the original appropriation or some later transfer. We further have to identify a counterfactual chain of just transfers (or of a just appropriation followed by just transfers) beginning at that point and leading up to the present. Compensation and redistribution must then be made so as to undo the harm and restore the state that would have obtained at the end point of the counterfactual chain. This proposal fails, because Nozick's theory does not uniquely specify just appropriations or just transfers. As long as they do not harm or coerce others, people are free to appropriate whatever they want, and to do as they please with their possessions. They can destroy their possessions, give them away, sell them for a profit, or consume them. For practical purposes, there is no way of telling which of these actions would have been chosen and what the further consequences would have been. Even for theoretical purposes, no plausible answer is forthcoming. Although we know that all presently existing societies are the result of massive injustice in the past, the rectification required by Nozick could not be carried out. And we should not say that the best we can do under these circumstances is to let present endowments remain as they are and apply the principle of justice in transfer from now onward. Any such idea would be a parody of justice. Yet, in practice, this is what we find many of Nozick's followers (although not Nozick himself) arguing.

Although Nozick's theory is a failure as a comprehensive account of justice, many of its elements appear in contexts of local justice. The principle of "finders keepers" is reflected in the use

---

[77] For a general analysis of these problems see Sunstein, "Legal Interference with Private Preferences."

of queuing, waiting lists, and seniority as principles of allocation. We have seen, however, that these principles can be open to two interpretations. On the one hand, they can be seen as expressing natural rights. On the other hand, they can be seen as maxims grounded in rule-utilitarian reasoning: the principle of "finders keepers" provides an incentive to look and hence leads to more things being found.

There is one particular right on which libertarians place a great deal of emphasis: the right to one's own bodily parts. Often, they will oppose consequentialist arguments for redistribution by such examples as the survival lottery. Yet the principle that bodily integrity should be respected could be a rule-utilitarian statement as well as the expression of a fundamental right. The right of families to their own children can be similarly reinterpreted in terms of uncertainty and incentive effects. It is more difficult to reinterpret people's alleged right to veto the use of their bodies for legal, medical, and scientific purposes after they are dead.[78] It may not be a coincidence that this right is both one that few people feel strongly about and one that cannot be given a simple rule-utilitarian foundation.

Issues of justice in transfer arise in many problems of local justice, when the government prohibits transactions that, on their face, appear to be voluntary, mutually beneficial, and involving no harm to third parties. In most countries, marketing human organs is a crime. One is allowed to donate a kidney to a sibling, not to sell it to a stranger. In France one can donate sperm, not sell it; in Great Britain, it used to be the case that one could donate blood, not sell it. Nor can one sell one's place on the waiting list for transplantation. To buy one's way out of the army by paying a substitute is no longer allowed in any Western countries. In many contexts, people are not allowed to waive their right to sue. Upon being admitted to an institution of higher education, one cannot sell the right to study there to another person. There are many reasons that can justify such prohibitions. In addition to collective action problems, lack of information, and weakness of will, one can cite the problems of rent-seeking and of adverse

---

[78] See, for instance, Hansman, "The Economics and Ethics of Markets for Human Organs."

selection.[79] In this case the study of local justice can help us to steer a middle path between two extreme views. On the one hand, there is no need to follow Nozick in his blanket endorsement of market transactions. On the other hand, the arguments against such transactions need not rest on Walzer's blanket appeal to shared understandings.

THE COMMONSENSE CONCEPTION OF JUSTICE

What follows is not the statement of a theory, but a series of largely unproven hypotheses about the principles of justice held by those who have given serious thought to the matter but who are not professional philosophers. In particular, I would expect these views to be widely held by lawyers, economists, and politicians, who are professional, secular all-round problem solvers. In systems of local justice, they constitute, roughly speaking, the first-order authorities. In Chapter 5, I said that these actors tend to be concerned with efficiency rather than equity. Here, I offer a somewhat more nuanced view. I give notice that what I am about to describe is a personal construct, in two senses. First, it represents *my* conception of the conceptions held by such people. Secondly, these are also conceptions to which I tend to subscribe myself (although with several exceptions). Hence I might be biased in ascribing them to others.

In addition to the views held by professional, all-round secular decision makers, several others may be distinguished. First, there are the views held by specialized secular problem solvers— second-order actors such as doctors or admissions officers. Next, there are the views held by nonsecular all-round problem solvers—rabbis, ministers, and priests. Because they have not come up in my case studies I have not had much to say about the last group, which is not to say that they could not be important. The implications of talmudic ethics for principles and practices of allocation, for instance, would be well worth studying, but it is not a

---

[79] Rent-seeking arises, as mentioned in Chapter 3, when in-kind allocation is combined with the possibility of post-allocation trade. Adverse selection can arise when people are allowed to sell their blood and sperm, thus creating an incentive to keep silent about acquired or inherited diseases.

task I can pursue here. Finally, there are the views that constitute public opinion—the views, roughly, of those who are not professional problem solvers.

The allocative views of second-order actors have been discussed throughout this book. They tend to be coherent but limited—with respect to the issues they address and the factors they deem relevant. Public opinion ranges more widely, but it is also considerably more fickle. Phenomena of framing loom very large in public perceptions of fairness,[80] which for that reason tend to be unstable and arbitrary. Also, public opinion tends to view issues one by one, essentially ignoring facts of scarcity. At the margin, there are no material constraints; but not all issues can be at the margin. The views of first-order authorities—what I call "the commonsense conception of justice"—range more widely than those of second-order actors, while more coherent and realistic than those of public opinion. Taken together, they add up to a view of global justice that seems worthwhile examining. As we saw in Chapter 5, these ideas of first-order authorities enter into the explanation of practices of local justice. More speculatively, since these ideas are grounded in the practice of allocative decision making rather than in intuitions about hypothetical cases, their empirical foundations might be more robust than those of philosophical theories.

The commonsense conceptions I shall examine are at an intermediate level of generality and abstractness. They are not intuitions about particular cases like the immorality of torturing small children, but "high-level intuitions" such as the idea that distribution should be sensitive to ambitions but not to endowments. I do not know how to derive them from a single, general conception of justice; indeed, it is possible that they are less than fully consistent with each other.[81] I discuss them here not to report work in

---

[80] Kahneman, Knetsch, and Thaler, "Fairness as a Constraint on Profit-seeking."

[81] We may distinguish between two forms of coherence. Strong coherence among a set of propositions obtains when all of them can be logically derived from a single noncontradictory set of premises. Weak coherence obtains when no contradiction can be derived from them. Philosophical theories aim at strong coherence. Common sense, while certainly not strongly coherent, may or may not be weakly coherent. Public opinion regularly violates even weak coherence.

progress on the foundations of justice, but to sketch a research program on the conceptions of justice held by centrally placed decision makers and problem solvers.

I shall divide the commonsense conception into principles of welfare, principles of rights, and principles of fairness. I begin with issues of welfare, which for practical purposes may be operationalized as income. (Special principles would govern support for the handicapped.) I believe there is wide consensus on the strong principle of Pareto-improvement: one should not pass up on any policy that holds out the prospect of welfare improvements for all, even if they do not improve by the same amount or in the same proportion. I believe there is an almost equally strong consensus on the weak principle: one should not pass up on any policy that improves the situation for some without making it worse for any. The fact that, in many cases, public opinion or interest groups force problem solvers to deviate from these principles does not show that they do not in fact hold them.

Many issues of welfare can be phrased in terms of protection of the poor. A common complaint against utilitarianism is that it does not take sufficient account of the welfare of the worst-off. An equally common complaint against maximin justice is that it takes too much account of their interest.[82] To maximize total welfare seems inhumane, to maximize minimum welfare seems inefficient. The commonsense conception of justice is somewhere in between these conceptions. One should maximize total welfare, subject to a fixed floor constraint on individual welfare.[83] If we ask about the determinants of the floor, common sense has no formula to offer. When philosophers discuss this idea, they tend to dismiss it as ad hoc because it does not contain a principle from which the floor could be deduced.[84] This dismissal is perhaps too rash. Using procedural criteria rather than a substantial formula, commonsense conceptions could define the right floor as

---

[82] For experimental evidence, see Yaari and Bar-Hillel, "On Dividing Justly."

[83] Frolich, Oppenheimer, and Eavey, "Laboratory Results on Rawls's Distributive Justice."

[84] Rawls, *A Theory of Justice*, pp. 316–317. For a different, and deeper, objection see § 38 of his *Justice as Fairness: A Restatement*.

one that has been chosen by a properly constructed democratic procedure. I return to this idea later.

Common sense would, nevertheless, be reluctant to embrace unconditional transfers to the poor.[85] A system that offered individuals who could find work the option of living on the unconditional grant would be widely perceived as exploitative. Rawlsian concerns for the worst-off must, so to speak, be tempered not only by utilitarian concerns with efficiency but also by Dworkin's view that we should not compensate people for low ambition levels. Yet Dworkin's position can also be criticized as inconsistent.[86] How can one escape the view that a low level of ambition or a high rate of time-discounting are also the products of social and genetic luck? If they are, why do they not provide grounds for compensation? This seems to be the central philosophical question in current controversies over the welfare state, with clear implications for local justice.

The beginning of an answer is provided by the fact that the modern welfare state is inserted into a political democracy, based among other things on the condition of publicity. To tell a citizen that he is entitled to welfare because he is not responsible for his preferences is pragmatically incoherent. One cannot at one and the same time treat the preferences of an individual as a handicap that justifies compensation, *and* treat them as a legitimate input to the political process; not in one and the same breath treat him as moved by psychic forces outside his control, *and* treat him as rational and open to arguments. Perhaps one might justify such practices to a third party, on the grounds that it is better to let irresponsible individuals have access to the political process than to cause political turmoil by excluding them. In a democratic society, however, a policy must be rejected if it cannot coherently be explained to the individuals in question. By withholding material benefits one protects the crucial values of concern and respect. Those who are able but unwilling to work should not receive support, nor should those who are able but unwilling to save be compensated for their incontinence.

---

[85] For a proposal for a guaranteed unconditional income, see van Parijs and van der Veen, "A Capitalist Road to Communism."

[86] See notably Roemer, "Equality of Talent."

Yet this austere principle is only the beginning of an answer. Applied to most contemporary societies, it would be widely and correctly perceived as unfair, because the economic and social means to form autonomous preferences are massively unequally distributed. In any society there will be individuals who for idiosyncratic reasons are deaf to incentives and who, in more serious cases, have to be supported by the state. In a society with fair background conditions the support would, however, not be offered as compensation; and the supported individuals would, like the mentally ill, be more or less randomly distributed across all social groups. Most contemporary societies do not approach this condition. They contain large groups whose members are systematically prevented, by poverty and lack of employment opportunities, from developing the mental attitude of holding themselves responsible for their actions.[87] To treat them as if the background conditions were just, telling them that they have only themselves to blame for their failure, would be a massive piece of bad faith. As long as the influence of genuinely arbitrary features such as wealth has not been eliminated, justice may require us to count as morally arbitrary some features which would be considered non-arbitrary in the absence of the former.

The commonsense conception of welfare may, then, be stated in four propositions, each of which modifies its predecessor. (1) Maximize total welfare. (2) Deviate from that goal if necessary to ensure that all achieve a minimum level of welfare. (3) Deviate from the requirement of a minimal level of welfare in the case of persons who fall below it because of their own choices. (4) Deviate from the principle of not supporting the persons identified in (3) if their failure to plan ahead and react to incentives is due to severe poverty and deprivation. Let me give an example to show what these propositions imply. In Norway, many young couples find themselves unable to service their mortgage. As a result, they are often bailed out by social assistance or the provision of cheap

---

[87]Some groups have a more ambiguous status. Consider the attitude of the welfare state toward gypsies in an affluent society like Norway. The only thing that prevents them from a life of regular work and schooling is their own attitude toward such things. They like to be free, to travel, and not to have to make plans for the future. Should society bail them out of trouble and more generally support their lifestyle, at the expense of other citizens?

loans. These practices violate the commonsense conception of the distribution of welfare, since few people in Norway live in such a state of deprivation or poverty as to be deaf to incentives. On the commonsense conception, couples who find themselves in this predicament should be left to their own devices, perhaps move into a smaller apartment, and not be supported by public funds.

Again, this may seem excessively austere. Two forces combine to create an almost irresistible pressure to help those who find themselves in a difficult situation due to their own lack of prudence. On the one hand, there is a simple urge of humanity: one should help those who suffer, regardless of the cause of their suffering. On the other hand, there is the natural tendency of politicians to think in act-utilitarian rather than rule-utilitarian terms. If young people who go through a difficult patch are not helped out, their future may be in jeopardy. They will be less productive as members of the work force, less happy as consumers, and more troublesome, perhaps, as citizens.[88] On rule-utilitarian grounds, one might argue that the unhappy incentive and precedent effects set by such practices will in the long run do more damage to society than the financial ruin of some couples. That argument, however, runs into objections grounded in conceptions of fairness, to which I return later.

Commonsense conceptions of rights exist on two levels. On the one hand, there is a conception of the source of rights. On the other hand, there is a conception of what the content of the rights should be. On the first issue, common sense is probably divided. Some rights are widely seen as natural, such as the right of parents to their children or of individuals to their bodies. The philosophical idea that these rights might be nothing more than rule-utilitarian prescriptions is foreign to common sense. Other rights are seen as having their source in the political system. Here I believe the views of John Hart Ely are representative.[89] He argues that the proper role of judicial review is not to lay down rights, but to ensure that the democratic rights-creating procedure is fair, unbiased, and unprejudiced.

---

[88] Note that this deviation from proposition (3) is based on (1) rather than on (4).
[89] *Democracy and Distrust.*

Let me illustrate these issues by the question of self-ownership.[90] What are people's rights with respect to the control, development, alienation, or destruction of their bodies? What rights do they have to the fruits of their labor? I shall argue that on the commonsense conception of justice people have natural rights of self-ownership in some respects but not in others.

I have already said that the right to one's own bodily parts is widely seen as a natural, inviolable right. This right minimally (and perhaps maximally) includes protection from forcible takings by others (as in the survival lottery). Commonsense is probably divided on other aspects of this right, such as the right to suicide and, more importantly for my purposes, the right to sell one's bodily parts. I do not believe the commonsensical conception would say that the right to sell parts of one's body is a natural one. It might, however, endorse it as one of the rights that ought to be guaranteed through the political process—or it might not. Arguments against allowing people this right would be analogous to those against allowing them to sell themselves into slavery for life, a practice that commonsense conceptions would certainly censure. The risk of coercion, free-rider problems, lack of information, and weakness of will might all be cited as grounds for denying people these rights.

Consider next people's right to develop and deploy their skills and talents, that is, their right to self-realization.[91] From society's point of view, it is desirable that people who possess rare and valued skills choose to develop and use those skills rather than others. From the individual's point of view, however, the prospect of being a poor and mediocre poet might be more attractive than that of being a wealthy engineer. Commonsense conceptions assert the right of self-realization as a natural right, and deny society the right to coerce people into socially valued occupations.[92] These conceptions would not, however, deny society the right to use inducements for the same purpose. Coercion in this case could

[90] For a good introduction to this topic, see Cohen, "Self-ownership, World Ownership and Equality: Part II."

[91] On this topic see my "Self-realization in Work and Politics."

[92] For discussions, see Appendix C to Barry, *Theories of Justice*, and A. Kronman, "Talent-pooling."

take the form of imposing a lump-sum tax on people according to their productive and income-earning *abilities* rather than on their actual earnings. The person who has been identified as a potential engineer would be taxed so heavily that he would have to become an engineer to afford to pay the tax, analogously with land taxes that are sometimes imposed to force the owners of the land to cultivate it. Common sense would object to this procedure, but not to large tax breaks to engineers for the purpose of inducing people to take up this profession.

Consider finally the right to retain the entire fruits of one's labor. I am confident that commonsense conceptions would not regard this as part of a natural right of self-ownership. The obvious need for taxation to finance public goods and ensure minimal welfare overrides this fragile philosophical idea. Also, in modern industrial economies the extensive economic cooperation and interdependence make it often impossible to identify the fruits of the labor of one particular individual. Commonsense conceptions regard taxation and restrictions on private property as merely pragmatic matters, to be resolved by considering welfare rather than rights, the main exception being the right to full compensation for expropriated property.

I conclude with some remarks on the commonsense conception of fairness. Although fairness is often used as a technical term in philosophical theories of justice, I am concerned here with a more amorphous idea, which can be broadly defined as the requirement of equal treatment and equal contribution. On the one hand, people should be treated equally. All who need a kidney should have a chance of receiving one, once they satisfy minimal medical requirements. Selective procedures are justified only if the authorities give reasons for their decision so as to reduce the risk of arbitrariness, caprice, or bias. The selection procedure must be fully public; those involved must have full access to all relevant documents; and there must be an instance to which those who are denied the good can appeal.

An important case is fairness based on legitimate expectations. Suppose that the government, using act-utilitarian reasoning, has set up transfers that later are found to have bad incentive effects (or not to have had the expected positive effects). Attempts to abolish the transfers will then often be resisted on grounds of fairness. The point is *not* that some would suffer because they would get less compared to earlier generations. Rather, it is that they would get less compared to what the practice toward the earlier generations had led them to expect for themselves. If the government proposes to change policy in midstream, arguments from fairness can often force it to withdraw the proposal. If the practice of supporting young couples in financial trouble is known to be general, the attempt to abolish it may similarly meet with objections from fairness. Changes in the system of admitting students to higher education are resisted if high school students had planned on the old system remaining in force. I believe that this general idea is an important part of the commonsense conception of justice.

On the other hand, people should contribute equally. The view that military service should either be fully voluntary or, if obligatory, be imposed on all is very strongly held in democratic societies. Selective procedures, once again, must be subject to rigorous scrutiny. As in the case of equal treatment, selection by lot might appear to be the best way of achieving fairness. Lotteries, however, do not allow decision makers to give reasons for their choice, nor do they make people feel that they have had a fair chance of presenting their case. Although the *randomness* of lotteries may be superior to the potential *capriciousness* of discretionary selection, both are often perceived as more unfair than a system in which cases are judged publicly on the basis of easily verifiable criteria. The proposal of deciding child custody cases by the toss of a coin, while in a sense fair to the parents and arguably best for the child, is widely rejected by commonsense conceptions because it does not ensure a proper hearing. The American demobilization system in World War II provides a good example of a procedure that was widely regarded as fair, for these reasons.

Lawyers, economists, and politicians will emphasize different parts of this bundle. Lawyers want to protect rights, economists want to promote welfare, and politicians have to be sensitive to considerations of fairness. I believe, nevertheless, that there is a rough consensus among this elite of decision makers. Their views remain distinct both from those of the public at large and from those who are professional philosophers, because they have been shaped by their all-round experience of making hard choices of allocation and selection. That experience also includes encounters with popular conceptions of justice. Sometimes the latter go into the shaping of their own views, as in the demand for procedural fairness. At other times their actions are merely constrained by popular ideas to which they do not themselves subscribe. One example is the idea that there is a "fair" price of electricity, based on historical costs of production rather than on current marginal cost.[93] Another is that direct wage subsidies to workers are degrading, but that indirect subsidies, for instance in the form of cheaper electricity to the firms that employ them, are not.[94] A third example is that politicians are sometimes constrained by weak envy: one should not provide to anyone what cannot be provided to everyone.

---

[93] For this and similar perceptions, see Zajac, "Perceived Economic Justice: The Example of Public Utility Regulation"; see also Kahneman, Knetsch, and Thaler, "Fairness as a Constraint on Profit-seeking."

[94] For a discussion of this case, see my "Is There (or Should There Be) a Right to Work?"

7 / Conclusion: Some Unexplored Issues

I shall not try to summarize the analyses in the previous chapters. Instead, I shall draw attention to some of the topics that I have not been able to treat as fully as I would have liked to. In doing so, I shall also suggest some directions for further research.

1. In the Introduction, I said that "One could write the fictional biography of a typical citizen, to depict his life as shaped by successive encounters with institutions that have the power to accord or deny him the scarce goods that he seeks." Toward the end of Chapter 4, I returned to the same theme, from a normative perspective. It seems to me that this idea would be worth exploring more fully. The central ideas in a study of this kind would be those of *life chances* and of *life cycle*. An intergenerational approach would be central. At various places in this work we have seen how the relations between children and parents give rise to problems of local justice. One topic that I have neglected, but which may become increasingly important in the years to come, is the selective admission to nursing homes for the elderly. As I briefly observed in Chapter 2, places in these homes form a scarce good not only for those who receive them, but also for their children.

2. The emphasis in this work on indivisible goods has blocked off a number of important issues. With respect to the allocation of scarce medical resources, for instance, I have largely limited myself to the issue of *whether* a patient should receive a certain treatment. Often, however, the more important question is *how much* he should receive. Admitting or refusing admission to an intensive care unit poses a question of the first kind. Deciding on when the patient should be transferred to the general ward raises the second question. I touched upon this issue in the comments on the norm of thoroughness (Chapter 5), but it deserves much more extensive treatment. The interaction between the two problems—and between the norms of compassion and of thoroughness—can be represented in the following diagram:

If there are several patients who need a scarce, livesaving drug, and the effect on their prospects is as indicated in Figure 7.1, doctors are faced with two choices. They can either give large doses to a few patients or smaller doses to many. And they can give priority either to the more or to the less critically ill patients. If both the norm of compassion and the norm of thoroughness operate, only very ill patients will receive the drug and few of

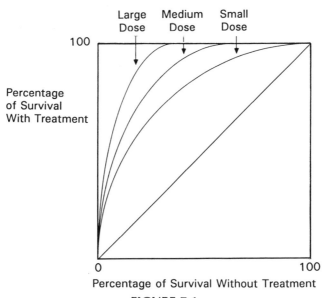

FIGURE 7.1

them will benefit. Considerations of instrumental efficiency would dictate that the drug be spread thinly over the moderately ill patients. If either the norm of compassion or the norm of thoroughness operates in the absence of the other, still different allocations would be observed.

3. Extension of the analysis to communities and corporate actors as recipients would, besides being of interest in its own right, probably lead to a sharper understanding of the individual-recipient case as well. In particular, the analysis of ethical individualism would certainly benefit from studies of the allocation of toxic waste to communities and of CO_2 emission quotas to countries. The latter question also raises issues related to ethical presentism: To what extent should past exploitation of the developing countries by the industrialized ones shape present allocation of rights to pollute? Also, the explanatory issues in such cases are likely to be quite different. In the absence of a world government, the allocation of emission quotas between countries will be more akin to the allocation of household work within the family than to the allocation of kidneys to patients. Matters of collective action and bargaining come to the forefront.

4. Intra-institutional politics, although briefly mentioned in Chapter 5, deserve a much fuller study. More generally, the present work would have been much improved had I known more about the sociology of complex organizations. In my exposition, the allocating institution has largely been treated as a black box, or identified with the values of its leading officers. This is simplification bordering on caricature. Although issues of costs and of incentives have been mentioned at various places, other questions have been neglected. What is the flow of information within the institution? To what extent is decision making centralized or decentralized? How do the trade unions that organize allocative personnel affect allocative policy?

5. In several cases, allocation is made by decentralized and local committees, constrained only by general and rather vague guidelines. Examples include draft boards, rationing boards, and laymen's committees for allocating scarce medical goods. The question then arises of the composition of such committees. Are the members elected or appointed? Do they have special expertise on, say, military or medical matters? Are they selected to form a

representative cross section of the population as a whole? Or a representative cross section of the potential recipients? Are they more like a jury or more like a panel of experts? In some cases, we may observe discretionary decisions by local boards combined with nondiscretionary principles for selecting members. In other cases, discretion may be allowed to reign supreme throughout the process, on the grounds that it takes expertise to recognize an expert.

6. In the American context, fear of litigation figures more prominently in shaping allocative practices than I have been able to convey. Many allocative processes take place "in the shadow of the law." The institution here is under double fire, from third-order actors as well as first-order ones. Private individuals can sue if they feel they have been unjustly denied the good; and the government may penalize institutions that do not respect federal rules. As a result, local justice has largely become a form of trench warfare between lawyers in different camps. Institutions take elaborate and costly precautions to protect themselves against litigation. This, too, is an aspect of allocation that needs much fuller treatment than I have been able to give here.

7. In previous chapters, the profit motive has been stressed mainly in the context of layoffs in private firms. Its operation, however, is more widespread. In many countries, some dialysis centers are run for profit, a fact that affects both the overall rate at which they refer patients for transplantation and the grounds for referring some patients rather than others. In Holland, where the sale of kidneys from living "donors" is legal, there is a private agency that makes money from matching donors with recipients. A closer look at such operations could be embedded in a larger study of the role of money in allocating scarce goods. The sociological and normative study of goods that cannot be bought for money—including the history of sumptuary laws—remains to be carried out on the scale it deserves.

8. The overall framework of the book has been static, with only brief comments on the evolution of allocative policies. A much fuller treatment of dynamics could be carried out. Although many changes are induced exogenously by changes in the economic, social, and political environment, allocative systems could also be subject to endogenous changes and cycles, driven by the fact,

mentioned in Chapter 5, that the faults of the system in place tend to be more vivid than the flaws of the alternatives. Some changes occur by drift or accretion; others by dramatic policy reversals. Diffusion of policies from one institution to another, from one arena to another, or from one country to another, would also be worth looking at. Perhaps one could find instances approximating natural selection of policies by differential survival.

I could go on like this, but I won't. If I have succeeded in presenting the basic issues and dilemmas, the reader should be able to think of further questions to be explored. There is an old saying that when the circle of light expands, so does the surrounding area of darkness. By turning the saying on its head, I can measure the success of my contribution by the extent to which the reader perceives that his ignorance has been extended.

References

Aaron, H. J., and W. B. Schwartz. *The Painful Prescription*. Washington, DC: The Brookings Institution, 1984.

Abraham, K., and J. L. Medoff. "Length of Service and Layoffs in Union and Nonunion Work Groups." *Industrial and Labor Relations Review* 38 (1984): 87–97.

Ainslie, G. *Picoeconomics: The Strategic Interaction of Successive Motivational States*. Cambridge, England: Cambridge University Press, 1992.

Angelos, C., and J. Jacobs. "Prison Overcrowding and the Law." *Annals of the American Academy of Political and Social Science* 478 (1985): 100–112.

Arrow, K. *Social Choice and Individual Values*. 2nd ed. New York: Wiley, 1963.

———. "Gifts and Exchanges." *Philosophy and Public Affairs* 1 (1972): 343–362.

———. "Review of Rawls's *A Theory of Justice*." *Journal of Philosophy* 70 (1973): 245–263.

———. "Extended Sympathy and the Possibility of Social Choice." *American Economic Review* 67 (1977): 219–225.

Austin, J. "Using Early Release to Relieve Prison Crowding: A Dilemma in Public Policy." *Crime and Delinquency* 32 (1986): 405–502.

Badeau, A. *Le village sous l'ancien régime*. Paris: Didier, 1882.

Bar-Hillel, M., and M. Yaari. "Judgments of Justice." Unpublished manuscript, Departments of Psychology and Economics, Hebrew University of Jerusalem, 1989.

Barry, B. "Is Democracy Special?" In P. Laslett and J. Fishkin, eds. *Philosophy, Politics and Society*, 5th series, pp. 155–196. Oxford, England: Blackwell, 1979.

———. Review of *Tragic Choices*. In his *Democracy, Power and Justice*, pp. 392–410. Oxford University Press, 1989.

———. *Theories of Justice*. Berkeley and Los Angeles: University of California Press, 1989.

Barry, B., and R. Hardin, eds. *Rational Man, Irrational Society*. Chicago: University of Chicago Press, 1982.

Bazerman, M. "Norms of Distributive Justice in Interest Arbitration." *Industrial and Labor Relations Review* 38 (1985): 558–570.

Beecher, H. K. "Scarce Medical Resources and Medical Advancement." *Daedalus* 98 (1969): 275–313.

Blum, A. "Soldier or Worker: A Reevaluation of the Selective Service System." *Midwest Quarterly* 13 (1972): p. 151.

de Bohigas, N. "Some Opinions on Exemption from Military Service in Nineteenth-century Europe." *Comparative Studies in Society and History* 10 (1968).

Boudon, R. "The Logic of Relative Frustration." In J. Elster, ed. *Rational Choice*, pp. 171–196. Oxford, England: Blackwell, 1986.

Boyes, W. J., and S. K. Happel. "Auctions as an Allocation Mechanism in Academia: The Case of Faculty Offices." *Journal of Economic Perspectives* 3 (1989): 37–40.

Briggs, V. *Immigration Policy and the American Labor Force*. Baltimore: Johns Hopkins University Press, 1984.

Brock, D. "Ethical Issues in Recipient Selection for Organ Transplantation." In D. Matthieu, ed. *Organ Substitution Technology*, pp. 86–99. Boulder, CO: Westview Press, 1988.

Broome, J. "Fairness and the Random Distribution of Goods." Unpublished manuscript, Department of Economics. Bristol, England: Bristol University, 1987.

Bureau of Labor Statistics, *Layoff, Recall, and Worksharing Procedures*. Bulletin 1425–13, 1972.

Burrell, A., ed. *Milk Quotas in the European Community*. C.A.B. International, 1989.

Cahn, E. *The Moral Decision*. Bloomington: Indiana University Press, 1955.

Calabresi, G., and P. Bobbit. *Tragic Choices*, New York: Norton, 1978.

Chambers, J. W. *To Raise an Army*. New York: The Free Press, 1987.

Childress, J. "Some Moral Connections Between Organ Procurement and Organ Distribution." *Journal of Contemporary Health Law and Policy* 3 (1987): 85–110.

Choisel, F. "Du tirage au sort au service universel." *Revue Historique des Armées* 37 (1981): 43–60.

Cohen, G. A. "Robert Nozick and Wilt Chamberlain." In J. Arthur and W. Shaw, eds. *Justice and Economic Distribution*, pp. 246–262. Englewood Cliffs, NJ: Prentice-Hall, 1978.

———. "Self-ownership, World Ownership and Equality, Part II." *Social Philosophy and Policy* 3 (1986): 77–96.

———. "Are Freedom and Equality Compatible?" In J. Elster and K. O. Moene, eds. *Alternatives to Capitalism*, pp. 113–126. Cambridge, England: Cambridge University Press, 1989.

———. "On the Currency of Egalitarian Justice." *Ethics* 99 (1989): 906–944.

Coleman, J. S. *Foundations of Social Theory*. Cambridge, MA: Harvard University Press, 1990.

Conley, P. "Local Justice and the Allocation of College Admissions." Working Paper # 9 from the Local Justice Project, Department of Political Science, University of Chicago, 1990.

Conley, P., M. Dennis, S. Laymon, and S. Romm. "The Use of Race as a Criterion in the Allocation of Scarce Resources: Case Studies of Health, Employment, Education and Housing." Working Paper # 10 from the Local Justice Project, Department of Political Science, University of Chicago, 1990.

Copeland, J. G., et al. "Selection of Patients for Cardiac Transplantation." *Circulation* 75 (1987): 1–9.

Creppell, I. "Democracy and Literacy: The Role of Culture in Political Life." *Archives Européennes de Sociologie* 30 (1989): 22–47.

Cwartosz, Z. "On Queuing." *Archives Européennes de Sociologie* 29 (1988): 3–11.

Dale, E. E. "Oklahoma's Great Land Lottery of 1832." *Great Plains Journal* 22 (1983): 2–41.

Davidson, D. *Essays on Actions and Events.* Oxford, England: Oxford University Press, 1980.

Dawes, R. "Social Selection Based on Multidimensional Criteria." *Journal of Abnormal and Social Psychology* 68 (1964): 104–109.

———. "A Case Study of Graduate Admission: Application of Three Principles of Human Decision Making." *American Psychologist* 26 (1971).

Dennis, M. "Reflections on the Unintended Consequences of Planning Local Justice: The Case of Organ Transplantation in the U.S." Working Paper # 11 from the Local Justice Project, Department of Political Science, University of Chicago, 1990.

Dequn, J. "Criteria for Land Distribution During the Second Revolutionary Civil War Period (1927–1937)." *Social Sciences in China* (1981).

Deutsch, M. "Equity, Equality and Need." *Journal of Social Issues* 31 (1975): 137–149.

Dworkin, R. "What Is Equality? Part 2: Equality of Resources." *Philosophy and Public Affairs* 10 (1981): 283–345.

"Early Retirement: Companies Move to Window Plans in Efforts to Stay Competitive." *BNA Pension Reporter* 14 (January 5, 1987), p. 8.

Einhorn, H. "The Use of Nonlinear, Noncompensatory Models in Decision Making." *Sociological Bulletin* 73 (1970): 221–230.

Elster, J. *Logic and Society.* Chichester, England: Wiley, 1978.

———. *Explaining Technical Change.* Cambridge, England: Cambridge University Press, 1983.

———. *Sour Grapes.* Cambridge, England: Cambridge University Press, 1983.

———. *Making Sense of Marx.* Cambridge, England: Cambridge University Press, 1983.

———. *Ulysses and the Sirens.* Rev. ed. Cambridge, England: Cambridge University Press, 1984.

———. "Weakness of Will and the Free-Rider Problem." *Economics and Philosophy* 1 (1985): 231–265.

———. "Self-realization in Work and Politics." *Social Philosophy and Policy* 3 (1986): 97–126.

———. "Is There (or Should There Be) a Right to Work?" In A. Guttman, ed. *Democracy and the Welfare State,* pp. 53–78. Princeton University Press, 1988.

———. *The Cement of Society.* Cambridge, England: Cambridge University Press, 1989.

———. *Solomonic Judgements.* Cambridge, England: Cambridge University Press, 1989.

———. *Nuts and Bolts for the Social Sciences.* Cambridge, England: Cambridge University Press, 1989.

———. "Local Justice." *Archives Européennes de Sociologie* 31 (1990): 117–140.

———. "Envy in Social Life." In R. Zeckhauser, ed. *Strategy and Choices.* pp. 49–82. Cambridge, MA: The M.I.T. Press, 1991.

———. "Arguing and Bargaining." Unpublished manuscript, Department of Political Science, University of Chicago, 1991.

———. *Political Psychology.* Forthcoming from Cambridge University Press.

Elster, J., and A. Hylland, eds. *Foundations of Social Choice Theory.* Cambridge, England: Cambridge University Press, 1986.

Elster, J., and J. Roemer, eds. *Interpersonal Comparisons of Wellbeing.* Forthcoming from Cambridge University Press.

Elster, J., and C. Sunstein. "When Ignorance Is Bliss." Unpublished manuscript, Department of Political Science, University of Chicago, 1990.

Ely, J. H. *Democracy and Distrust.* Cambridge, MA: Harvard University Press, 1980.

Entscheidungen des Bundesarbeitsgerichts. Vol. 42. Berlin and New York: De Gruyter, 1985.

Esposito, J. L. *The Obsolete Self: Philosophical Dimensions of Aging.* Berkeley: University of California Press, 1987.

Evans, R. W., and C. R. Blagg. "Lessons Learned from the End-Stage Renal Disease Experience: Their Implications for Heart Transplantation." In D. Mathieu, ed. *Organ Substitution Technology,* pp. 175–197. Boulder, CO, and London: The Westview Press, 1988.

Evans, R. W., and D. L. Manninen. "U.S. Public Opinion Concerning the Procurement and Distribution of Donor Organs." *Transplantation Proceedings* 20 (1988): 781–785.

Farrand, M., ed. *The Records of the Federal Convention of 1787.* New Haven: Yale University Press, 1966.

Feinberg, J. "Noncomparative Justice." *Philosophical Review* 83 (1974): 297–338.

Feller, W. *An Introduction to Probability Theory and Its Applications.* Vol. 1, 3d ed. New York: Wiley, 1968.

Fellner, I. "Recruiting Adoptive Applicants." *Social Work* 13 (1968): 92–100.

Fienberg, S. "Randomization and Social Affairs: The 1970 Draft Lottery." *Science* 171 (1971): 255–261.

Freeman, R. B., and J. Medoff. *What Do Unions Do?* New York: Basic Books, 1984.

Frolich, N., J. Oppenheimer, and C. Eavey. "Laboratory Results on Rawls's Distributive Justice." *British Journal of Political Science* 17 (1987): 1–21.

Gale, D., and L. Shapley. "College Admissions and the Stability of Marriages." *American Mathematical Monthly* 69 (1962): 9–15.

Gennard, J. "Great Britain." In E. Yemin, ed. *Workforce Reductions in Undertakings,* pp. 107–140. Geneva: International Labour Office, 1982.

Gerhardt, J. *The Draft and Public Policy: Issues in Military Manpower Procurement 1945–1970.* Columbus: Ohio State University Press, 1971.

Gersuny, C. "Origins of Seniority Provisions in Collective Bargaining." *Labor Law Journal* 33 (1982): 518–524.

Gersuny, C., and G. Kaufman. "Seniority and the Moral Economy of U.S.

Automobile Workers, 1934–1946." *Journal of Social History* 18 (1985): 463–475.

Gettell, R. G. "Rationing: A Pragmatic Problem for Economists." *American Economic Review* 33 (1943): 260–271.

Geuss, R. *The Idea of a Critical Theory*. Cambridge, England: Cambridge University Press, 1981.

Gibbard, A. "Manipulation of Voting Schemes." *Econometrica* 41 (1973): 587–601.

———. *Wise Choices, Apt Feelings*. Cambridge, MA: Harvard University Press, 1990.

Goldberg, V. "Bridges over Contested Terrain: Exploring the Radical Account of the Employment Relationship." *Journal of Economic Behavior and Organization* 1 (1980): 249–274.

Golden, M. "A Comparative Inquiry into Systems for Allocating Job Loss." Unpublished manuscript, Department of Political Science, University of California, Los Angeles, 1990.

Goldstein, J., A. Freud, and A. Solnit. *Before the Best Interests of the Child*. New York: The Free Press, 1979.

Gottfredson, S., and D. Gottfredson. "Selective Incapacitation?" *Annals of the American Academy of Political and Social Science* 478 (1985): 135–149.

Greenberg, E. R. "Downsizing and Worker Assistance: Latest AMA Survey Results." *Personnel* 65 (1988): 49–53.

Grether, D. M., R. M. Isaac, and C. R. Plott. *The Allocation of Scarce Resources: Experimental Economics and the Problem of Allocating Airport Slots*. Boulder, CO: Westview Press, 1989.

Halper, T. *The Misfortunes of Others: End-Stage Renal Disease in the United Kingdom*. Cambridge, England: Cambridge University Press, 1989.

Hammermesh, D. S. "What Do We Know about Worker Displacement in the U.S.?" *Industrial Relations* 28 (1989): 51–59.

Handler, J. F. *The Conditions of Discretion*, New York: Russell Sage Foundation, 1986.

Hans, V. P., and N. Vidmar. *Judging the Jury*. New York: Plenum Publishing, 1986.

Hansman, H. "The Economics and Ethics of Markets for Human Organs." *Journal of Health Politics, Policy, and Law* 14 (1989): 57–86.

Harris, J. "The Survival Lottery." *Philosophy* 50 (1975): 81–87.

Harris, R. J. "Pinning down the Equity Formula." In D. M. Messick and K. Cook, eds. *Equity Theory*, pp. 207–242. New York: Praeger, 1983.

Harsanyi, J. "Cardinal Welfare, Individualistic Ethics and Interpersonal Comparisons of Utility." *Journal of Political Economy* 63 (1955): 309–321.

———. "Can the Maximum Principle Serve as a Basis for Morality?" *American Political Science Review* 69 (1976): 594–606.

———. "Rule Utilitarianism and Decision Theory." *Erkenntnis* 11 (1977): 25–53.

Harsanyi, J., and R. Selten. *A General Theory of Equilibrium Selection in Games*. Cambridge, MA: M.I.T. Press, 1988.

Hernandez, B. E. "Title VII v. Seniority: The Supreme Court Giveth and the Supreme Court Taketh Away." *American University Law Review* 35 (1986): 339–386.

Herpin, N. "Le don de sperme." *Archives Européennes de Sociologie* 31 (1990): 141–173.

Higham, J. *Strangers in the Land: Patterns of American Nativism 1860–1925.* 2d ed. New Brunswick, NJ: Rutgers University Press, 1988.

Hofstee, W. "The Case for Compromise in Educational Selection and Grading." In S. B. Anderson and J. S. Helmick, eds. *On Educational Testing,* pp. 109–127. San Francisco: Jossey-Bass, 1983.

———. "Allocation by Lot: A Conceptual and Empirical Analysis." *Social Science Information* 29 (1990): 745–763.

Holt, C. A., and R. Sherman. "Waiting-Line Auctions." *Journal of Political Economy* 90 (1982): 280–294.

Houseman, S. "Allocating the Costs of Economic Change: Work Force Reductions and Restructuring in Steel." Unpublished manuscript, W. E. Upjohn Institute for Employment Research, 1989.

Hutchinson, E. P. *Legislative History of American Immigration Policy 1798–1965.* Philadelphia: University of Pennsylvania Press, 1981.

Hylland, A., and R. Zeckhauser. "The Efficient Allocation of Individuals to Positions." *Journal of Political Economy* 87 (1979): 293–314.

Iversen, T. "A Simple Model of Waiting List Generating Incentives." Unpublished manuscript, Senter for Helseadministrasjon, University of Oslo, 1988.

Jakobovits, I. *Jewish Medical Ethics.* New York: Bloch, 1975.

Jensen, A. "The Representative Method in Practice." *Bulletin of the International Statistical Institute* 22 (1926): 381–439.

Johansen, L. "The Bargaining Society and the Inefficiency of Bargaining." *Kyklos* 32 (1979): 497–522.

———. "Queues (and 'Rent-seeking') as Non-cooperative Games." In his *Collected Papers,* Vol. 2, pp. 827–876. Amsterdam: North-Holland, 1987.

Kahneman, D., and A. Tversky, "Prospect Theory." *Econometrica* 47 (1979): 263–291.

Kahneman, D., J. Knetsch, and R. Thaler. "Fairness as a Constraint on Profit-seeking." *American Economic Review* 76 (1986): 728–741.

Kamm, F. M. "The Report of the U.S. Task Force on Organ Transplantation: Criticisms and Alternatives." *The Mount Sinai Journal of Medicine* 56 (1989): 207–220.

Karellis, C. "Distributive Justice and the Public Good." *Economics and Philosophy* 2 (1986): 101–126.

Kasperson, R., ed. *Equity Issues in Radioactive Management Waste.* Cambridge, MA: Oelgeschlager, Gunn, 1983.

Keeney, R., and H. Raiffa. *Decisions with Multiple Objectives: Preferences and Value Tradeoffs.* New York: Wiley, 1976.

Kellerhals, J., J. Coenen-Huther, and M. Modak. "Justice and the Family." *Archives Européennes de Sociologie* 31 (1990): 174–184.

Kelley, M. R. "Discrimination in Seniority Systems—A Case Study." *Industrial and Labor Relations Review* 36 (1982): 40–55.

Kilner, J. F. "A Moral Allocation of Scarce Lifesaving Medical Resources." *Journal of Religious Ethics* 9 (1981): 245–271.

———. *Who Lives? Who Dies?* New Haven: Yale University Press, 1990.

Kjellstrand, M. "Age, Sex, and Race Inequality in Renal Transplantation." *Archives of Internal Medicine* 148 (1988): 1305–1309.

Klag, M. J., et al. "The Association of Skin Color with Blood Pressure in U.S. Blacks with Low Socioeconomic Status." *Journal of the American Medical Association* 265 (1991): 599–602.

Klitgaard, R. *Choosing Elites.* New York: Basic Books, 1985.

————. *Elitism and Meritocracy in Developing Countries.* Baltimore: Johns Hopkins University Press, 1986.

Knesper, D. J., D. J. Pagnucco, and J. R. C. Wheeler. "Similarities and Differences Across Mental Health Services Providers and Practice Settings in the United States." *American Psychologist* 40 (1985): 1352–1369.

Kolm, S.-C. *The General Theory of Justice.* Unpublished manuscript, Ecole des Hautes Etudes en Sciences Sociales, Paris, 1989.

Kronman, A. "Talent-pooling." In J. R. Pennock and J. W. Chapman, eds. *Nomos XXIII: Human Rights,* pp. 58–79. New York: New York University Press, 1981.

Krouse, R., and M. McPherson. "Capitalism, 'Property-owning Democracy,' and the Welfare State." In A. Guttman, ed. *Democracy and the Welfare State,* pp. 79–106. Princeton University Press, 1988.

Kuran, T. "Behavioral Norms in the Islamic Doctrine of Economics." *Journal of Economic Behavior and Organization* 4 (1983): 353–379.

————. "On the Notion of Economic Justice in Contemporary Islamic Thought." *International Journal of Middle East Studies* 21 (1989): 171–191.

Lane, M. P. "The Case for Early Release." *Crime and Delinquency* 32 (1986): 399–403.

Leibniz, Gottfried. *Philosophische Schriften.* C. J. Gerhardt, ed. Berlin, 1875–1890.

Leiman, S. Z. "Therapeutic Homicide: A Philosophic and Halakhic Critique of Harris's Survival Lottery." *Journal of Medicine and Philosophy* 8 (1983): 257–267.

Loewenstein, G. "Anticipation and the Valuation of Delayed Consumption." *Economic Journal* 97 (1987): 667–684.

Lorentzen, H. "Admission to Medical Schools in Norway 1970–1988." Unpublished manuscript, Institute for Social Research, Oslo, 1989.

Luce, R. D., and H. Raiffa. *Games and Decisions.* New York: Wiley, 1957.

MacDowell, D. M. *The Law in Classical Athens.* Ithaca, NY: Cornell University Press, 1978.

Mackie, G. "U.S. Immigration Policy and Local Justice." Unpublished manuscript, Department of Political Science, University of Chicago, 1990.

————. "Frustration, Preference Changes, and Immigration Demand." Unpublished manuscript, Department of Political Science, University of Chicago, 1990.

McPherson, M., and M. Shapiro. *Selective Admission and the Public Interest.* New York: College Entrance Examination Board, 1990.

Maidment, S. *Child Custody and Divorce.* London: Croom Helm, 1984.

Martin, C. D. *Beating the Adoption Game.* Rev. ed. San Diego: Harcourt Brace Jovanovich, 1988.

Matthieu, D. "Introduction to Part 2." In D. Matthieu, ed. *Organ Substitution Technology,* pp. 33–51. Boulder, CO: Westview Press, 1988.

————. "Introduction to Part 3." In D. Matthieu, ed. *Organ Substitution Technology,* pp. 133–152. Boulder, CO: Westview Press, 1988.

Maxwell, J. A., and M. N. Balcom. "Gasoline Rationing in the United States, I." *Quarterly Journal of Economics* 60 (1946): 561–587.

————. "Gasoline Rationing in the United States, II." *Quarterly Journal of Economics* 61 (1946): 125–155.

Meehl, P. *Clinical versus Statistical Prediction*. Minneapolis: University of Minnesota Press, 1954.
Mellers, B., and E. Hartka. "Fair Selection Decisions." *Journal of Experimental Psychology* 14 (1988): 572–581.
Merritt, W. T. President of the National Association of Black Social Workers. "Barriers to Adoption." Testimony in Senate Hearings, Committee on Labor and Human Resources, Tuesday, June 25, 1985.
Milford, E. L., L. Ratner, and E. Yunis. "Will Transplant Immunogenetics Lead to Better Graft Survival in Blacks?" *Transplantation Proceedings* 19 (1987): 30–32.
Mollat, G. *Mittheilungen aus Leibnizens ungedruckten Schriften*. Leipzig, 1893.
Morris, P. J. "Results of Renal Transplantation." In P. J. Morris, ed. *Kidney Transplantation*. 3d ed. Philadelphia: Saunders, 1988.
Nalebuff, B., and A. Dixit. "Making Strategies Credible." In R. Zeckhauser, ed. *The Strategy of Choice*. Cambridge, MA: The M.I.T. Press, 1992.
National Committee on Adoption. *Adoption Factbook: United States Data, Issues, Regulations, and Resources*. Washington DC, 1985; National Committee on Adoption.
Neumann, J. von, and O. Morgenstern. *The Theory of Games and Economic Behavior*. 2nd ed. Princeton University Press, 1947.
Nozick, R. *Anarchy, State and Utopia*. New York: Basic Books, 1974.
Okun, A. M. *Equality and Efficiency: The Big Trade-off*. Washington, DC: The Brookings Institution, 1975.
Opelz, G. "Allocation of Cadaver Kidneys for Transplantation." *Transplantation Proceedings* 20 (1988): 1028–1032.
Oren, D. A. *Joining the Club: A History of Jews and Yale*. New Haven: Yale University Press, 1985.
Parijs, P. van, and R. van der Veen. "A Capitalist Road to Communism." *Theory and Society* 15 (1986): 635–656.
Paterson, F. "Enquête sur la justice locale: La transplantation rénale." Unpublished manuscript, 1989.
Pauly, M. V. "Equity and Costs." In D. Matthieu, ed. *Organ Substitution Technology*, pp. 171–174, Boulder, CO: Westview Press, 1988.
Perez, L. M., A. J. Matas, and V. A. Tellis. "Organ Donation in Three Major U.S. Cities by Race/Ethnicity." *Transplantation Proceedings* 20 (1988): 815.
Perraud, D. et al. *Quotas Laitiers*. Special issue of *Cahiers d'Economie et Sociologie Rurales* 7 (1988).
Peters, D. "A Unified Approach to Organ Donor Recruitment, Organ Procurement, and Distribution." *Journal of Law and Health* 3 (1989): 157–187.
Petersen, R. "Rationality, Ethnicity and Military Enlistment." *Social Science Information* 28 (1989): 563–598.
Raiffa, H. *The Art and Science of Negotiation*. Cambridge, MA: Harvard University Press, 1982.
Rasch, B. E. "Barnas Beste? Om Fordeling av Barnehageplasser." ("In the Best Interest of Children? On the Allocation of Places in Kindergarten.") Working Paper # 3, 1990, Institute for Social Research, Oslo.
Rawls, J. *A Theory of Justice*. Cambridge, MA: Harvard University Press, 1971.
———. "Justice as Fairness: Political Not Metaphysical." *Philosophy and Public Affairs* 14 (1985): 223–251.
———. *Justice as Fairness: A Restatement*. Unpublished manuscript, Department of Philosophy, Harvard University, 1990.

Robertson, J. A. "Supply and Distribution of Hearts for Transplantation: Legal, Ethical, and Policy Issues." *Circulation* 75 (1987): 77–87.

Roemer, J. "Should Marxists Be Interested in Exploitation." *Philosophy and Public Affairs* 14 (1985): 30–65.

——. "Equality of Talent." *Economics and Philosophy* (1985): 151–188.

Romm, S. "Local Justice and Layoffs." Working Paper # 3 from the Local Justice Project, Department of Political Science, University of Chicago, 1990.

Rosner, F. *Modern Medicine and Jewish Ethics.* New York: Yeshiva University Press, 1966.

Roth, A. "The Evolution of the Labor Market for Medical Interns and Residents." *Journal of Political Economy* 92 (1984): 991–1016.

——. "New Physicians: A Natural Experiment in Market Organization." *Science* 250 (1990): 1524–1528.

Roth, A., and M. Sotomayor. *Two-sided Matching: A Study in Game-Theoretic Modelling and Analysis.* Cambridge, England: Cambridge University Press, 1990.

Sah, R. K. "Queues, Rations and Markets: Comparisons of Outcomes for the Poor and the Rich." *American Economic Review* 77 (1987): 69–77.

"Scarce Medical Resources." *Columbia Law Review* 69 (1969): 621–692.

Scheffler, S. *The Rejection of Consequentialism.* Oxford University Press, 1982.

Schelling, T. C. *The Strategy of Conflict.* Cambridge, MA: Harvard University Press, 1960.

Schmidt, V. "Local Justice in West Germany." Paper prepared for the meeting of the Local Justice project groups in Paris, June 11–13, 1990.

Selten, R. "The Equity Principle in Social Behavior." In H. Gottinger and W. Leinfellner, eds. *Decision Theory and Social Ethics,* pp. 289–301. Dordrecht: Reidel, 1978.

Sen, A. *Collective Choice and Social Welfare.* San Francisco: Freeman, 1971.

——. *On Economic Inequality.* Oxford, England: Blackwell, 1973.

——. "Utilitarianism and Welfarism." *Journal of Philosophy* 76 (1979): 463–486.

——. "Rights and Agency." *Philosophy and Public Affairs* 11 (1982): 3–39.

——. "Equality of What?" In his *Choice, Welfare and Measurement,* pp. 353–369. Oxford, England: Blackwell, 1982.

——. *Commodities and Capabilities.* Amsterdam: North-Holland, 1985.

Shapiro, C., and J. Stiglitz. "Equilibrium Unemployment as a Worker Discipline Device." *American Economic Review* 74 (1984): 433–444.

Sher, G. "Antecedentialism." *Ethics* 94 (1983): 6–17.

——. *Desert.* Princeton University Press, 1987.

Simpson, A. W. *Cannibalism and the Common Law.* University of Chicago Press, 1984.

Singer, D. E., et al. "Rationing Intensive Care—Physician Responses to a Resource Shortage." *New England Journal of Medicine* 309 (1983): 1155–1160.

Singer, P. "Utility and the Survival Lottery." *Philosophy* 52 (1977): 218–222.

Spence, J. *The Search for Modern China.* London: Hutchinson, 1990.

Starzl, T., et al. "A Multifactorial System for Equitable Selection of Cadaver Kidney Recipients." *Journal of American Medical Association* 257 (1987): 3073–3075.

Stouffer, S., et al. *The American Soldier.* Vols. 1–2. Princeton University Press, 1949.

Strom, T. "Letter to the Editor." *New England Journal of Medicine* 319 (1988): 1420.

Sunstein, C. "Legal Interference with Private Preferences." *University of Chicago Law Review* 53 (1986): 1129–1174.

———. "Three Civil Rights Fallacies." *University of California Law Review* 79 (1991): 751–774.

———. "Why Markets Won't Stop Discrimination." *Social Philosophy and Policy* 8 (1991): 22–37.

Swazey, J. P., and R. C. Fox. *The Courage to Fail.* Chicago, IL: University of Chicago Press, 1974.

Taylor, R., et al. "Individual Differences in Selecting Patients for Regular Hemodialysis." *British Medical Journal* 17 (1975): 38–81.

Teitelbaum, M. "Right Versus Right: Immigration and Refugee Policy in the United States." *Foreign Affairs* 59 (1980): 21–59.

———. "Skeptical Noises about the Immigration Multiplier." *International Migration Review* 23 (1989): 893–899.

Thaler, R. "Towards a Positive Theory of Consumer Choice." *Journal of Economic Behavior and Organization* 1 (1980): 39–60.

Thompson, J. J. *The Realm of Rights.* Cambridge, MA: Harvard University Press, 1990.

Thresher, B. A. *College Admission and the Public Interest.* New York: College Entrance Examination Board, 1966.

Tobin, J. "On Limiting the Domain of Inequality." *Journal of Law and Economics* 13 (1970): 263–267.

de Tocqueville, A. *L'Ancien régime et la révolution.* In Tocqueville, *Oeuvres Complètes.* Vol. 2. Paris: Gallimard, 1952.

———. *Souvenirs.* In Tocqueville, *Oeuvres Complètes.* Vol. 12. Paris: Gallimard, 1964.

———. *Democracy in America.* New York: Anchor Books, 1969.

Toft, M. "Adoption as an Issue of Local Justice." Unpublished manuscript, Department of Political Science, University of Chicago, 1990.

Tong, J. "Allocation of Disaster Relief in China's Qing Dynasty, 1644–1911." Unpublished manuscript, Department of Political Science, University of California, Los Angeles, 1989.

Tresher, B. A. *College Admission and the Public Interest.* New York: College Entrance Examination Board, 1966.

Tversky, A., and D. Kahneman. "Judgment under Uncertainty." *Science* 185 (1974): 1124–1130.

———. "The Framing of Decisions and the Psychology of Choice." *Science* 211 (1981): 453–458.

UCLA Freshman Admissions in the 1990s: A Decade of Rapid Change. Presentation to the University of California Regents, July 20, 1990.

"UNOS Policy Regarding Utilization of the Point System for Cadaveric Kidney Allocation." Richmond, Virginia: United Network for Organ Sharing, April 7, 1989.

Veyne, P. *Le pain et le cirque.* Paris: Editions du Seuil, 1976.

Walder, A. *Communist Neo-Traditionalism.* Berkeley: University of California Press, 1986.

Walzer, M. *Spheres of Justice.* New York: Basic Books, 1983.

Welch, H. G., and E. Larson. "Dealing with Limited Resources: The Oregon

Decision to Curtail Funding for Organ Transplantation." *New England Journal of Medicine* 319 (1988): 171–173.

Westen, P. *Speaking of Equality*. Princeton University Press, 1990.

Weymark, H. "A Reconsideration of the Harsanyi-Sen Debate on Utilitarianism." In J. Elster and J. Roemer, eds. *Interpersonal Comparisons of Wellbeing*. Forthcoming from Cambridge University Press.

Wikler, D. "Personal Responsibility for Illness." In D. VanDeVeer and T. Regan, eds. *Health Care Ethics*, pp. 326–358. Philadelphia: Temple University Press, 1987.

Wilms, D. C. "Georgia's Land Lottery of 1832." *The Chronicles of Oklahoma* 52 (1974): 52–60.

Wingard, D. "Trends and Characteristics of California Adoptions: 1964–1982." *Child Welfare* 66 (1987): 303–314.

Winslow, G. R. *Triage and Justice*. Berkeley: University of California Press, 1982.

Wood, G. *The Creation of the American Republic*. New York: Norton, 1972.

Yaari, M., and M. Bar-Hillel. "On Dividing Justly." *Social Choice and Welfare* 1 (1984): 1–25.

Yemin, E., ed. *Workforce Reductions in Undertakings*. Geneva: International Labour Office, 1982.

Young, H. P. "Equitable Selection of Kidney Recipients." *Journal of American Medical Association* 26 (1989): p. 2957.

———. "Sharing the Burden of Global Warming." Working Paper # 4 from the Equity and Global Climate Change Project, School of Public Affairs, University of Maryland, 1990.

Zajac, E. P. "Perceived Economic Justice: The Example of Public Utility Regulation." In H. P. Young, ed. *Cost Allocation*, pp. 119–153. Amsterdam: North-Holland, 1985.

Zeckhauser, R., and D. Shepard. "Where Now for Saving Lives?" *Law and Contemporary Problems* 40 (1976): 5–45.

Index

renal disease, 94; end-stage (ESRD), 35, 222. *See also* dialysis
residence, 82
resources, 5, 210; allocation of fungible, 140; productive, 186. *See also* goods; medical resources
retirement, early, 25–26
retransplantation: of hearts, 95–96; low priority of, for substance abusers, 142; success rates for, 148
rewards, 99–100
rich, 13*n*, 213*n*, 214; interaction of poor and, 231–232; purchase of goods by, 101; purchase of medical treatments by, 13; transfers from, 206, 214. *See also* wealth
rich countries, 224
rights, 238; -based theories, 210; commonsense conceptions of, 241–242; individual, 210, 224; natural, 235; of self-ownership, 243; of self-realization, 242. *See also* bodily parts; procreation rights
risk, 196, 221
Robertson, J.A., 96*n*
Roemer, John, 181*n*, 203*n*, 218*n*, 231*n*, 239*n*
Romm, Stuart, 40*n*, 75*n*, 125*n*
Roosevelt, Theodore, 123, 124
Rosner, F., 71*n*
rotation, 73
Roth, Alvin, 45*n*, 130*n*, 131–132, 131*n*

S

Sah, R.K., 109*n*
Salinas v. *Roadway Express*, 41*n*
salvation, 26, 27, 99
scandals, 6, 181, 182
scarcity, 16, 21–23, 21*n*, 26, 237; alleviation of, 165
Schaefer v. *Tannian*, 41*n*
Scheffler, S., 209*n*
Schelling, T.C., 70*n*, 175*n*
Schmidt, V., 44*n*
schools, 32*n*, 46–47, 90. *See also* colleges; kindergarten; medical school; nursery school
Schwartz, William B., 6, 65*n*, 77*n*, 102*n*, 150*n*

Sears v. *Atchinson*, 42*n*
Seattle, 63; access to dialysis in, 101, 156
Seattle Artificial Kidney Center, 156–157
Seattle God committee, 156, 182
secondary effects, 113, 114, 120; of immigration law, 121–124; instances of debated, 115
seduction, 140, 140*n*
selection, 16, 236, 245; delay between time of service and time of, 20; discretionary, 167–168, 169, 244; by lot, 156, 160, 244; procedure, 24, 27, 156, 243, 244; random, 64; of students, 44, 45, 119. *See also* applicants for college; individuals; military service; soldiers
selective incapacitation, 57
Selective Service: Headquarters, 31; System, 32, 33, 60
self-exclusion, 78, 78*n*, 79
self-interest, 162, 173, 180–184
self-mutilation, 159–160, 171
self-ownership, 203, 242, 243
self-respect, 77, 186, 225, 229
self-selection, 44, 45, 66*n*
Selten, R., 63*n*, 192*n*
Sen, Amartya, 187, 187*n*, 196*n*, 209*n*, 210*n*, 216*n*, 226*n*, 228*n*
seniority, 2, 27, 74–76, 104–105; alliance for, 173; clauses for, 39–40; in Europe and U.S., 150; "finders keepers" principle reflected in, 235; interaction of age and, 77–78; in layoff situations, 3, 39–40, 75, 125, 163, 173, 215; overriding of, 223; principle of, 42–43; systems, 40–42, 64, 120, 121*n*, 210; use of, as tiebreaker, 106. *See also* workers
sentencing, 56, 57
sexual orientation, 79
Shapiro, C., 125*n*
Shapiro, M., 44*n*
Shapley, L., 130*n*
Shepard, D., 220*n*, 222*n*
Sher, G., 210*n*
Sherman, R., 128*n*
Simpson, A.W., 9*n*, 72*n*, 107*n*
Singapore: law, 161; system, 197